The Complete Resource Book

The Complete Resource Book

The Complete Resource Book

An Early Childhood Curriculum

Over 2000 Activities and Ideas!

Pam Schiller
Kay Hastings

Illustrations by Joan Waites

gryphon house
Beltsville, Maryland

Dedication

To Sam Marotta, intuitive teacher, extraordinary father and friend to all children

To Jim and Madison, my inspiration and my joy

Published by Gryphon House, Inc.
10726 Tucker Street, Beltsville, MD 20705

World Wide Web: http://www.ghbooks.com

Library of Congress Cataloging-in-Publication Data

Schiller, Pamela Byrne.
  The complete resource book : an early childhood curriculum : over 2000 activities and ideas / Pam Schiller and Kay Hastings.
      p.   cm.
    Includes bibliographical references and index.
    ISBN 0-87659-195-0
    1. Education, Preschool--Curricula--Handbooks, manuals, etc.
  2. Education, Preschool--Activity programs--Handbooks, manuals, etc.
  3. Classroom learning centers--Handbooks, manuals, etc.
  4. Child development--Handbooks, manuals, etc.   I. Hastings, Kay,– .
  II. Title.
  LB1140. 4. S35   1998   98-11802
  372.21--dc21   CIP

Table of Contents

Introduction

The Complete Resource Book is a gigantic collection of 25 two-week themes. Each theme features ten daily plans that include a primary focus activity (for morning circle time), six learning center ideas, and music and story suggestions for 250 days of learning. Two one-week themes—School Bells Ring and Summertime Fun—are included as a bonus. That's a full year of curriculum! *The Complete Resource Book* is filled with developmentally appropriate activities for three, four and five year olds and is designed to be easily integrated into any teacher's daily schedule.

The Theme Units

Each theme begins with a description of the theme and a table of the unit at a glance. This page lets you see in a minute the focus for each day and the suggestions for center activities, story circle, and music and movement activities.

We arranged the themes in this book in an order that makes sense to us. Our goal was to teach those themes or concepts that were most relevant or closest to the child first. Therefore, we begin with self-awareness and move to family and then friends. Themes like farms and transportation may be a little bit removed from the child's immediate world, so we introduce them later in the year.

Use our sequence or one that matches your existing curriculum and/or children's interests. Repeat or expand a theme if children remain interested after two weeks. The index in this book is a terrific resource for locating ideas that enrich the themes in this book and activities you are likely already using in your classroom.

Daily Schedules

Activities in *The Complete Resource Book* were developed to use in a typical half-day schedule or a complete day schedule.

Half-Day Schedule

8:30—8:50	Morning Circle	(PLANNING)
8:50—9:30	Learning Centers	(DOING)
9:30—10:00	Outdoor Play	
10:00—10:20	Story Circle	
10:20—11:00	Learning Centers	
11:00—11:15	Creative Movement	
11:15—11:30	Snack	
11:30—12:00	Closing Circle	(REVIEWING)

Full-Day Schedule

8:00—8:10	Welcome and Quiet Activities	
8:10—8:30	Morning Circle	(PLANNING)
8:30—9:20	Learning Centers	(DOING)
9:20—9:50	Outdoor Play	
9:50—10:10	Story Circle	
10:10—11:00	Learning Centers	(DOING)
11:00—11:15	Music and Movement	
11:15—11:30	Closing Circle	(RECAP THE MORNING)
11:30—12:00	Lunch	
12:00—12:15	Story Circle (select from list of additional books at the end of each chapter)	
12:15—2:30	Rest	
2:30—2:45	Transition (put away mats, etc.)	
2:45—3:00	Snack	
3:00—4:00	Learning Centers	(DOING)
4:00—5:00	Outdoor Play	
5:00—5:20	Story Circle (children's choice)	(RECAP THE DAY)
5:20—6:00	Choice of Quiet Activities	

Note: Schedules are for reference only. Please modify to suit the needs of the children in your care.

For each day there is a focus activity (which we assume will take place in the morning circle), suggestions for six learning centers, a book to read during the story circle and a creative movement activity. Programs using a full-day schedule would include lunch, rest time, snack time and a repeat of the learning center activities in the afternoon.

Closing circle is used to recap and review the day's activities. It helps children assimilate and evaluate what they've done at school, and it prepares them for the inevitable question, "What did you do at school today?"

Why Learning Centers?

Learning centers provide opportunities for hands-on reinforcement of concepts and skills that have been introduced in a whole-group setting. Because young children learn best through active exploration and concrete experience, learning centers make up the biggest portion of the daily schedule in the early childhood classroom.

Learning centers are not just free play. They are planned and organized to give support to themes, skills and concepts. When setting up learning centers, you must decide which centers best support your goals, what you want to accomplish in each center and what materials you will need. As you plan for learning centers, consider the ages, interests, needs and abilities of all your children. It is not necessary to open every center every day. In fact, it is important to rotate and change centers on a regular basis to avoid over-saturation.

Getting Started: Setting Up Learning Centers

Consider the physical layout of your room. Divide your room into distinct areas. Keep noisy centers, such as blocks, away from quiet ones, such as language and writing. Sand and water tables and art centers should be placed in an area that is close to water, if possible, and not carpeted. Blocks should be placed on carpet and completely enclosed to prevent cars and blocks from rolling into other areas. If you use bookshelves to create a T or an X in the center of your classroom, you will increase the options for creating centers (see illustration below). This arrangement also helps control traffic by eliminating wide open spaces children might be tempted to run through.

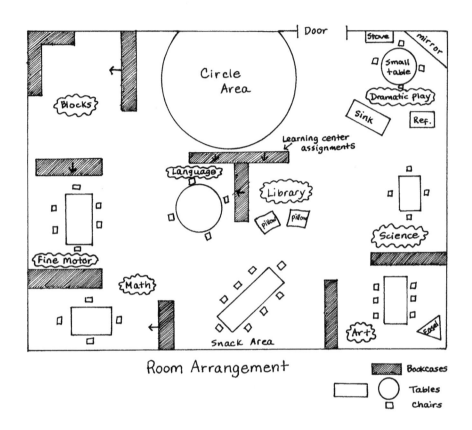

Room Arrangement

Decide which and how many centers you want to establish.
Generally, six to eight centers are sufficient. For larger classes you may want more. If you divide four into the number of children in the class, you will come up with a number that will most adequately accommodate your class. The most popular centers (sometimes considered core centers) are Art, Language, Science, Math, Fine Motor, Blocks and Dramatic Play. Other centers, such as Construction, Discovery, Game, Listening, Music, Library and Sand and Water, may be used as either core centers or rotation centers.

Label centers clearly.
Children need to be able to identify which center is which and where the boundaries of each center are. It's a good idea to color-code centers and to place a descriptive illustration in each center so that children will recognize it. (Enlarge the illustrations on appendix pages 439-440 to place in the centers.) You may want to include a list of skills normally developed in that center as a way of helping to educate parents.

Determine ground rules.
Set your rules of operation early. Keep them as simple as possible. For example:
You must have a necklace to enter the center.
Put away materials before you leave a center.
Keep materials in the center where they belong.

Managing Learning Centers

During the first two to three weeks of the school year, introduce the learning centers, lay the ground rules and invite the children to explore the different centers. After the children are familiar with the room arrangement and the materials in the centers, you may want a more formal monitoring system. Here's one suggestion for such a system:

1. Decide how many children you can allow in each center. As an example, the optimum number of children for each center is: Art (5), Math (4), Science (4), Fine Motor (5), Language (4), Blocks (3), Dramatic Play (3), Sand and Water (2), Discovery (2), Construction (2), Games (4), Music (2), Listening (2-3) and Library (2-3).

2. Make a sign for each center and assign a color code to it. Make color necklaces to correspond with each center's color code and with the number of children that center will accommodate (e.g., if your Block Center will accommodate four children, make four necklaces for it). Hang necklaces for each center in that center.

3. Use index cards or luggage tags to create a card for each child. Take a photograph of the child and then photocopy it so that you have two pictures. Tape or glue a picture to each side of the card. (Note: You can usually get three children in one photograph. Cut that photo into the three individual pictures and photocopy. This saves film.) Write the child's name on each side of the card. Next make colored circles to correspond with your center colors across the bottom of each side. (If you have six centers, make three different-colored circles on each side. If you have eight centers, make four circles on each side. Note: Make sure every child's card has the colored circles arranged in the same way.) Laminate and punch a hole in the top of each card.

4. Hang the cards on hooks on the back of a bookcase or on a pegboard. It works best to have the cards near your circle area. When placing the cards on the board, it's a good idea to turn them so that every other one has the same colored circles facing out. This way, if children try to turn a card over to get a different center (and they will), you can spot it right away. (Note: The cards always stay on the hooks.)

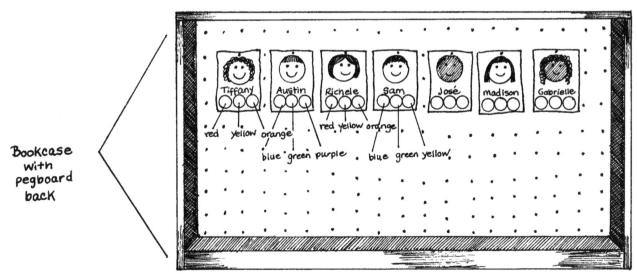

Card Assignment

5. Dismiss children from morning circle a few at a time to begin their learning center work. Have them find their cards and select a center that corresponds with one of the colored circles showing. Encourage each child to select a necklace for the chosen center and begin play. If no necklace is available (meaning the center is full), the child must make a second choice. Children can change centers as often as they wish as long as they follow the ground rules. This system allows you to help children make better decisions by limiting their number of options. It also allows you to separate children who have difficulty playing together by turning their cards to offer opposite choices.

6. After the first session of centers is over (see schedule), turn the cards over to expose the other side. Next time children go to centers, they will be able to choose from a different set.

7. You can use the assignment cards for a variety of other management needs. For example, place paper clips or clothespins on the cards as a means of record-keeping (e.g., to show who has made an invitation for the parent tea, who has already had a sharing opportunity this week, or who has been in an area where you are doing assessment). If you laminate the cards, you can place masking tape over any colored circle representing an area that is closed to the child because of inappropriate behavior. For example, Gabrielle is not allowed to play in the Art Center today because she deliberately broke crayons there this morning. You can arrange the cards so a specific group of children (perhaps more advanced children) are grouped to come to the math center during the first learning center session and another group during the next session.

This system allows you to have both flexibility and control over classroom activities. At the same time, it provides a mechanism that empowers children by allowing them to make choices based on their interests, needs and abilities.

Appendix

The appendix includes useful stories, recipes, directions for games, patterns and words to fingerplays, songs and chants that will help you make better use of the activities in *The Complete Resource Book*. Many of the patterns, such as those for the concentration games, can be used in a variety of ways. For example, individual squares can be enlarged to create puzzles or attached to potato chip cans (such as Pringles) for bowling or ring toss games, or each set of cards can be turned into a simple matching game. Many appendix materials are referenced in the daily lessons.

This book was written just for you. So get out your lesson plans—with more than 2000 ideas in *The Complete Resource Book*, you've got more time for teaching.

School Bells Ring

The first week of school is filled with new rules and new experiences. This unit will help you acquaint children with their new environment and routine.

Unit at a Glance

Day	Focus	Centers	Story Circle	Music/Movement
1	First Day	Crayon Drawings Block Building Puppets Playdough Puzzles Magnet Exploration	My Teacher Sleeps in School	Circle Dance
2	Schedule	Fingerpainting Build a Highway Homemaking Flannel Board Story Junk Boxes Magnificent Plants	My First Day of School	Marching
3	Rules	Collage Build a Town Playing With Dolls Scooping Beans Cards and Puzzles Scales and Weights	How to Lose All Your Friends	Punchinello
4	Friends	Watercolors Cardboard Boxes Grocery Store Friendship Bracelets School Books Tracing	Will I Have a Friend?	Partner Dance
5	School Helpers	Easel Painting Cans and Baskets Stringing Beads More Junk Magnifiers and More Chalkboard Writing	Monster Goes to School	Rhythm Band

First Day

Materials

flannel board story, "My First Day of School" (see the appendix, pages 380-381), flannel board, flannel board pieces for "My First Day of School"

Morning Circle

1. In advance, cut up greeting cards to make a simple puzzle for each child. The puzzles will provide something for children to do until everyone arrives and settles in.
2. Ask the children if they've been to school before and encourage them to tell stories about their experiences.
3. Talk about activities the children will do at school every day.
4. Tell the story, "My First Day of School," with the flannel board and flannel board pieces.

Story Circle

My Teacher Sleeps in School by Ellen Weiss

Music and Movement

"Circle Dance" from *Getting to Know Myself* by Hap Palmer

Learning Centers

Art

Crayon Drawings
Set out crayons and drawing paper for the children. Let them draw and color freely.

Fine Motor

Playdough
Provide playdough for the children to play and sculpt with.

Blocks

Block Building
Put out two or three kinds of blocks (wooden, plastic interlocking, hollow cardboard, etc.). Encourage the children to build with the blocks.

Language

Puzzles
Place the greeting card puzzles in the center. Invite the children to tell stories about each puzzle as they put them together.

Dramatic Play

Puppets
Encourage the children to use puppets to show and/or tell about their school experiences.

Science

Magnet Exploration
Put magnets and a variety of metal and nonmetal objects in the center. Encourage the children to experiment with the objects.

Schedule

Materials
enlarged class schedule with photographs or pictures on it

Morning Circle
1. Talk with the children about the schedule they will follow each day.
2. Mount an enlarged copy of the schedule on chart paper. Use pictures, rebus drawings and photographs to show what happens during each time period.
3. If you use one color to identify each of the centers, show the children where they can find the color in each area.
4. Tour the room, providing names for materials and areas.

Story Circle
"My First Day of School," flannel board story from Day 1 (see the appendix, pages 380–381)

Music and Movement
Play marching music (such as "Stars and Stripes Forever" by John Philip Sousa) and invite the children to march.

Learning Centers

Art

Fingerpainting
Provide fingerpaint and paper and encourage the children to create a picture.

Language

Flannel Board Story
Provide a flannel board and felt pieces. Encourage the children to retell the flannel board story, "My First Day of School."

Blocks

Build a Highway
Add cars to the center and encourage the children to build a highway for them.

Math

Junk Boxes
Encourage the children to explore the characteristics of the junk materials, such as keys, assorted buttons, spools and colored tiles, in the center.

Dramatic Play

Homemaking
Invite the children to explore the homemaking materials in the center.

Science

Magnificent Plants
Invite the children to examine seeds and plants with magnifying glasses.

Rules

Materials
chart paper and marker

Morning Circle
1. Let the children help set up class rules. Depending on the ages and experiences of the children, you may need to take the lead in the discussion.
2. Write the rules on chart paper and read them back to the children.
3. You may want to suggest that all the rules be condensed into one easy-to-remember rule: You can do anything that doesn't hurt yourself or someone else. It covers everything!

Story Circle
How to Lose All Your Friends by Nancy Carlson

Music and Movement
Sing "Punchinello" (see the appendix, pages 397-398).

Learning Centers

Art

Collage
Provide materials such as scraps of paper, glue, tape, glitter, sticky dots, fabric scraps and markers for the children to create a collage.

Blocks

Build a Town
Add plastic people and animals to the center. Invite the children to build a town.

Dramatic Play

Playing With Dolls
Add dolls to the center for the children to role-play with.

Fine Motor

Scooping Buttons
Give the children large buttons, small brushes and a scoop. Encourage the children to sweep the buttons into the scoop.

Language

Cards and Puzzles
Invite the children to use sequence cards, association cards, puzzles and other materials in the center. Encourage explanation and discussion.

Science

Scales and Weights
Provide scales and a variety of objects for the children to weigh and balance.

Friends

Materials
none

Morning Circle
1. Sing "The More We Get Together" (see the appendix, page 396).
2. Talk with the children about how the class is like a family and how you are all friends to each other.
3. Divide the class into pairs. Encourage the children to work with their partners today.

Story Circle
Will I Have a Friend? by Miriam Cohen

Music and Movement
Invite children to make up a partner dance to "The More We Get Together" or another friendly song.

Learning Centers

Art

Watercolors
Provide watercolors, brushes and paper for the children to explore.

Fine Motor

Friendship Bracelets
Provide beads, pipe cleaners and straws cut into 1" (3 cm) lengths. Invite the children to make friendship bracelets.

Blocks

Cardboard Boxes
Add cardboard boxes to the center for creative building. Invite the children to build with boxes and blocks.

Library

School Books
Fill the library with books about school and school friends.

Dramatic Play

Grocery Store
Provide props for the children to set up a grocery store (e.g., food cans and boxes, grocery sacks, cash register, shopping basket, etc.).

Writing

Tracing
Provide tracing paper and crayons. Encourage the children to select flat objects from the classroom to trace.

School Helpers

Materials

Morning Circle

1. Talk about all the people who help around the school, such as the director, administrator, nurse, custodian, cook, librarian and so on.
2. Take a tour of the school. Introduce the children to each of the people you talked about.

Story Circle

Monster Goes to School by Virginia Mueller

Music and Movement

Introduce rhythm band instruments and encourage the children to play them.

Learning Centers

Art

Easel Painting
Provide tempera paints and drawing paper. Invite the children to paint at the easel.

Math

More Junk
Add more junk items for the children to explore, sort, classify and seriate.

Blocks

Cans and Baskets
Add cans and baskets to the center. Show the children how to make signs and labels with crayons and paper.

Science

Magnifiers and More
Add leaves, locust skins, flowers and other interesting objects. Put out the magnifying glasses again.

Fine Motor

Stringing Beads
Give the children shoelaces or yarn and beads for stringing.

Writing

Chalkboards
Invite the children to write or draw on a small chalkboard.

Additional Books for School Bells Ring

All My Feelings at Preschool: Nathan's Day by Susan Colin and Susan Levine Friedman

Annabelle Swift, Kindergartner by Amy Schwartz

Arthur Goes to School by Marc Brown

Carl Goes to Day Care by Alexandra Day

Chrysanthemum by Kevin Henkes

Friends at School by Rochelle Bunnett

Jessica by Kevin Henkes

The Kissing Hand by Audrey Penn

Little Critter's This Is My School by Mercer Mayer

Marcellus by Lorraine Simeon

Miss Bindergarten Gets Ready for Kindergarten by Joseph Slate

Miss Nelson Is Back by Harry Allard

Miss Nelson Is Missing by Harry Allard

My Nursery School by Harlow Rockwell

Never Spit on Your Shoes by Denys Cazet

School Bus by Donald Crews

Starting School by Janet and Allan Ahlberg

The Day the Teacher Went Bananas by James Howe

This Is the Way We Go to School by Edith Baer

What Will Mommy Do When I'm at School? by Delores Johnson

Will You Come Back for Me? By Ann Tompert

Gotta Be Me

Each person is unique. This unit looks at how we are different and how we are alike. Children explore their physical features, their feelings and their senses.

Unit at a Glance

Day	Focus	Centers	Story Circle	Music/Movement
1	Physical Me	Me Puppets Dress Up Body Parts Bingo Self-Portraits Eye Color Graph Thumbprints	I'm Terrific	I Am Special
2	Physical Me	Body Tracers Me Towers Twister Me Books Felt Faces Growth Records	All By Myself	Everybody's Different
3	Thinking Me	Doodle Art Paper Clip Pick-Up What's Missing? Patterns Solid Sort Mystery Footprints	Oh! The Thinks You Can Think	Let's Pretend
4	Feeling Me	Fingerpainting Happy Pictures Pizza Faces Me Puppets Things I Like Feelings Concentration	Feelings	A Really Good Feeling
5	Celebrating Me	Birthday Hats Cupcakes Birthday Party Gift Wrapping Making Invitations Candle Sort	Moira's Birthday	Special Day

Day	Focus	Centers	Story Circle	Music/Movement
6	My Sense of Touch	Textured Fingerpaints Textured Building Sand Drawing Hand Books Finger Patterns Feely Box	I Can Tell by Touching	Where Is Thumbkin?
7	My Sense of Sound	Bell Ringers Jingle Bracelets Listen and Tell Sound Canisters Rhythm Band Sound Jars	The Listening Walk	Play Your Instruments
8	My Sense of Smell	Smelly Art Scratch and Sniff Potpourri Bags Scented Playdough Fragrance Graph Smelly Jars	Smell	Popcorn
9	My Sense of Sight	Magnified Pictures Sunglass Views Pin the Tail on the Donkey Finger Spelling Eye Sort Up-Close Eyes	Take Another Look	I Spy
10	My Sense of Taste	Favorite Food Pictures Restaurant Peanut Butter Playdough Recipe Dictation Food Classification Substance Sort	Taste	Make Myself Some Cookies

Physical Me

Materials
none

Morning Circle

1. Ask two children to stand up. Ask the group to look at the children and describe ways they are alike and ways they are different. Do this activity with other pairs of children. Be sensitive to characteristics that might embarrass some children (e.g., short, fat, skinny, etc.).
2. Ask all the children to tell you something about themselves, such as their eye color, hair color, skin color, etc.
3. Explain to the children that our physical characteristics are some of the things that make each of us special and unique.

Story Circle
I'm Terrific by Marjorie Weinman Sharmat

Music and Movement
"I Am Special" from *I Am Special* by Thomas Moore

Learning Centers

Art

Me Puppets
Encourage the children to make Me Puppets. Use 6" (15 cm) paper plates as faces and tongue depressors as holders. Provide yarn, crayons, markers, scissors, stapler and glue.

Language

Self-Portraits
Encourage the children to draw pictures of themselves and to dictate lists of words that describe them.

Dramatic Play

Dress Up
Fill the center with dress-up clothes and a mirror. Encourage the children to put on the clothes.

Math

Eye Color Graph
Make a graph to illustrate blue, brown, green and gray eyes. Let each child look in a mirror and then mark the appropriate square on the graph using stickers, colored dots or name labels.

Games

Body Parts Bingo
Invite the children to play Body Parts Bingo. Make Bingo game boards and matching cards (see the directions in the appendix, pages 418-421).

Science

Thumbprints
Provide an ink pad and paper. Let the children make thumbprints and examine them with magnifying glasses.

24 • • • GOTTA BE ME

Physical Me

Day 2

Materials
small mirrors

Morning Circle
1. Invite the children to look at themselves in the mirrors. Discuss eye and hair color and kinds of noses, mouths, hair, etc.
2. Use physical characteristics (e.g., eye color, hair color, number of legs) to group the children. Be sensitive to characteristics that might embarrass some children (e.g., short, fat, skinny, etc.).
3. Regroup the children several times, using different criteria each time.

Story Circle
All By Myself by Mercer Mayer

Music and Movement
"Everybody's Different" from *Songs for You and Me* by Jane Murphy

Learning Centers

Art

Body Tracers
Ask each child to lie down on a large sheet of bulletin board paper. Use a crayon or marker to trace around the body. Encourage the children to color in their clothes, hair, eyes, etc.

Blocks

Me Towers
Encourage the children to build towers as tall as they are.

Games

Twister
Play Twister, using either the commercial version or your own creation.

Language

Me Books
Encourage the children to make books about themselves. Provide paper and markers. Help the children get started by suggesting that they make a list of things they can do.

Math

Felt Faces
Provide felt-covered coffee cans and different sizes, shapes and colors of felt cutouts. Encourage the children to use the cutouts to make faces on the cans.

Science

Growth Records
Provide a measurement chart and scales for the children to measure their height and weight. Help them record their findings.

Thinking Me

Day 3

Materials
Swimmy by Leo Lionni

Morning Circle
1. Read *Swimmy* to the children.
2. Let the children discuss how Swimmy solves his problem. Ask questions like, "How would the story be different if Swimmy were a big fish?" and "What do you think might have happened if Swimmy hadn't found a solution to his problem?"

Story Circle
Oh! The Thinks You Can Think by Dr. Seuss

Music and Movement
Let's Pretend by Hap Palmer

Learning Centers

Art

Doodle Art
Make doodles on sheets of paper. Encourage the children to make pictures from them, then draw their own doodles and make them into pictures.

Fine Motor

Paper Clip Pick-Up
Spill a pile of paper clips on the table. Provide a small whisk broom, a magnet and a pair of tweezers. Ask the children to find the easiest way to pick up the clips.

Language

What's Missing?
Display five familiar objects. Ask one child to remove one object while the others cover their eyes. Invite the children to look again and tell which object is missing.

Math

Patterns
Create several patterns with multi-link cubes, blocks or other classroom objects and invite the children to extend the patterns or create their own.

Sand and Water Table

Solid Sort
Provide a strainer, a colander, three empty bowls and a mixture of birdseed, marbles and sand. Ask the children to separate the marbles, sand and birdseed. Scatter the birdseed outside when finished.

Science

Mystery Footprints
Cut out several sets of bird footprints and cat paw prints. Attach a set of cat prints, then a set of bird prints, to the floor. At the end, have just cat prints. Ask, "What do you think happened to the bird?"

Feeling Me

Day 4

Materials

6" (15 cm) paper plate for each child with a smiling face drawn on one side and a frowning face on the other

Morning Circle

1. Sing "If You're Happy and You Know It" with the children (see the appendix, pages 394-395).
2. Give each child one of the paper plates.
3. Make a series of statements and ask the children to respond by showing the side of the plate that represents how they feel about the statement. If they feel neither happy nor sad about a statement, they keep the plate in their laps.

Story Circle

Feelings by Aliki

Music and Movement

"A Really Good Feeling" from *Bert and Ernie's Sing Along*

Learning Centers

Art

Fingerpainting

Invite the children to fingerpaint to different kinds of music (e.g., rock and roll, jazz, classical, country, blues).

Art

Happy Pictures

Encourage the children to draw pictures of things that make them feel happy.

Cooking and Snack

Pizza Faces

Let the children make Face Pizzas on English muffins. Encourage them to arrange the toppings (such as green peppers, pimentos, cheese, olives, etc.) to look like different facial expressions.

Dramatic Play

Me Puppets

Take photographs of the children and enlarge them to 8" x 10" (20 cm x 25 cm) size. Cut out and mount the pictures on popsicle sticks. Encourage the children to stage a puppet show.

Fine Motor

Things I Like

Invite the children to cut out magazine pictures of things they like.

Games

Feelings Concentration

Encourage the children to play Feelings Concentration (see directions in the appendix, pages 406).

Celebrating Me

Materials

butcher paper or poster board, markers

Morning Circle

1. Make a birthday graph on butcher paper or a large sheet of poster board.
2. Let each child place an X under the month he or she was born.
3. Make comparisons (e.g., more children born in November than in December, no birthdays in April).
4. Why are birthdays special? Explain to the children that a birthday is a celebration of beginning life.
5. Tell the children, "Today we are going to celebrate all our birthdays together. It's the Giant Birthday Celebration!"

Story Circle

Moira's Birthday by Robert Munsch

Music and Movement

"Special Day" from *Songs for the Whole Day* by Thomas Moore

Learning Centers

Art

Birthday Hats
Provide construction paper, staplers, stickers, streamers and markers to make birthday hats.

Fine Motor

Gift Wrapping
Provide a variety of boxes and wrapping paper for the children to practice wrapping presents.

Cooking and Snack

Cupcakes
Let the children decorate cupcakes with icing, sprinkles, shredded coconut, etc.

Language

Making Invitations
Encourage the children to make party invitations with construction paper, crayons and decorative scraps.

Dramatic Play

Birthday Party
Provide paper plates, playdough, wrapped boxes and party hats to role-play a birthday party.

Math

Candle Sort
Encourage the children to sort and classify an assortment of birthday candles.

My Sense of Touch

Materials

variety of objects with different textures, chart paper and marker

Morning Circle

1. Bring in several objects with different textures (e.g., satin, sandpaper, net, cotton).
2. Pass the objects around and ask the children to describe how each item feels.
3. How do we know the difference in materials? Encourage the children to understand that we use our hands to touch and feel.
4. Make a list of other things we do with our hands.

Story Circle

I Can Tell By Touching by Carolyn Otto

Music and Movement

"Where Is Thumbkin?" from *Where Is Thumbkin?* by The Learning Station

Learning Centers

Art

Textured Fingerpaints
Mix fingerpaint or tempera paint with sand, sawdust or salt. Invite the children to fingerpaint with the textured paints.

Language

Hand Books
Let the children trace around their hands to make Hand Book pages. On each page, they draw or write about something they do with their hands.

Blocks

Textured Building
Provide a variety of textured materials (e.g., carpet squares, corrugated cardboard, pie tins, egg cartons and baskets) for building.

Math

Finger Patterns
Provide the children with small rubber bands of different colors and encourage them to make patterns on a cut-out pattern of their fingers (e.g., two red, one blue or red-blue-red-blue).

Fine Motor

Sand Drawing
Sprinkle salt or sand on a cookie sheet or shallow pan and encourage the children to draw in it with their fingers.

Science

Feely Box
Place objects with different textures in a bag or a box with a hole cut in one end. Have the children reach in and describe the objects they touch, or match objects with the same texture.

My Sense of Sound

Materials
a variety of musical instruments, chart paper and marker

Morning Circle
1. Bring a variety of musical instruments to the circle.
2. Let the children play the instruments and compare the sounds they make.
3. Ask them how we are able to hear the differences in the sounds.
4. Make a list of all the things we can hear.

Story Circle
The Listening Walk by Paul Showers

Music and Movement
"Play Your Instruments" from *Play Your Instruments and Make a Pretty Sound* by Ella Jenkins

Learning Centers

Blocks

Bell Ringers
Hang bells from the ceiling with yarn in an out-of-the-way place in the classroom. Encourage the children to toss beanbags and try to ring the bells.

Fine Motor

Jingle Bracelets
Provide yarn and jingle bells of different sizes for the children to make bracelets. Put pipe cleaners on the yarn ends to make stringing easier.

Games

Listen and Tell
Play Listen and Tell. Blindfold one child. Invite a second child to make a noise. Ask the blindfolded child to point in the direction of the sound.

Listening

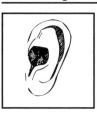

Sound Canisters
Make sound canisters by filling empty film canisters with things like bells, paper clips and sand. Make two of each and let the children match sounds that are alike.

Music

Rhythm Band
Invite the children to experiment with rhythm band instruments.

Science

Sound Jars
Provide glasses or baby food jars with varying amounts of water inside. Encourage the children to tap the glasses with spoons to make different sounds and pitches.

My Sense of Smell

Day 8

Materials

orange and grapefruit, cutting board and knife (optional), potpourri, plastic bottle,
glue, nail and hammer (for teacher only)

Morning Circle

1. Bring an orange and a grapefruit to the circle. If the smell of each is not strong, cut the fruits in half. Pass both around the circle for each child to smell.
2. Ask one child to close her eyes. Hand one of the fruits to her and ask her to identify it.
3. Ask the child, "How did you know? What other things do we smell each day?"
4. Fill a plastic bottle with potpourri and glue the lid on. Punch holes in the bottle and then pass it around the circle so the children can smell the potpourri.

Story Circle

Smell by J. M. Parramon and J. J. Puig

Music and Movement

"Popcorn" from *We All Live Together* by Greg and Steve

Learning Centers

Art

Smelly Art
Provide scented markers and encourage the children to draw pictures illustrating their favorite smells.

Discovery

Scratch and Sniff
Let the children use wet cotton swabs to spread flavored, powdered gelatin on paper. Let dry, then scratch and sniff.

Fine Motor

Potpourri Bags
Provide spices such as cloves, cinnamon sticks and mint leaves and 8" (20 cm) squares of net. Invite the children to fill each square with the spices and tie together with ribbon.

Fine Motor

Scented Playdough
Make playdough (see the recipe in the appendix, page 388). Add extracts and oils to create scented playdough. Substituting massage oil for vegetable oil in the recipe works great.

Math

Fragrance Graph
Spray different fragrances on three index cards. Let the children smell the cards and vote for their favorite. Graph the results.

Science

Smelly Jars
Prepare Smelly Jars for the children to smell. Soak cotton balls in flavorings (e.g., lemon, peppermint, orange). Put each "flavor" in a baby food jar and punch holes in the lid.

My Sense of Sight

Materials
Brown Bear, Brown Bear by Bill Martin Jr., chart paper and marker

Morning Circle
1. Ask the children to describe things they saw on the way to school.
2. Make a list of the things they describe.
3. Talk about things the children would miss if they were asleep or blindfolded.
4. Read *Brown Bear, Brown Bear* to the children.

Story Circle
Take Another Look by Tana Hoban

Music and Movement
Invite the children to play I Spy (see the directions in the appendix, page 403).

Learning Centers

Art

Magnified Pictures
Encourage the children to draw pictures while looking through a magnifying glass.

Language

Finger Spelling
Help the children learn to finger spell their names using the American Manual Alphabet (for letter formations, see the appendix, pages 439–440).

Dramatic Play

Sunglass Views
Provide a variety of sunglasses for pretend play. Make more colored lenses with colored cellophane. How does the world look different?

Math

Eye Sort
Provide different sizes and colors of wiggly eyes for the children to sort.

Games

Pin the Tail on the Donkey
Invite the children to play Pin the Tail on the Donkey.

Science

Up-Close Eyes
Provide close-up pictures of human and animal eyes for the children to examine. Fill a clear, empty soda bottle with hair gel (such as Dippity-Do) and wiggle eyes. Add it to the center just for fun.

My Sense of Taste

Materials
dill pickles, sugar cookies, plates, mirror

Morning Circle
1. Pass a plate of dill pickles around and invite each child to eat one.
2. Ask the children to describe the taste.
3. Pass sugar cookies around. Let each child eat one and describe that taste.
4. Ask the children to compare the two tastes.
5. Tell the children that the taste buds on our tongue distinguish tastes for us. Pass a mirror around and let the children look at their taste buds.

Story Circle
Taste by J. M. Parramon and J. J. Puig

Music and Movement
"Make Myself Some Cookies" from *I Am Special* by Thomas Moore

Learning Centers

Art

Favorite Food Pictures
Invite the children to draw pictures of things they like to eat.

Language

Recipe Dictation
Invite the children to dictate recipes for their favorite foods.

Dramatic Play

Restaurant
Provide props for the children to set up a restaurant, such as menus, trays, dishes, aprons and order forms.

Math

Food Classification
Provide magazine pictures of foods and let the children classify them according to whether they like or dislike the food pictured or according to categories such as fruit, meat, vegetable, dairy product.

Fine Motor

Peanut Butter Playdough
Let the children make and eat peanut butter playdough (see the recipe in the appendix, page 390).

Science

Substance Sort
Provide substances that look alike, such as salt and sugar, vinegar and water, flour and baking soda. Let the children sample each to determine the differences. Encourage them to describe how they taste and look (same or different).

Additional Books for Gotta Be Me

Arthur's Eyes by Marc Brown

Bright Eyes, Brown Skin by Cheryl Willis Hudson and Bernette G. Ford

Brown Bear, Brown Bear, What Do You See? by Bill Martin, Jr.

Don't Touch! by Suzy Kline

The Ear Book by Al Perkins

Everybody Has Feelings by Charles E. Avery

The Five Senses: Hearing by Maria Ruis

The Five Senses: Sight by Maria Ruis

The Five Senses: Smell by Maria Ruis

The Five Senses: Taste by Maria Ruis

The Five Senses: Touch by Maria Ruis

Here Are My Hands by Bill Martin, Jr. and John Archambault

I Can Do It Myself by Lessie Jones Little

I Like Me! by Nancy Carlson

Indoor Noisy Book by Margaret Wise Brown

The Joy of Signing by Lottie Riekehof

My Feet by Aliki

My Five Senses by Aliki

My Hands by Aliki

The Nose Book by Al Perkins

Polar Bear, Polar Bear, What Did You Hear? by Bill Martin Jr.

Sense Suspense by Bruce McMillan

Smelling by Kathy Billingslea Smith & Victoria Crenson

Something Special by David McPhail

Sounds All Around by Fay Robinson

The Touch Me Book by Pat and Eve Witte

When I Get Bigger by Mercer Mayer

The More We Get Together

Family and friends are an important part of every child's life. This unit celebrates family and friends.

Unit at a Glance

Day	Focus	Centers	Story Circle	Music/Movement
1	**Family Members Help Each Other**	Family Portraits Family Dinner Family Pictures Washing Dishes Silver Sort Family Names	A Chair for My Mother	The Farmer in the Dell
2	**Families Come in All Shapes and Sizes**	Building Homes Stick Puppets Wash the Baby Family Puzzles Family Puppet Show One-to-One	Blueberries for Sal	Where Is Thumbkin?
3	**Families Have Roots**	Tempera Trees No-Bake Cookies Family Dress-Up Family Concentration Family Trees Animal Families	Granpa	Grandmother, May I?
4	**Families Celebrate Together**	Celebration Pictures Icing on the Cupcake Birthday Party Table Games Celebration Stories Greeting Cards	The Relatives Came	She'll Be Comin' 'Round the Mountain
5	**Our Family Members Are Our Friends**	Laundry Fold Helping Hands Helping Pictures Family Puppets Story Time Matching Socks	Owl Moon	Mulberry Bush

Day	Focus	Centers	Story Circle	Music/Movement
6	Friends Help Each Other	Friends at the Easel Tower Building Tic-Tac-Toe Copy Patterns Three-Legged Race Identify by Touch	That's What a Friend Is	Friendship March
7	Friends Come in All Sizes	Friendly Fun Pictures Friendship Mobile Friends Dress-Up Body Tracing Find a Friend People Sort	The Lion and the Mouse	Partner Dance
8	Friends Have Fun Together	Fingerpaints Playdough Table Games Puppet Show Friends Book Dance	Chester's Way	Belly Laughs
9	Friends Can Live Far Away	Red and Green Auto Transport Pack for a Trip Magnetic Maze Pen Pals Can Telephones	Arthur's Pen Pal	Red Light, Green Light
10	Friends Share	Community Crayons Friendship Soup Friendship Bracelets Friendly Stories Tricycle Timer Bubbles for Two	Amos and Boris	Cooperative Musical Chairs

Family Members Help Each Other

Day 1

Materials
chart paper, pen

Morning Circle
1. Ask the children to describe or define what a family is.
2. As definitions emerge, help the children focus on the aspect of family members helping each other.
3. Make a list of ways family members help each other.
4. Encourage the children to bring family photographs to school tomorrow.

Story Circle
A Chair for My Mother by Vera B. Williams

Music and Movement
Sing and play "The Farmer in the Dell" (see the directions in the appendix, page 402).

Learning Centers

Art

Family Portraits
Encourage the children to draw family portraits.

Math

Washing Dishes
Provide plastic dishes for the children to wash, dry and arrange on the table from smallest to largest.

Dramatic Play

Family Dinner
Invite the children to assume family roles and work together to "cook" and serve dinner.

Math

Silver Sort
Provide silverware for the children to arrange into trays.

Fine Motor

Family Pictures
Provide scissors and magazines. Invite the children to cut out pictures of family members helping each other.

Writing

Family Names
Write names of family members (Mom, Dad, Brother, Sister, etc.) on index cards. Provide tracing paper and pencils for the children to trace.

Families Come in All Shapes and Sizes

Materials
chart paper, pen or marker (optional)

Morning Circle
1. Ask the children about the members of their families.
2. You may want to record their descriptions on chart paper, or make a chart of the number of family members using tally marks for each family member.
3. Help the children see that families come in all sizes and configurations. You may want to place emphasis on a new baby if one child in the class has a new brother or sister, or talk about aspects of the family that the children are interested in.

Story Circle
Blueberries for Sal by Robert McCloskey

Music and Movement
"Where Is Thumbkin?" from *Where Is Thumbkin?* by The Learning Station

Learning Centers

Blocks

Building Homes
Invite the children to build family homes.

Games

Family Puzzles
Make photocopies of the children's family portraits. Laminate and cut into puzzle pieces for the children to put together.

Construction

Stick Puppets
Invite the children to decorate tongue depressors to represent their family members.

Language

Family Puppet Show
Provide puppets for the children to put on a show about a family. Use illustrations from Family Concentration (see the appendix, page 407) to make the puppets.

Dramatic Play

Wash the Baby
Provide a baby doll, wash tub, wash cloth and towel. Encourage the children to bathe the baby.

Math

One-to-One
Invite the children to put one button for each family member in a resealable plastic bag. Send the bags home with a note for families to verify that the one-to-one correspondence is correct.

Families Have Roots

Materials
Family Tree pattern (see the appendix, page 425)

Morning Circle
1. Use a copy of the Family Tree pattern to trace your family back to your grandparents. Write in the names of all your family members.
2. Show and explain your family tree to the children.
3. Ask the children about their parents and grandparents.
4. Give each child a copy of the Family Tree pattern to take home for parents to fill out.

Story Circle
Granpa by John Burningham

Music and Movement
Invite the children to play Grandmother, May I? like Mother, May I? (see the directions in the appendix, page 404).

Learning Centers

Art

Tempera Trees
Provide tempera paints at the easel. Encourage the children to paint pictures of trees.

Games

Family Concentration
Invite the children to play Family Concentration (see the appendix, page 407).

Cooking and Snack

No-Bake Cookies
Encourage the children to make No-Bake Cookies to share with their families (see the recipe in the appendix, page 389).

Language

Family Trees
Encourage the children to dictate a sentence about each family member in the tree.

Dramatic Play

Family Dress-Up
Provide dress-up clothes for the children to dress up like different family members.

Science

Animal Families
Provide pictures of animal families for the children to look at.

Families Celebrate Together   Day 4

Materials
photos or magazine pictures of family celebrations (optional), chart paper, marker

Morning Circle
1. Discuss family celebrations with the children. Show the pictures of family celebrations.
2. Ask the children to describe their family celebrations (e.g., birthdays, holidays, picnics).
3. Make a word web showing different things a family might celebrate.

Story Circle
The Relatives Came by Cynthia Rylant

Music and Movement
"She'll Be Comin' 'Round the Mountain" from *Where Is Thumbkin?* by The Learning Station

Learning Centers

Art

Celebration Pictures
Invite the children to draw pictures of family celebrations.

Games

Table Games
Encourage the children to play easy card games and board games that a family might play, such as Go Fish.

Cooking and Snack

Icing on the Cupcake
Provide colored icing for the children to decorate cupcakes or graham crackers.

Language

Celebration Stories
Place the family celebration pictures in the center and encourage the children to dictate stories about them.

Dramatic Play

Birthday Party
Provide props for a picnic or birthday party.

Writing

Greeting Cards
Provide construction paper, crayons and markers, glue, scissors and recycled greeting cards. Invite the children to create greeting cards for special family members.

Our Family Members Are Our Friends

Materials
none

Morning Circle
1. Ask questions that will help the children determine what a friend is. For example, "Who do you enjoy spending time with? Who helps you when you need help?"
2. Encourage the children to discuss times when their family members are also their friends.

Story Circle
Owl Moon by Jane Yolen

Music and Movement
Invite the children to sing "Mulberry Bush" (see the appendix, page 397).

Learning Centers

Dramatic Play

Laundry Fold
Provide assorted items of clothing so the children can fold the laundry.

Language

Family Puppets
Provide family puppets and encourage the children to act out situations where family members are friends.

Fine Motor

Helping Hands
Invite the children to find and cut out a magazine picture showing something they do to help at home. Encourage them to trace around a hand and glue the picture in the center of the hand.

Listening

Story Time
Record *Owl Moon* on tape and place it in the center for the children to enjoy.

Language

Helping Pictures
Encourage the children to draw a picture of a family member being a friend and dictate a sentence about the picture.

Math

Matching Socks
Provide several pairs of socks for the children to match and roll together.

Friends Help Each Other · Day 6

Materials
The Enormous Carrot by Vladimir Vagin

Morning Circle
1. Read the story to the children.
2. Help the children act out the story of the giant carrot.
3. Ask the children how they were able to pull the carrot out of the ground.
4. Invite the children to describe ways that they have helped friends and ways friends have helped them. Don't forget community friends.

Story Circle
That's What a Friend Is by Patrick Hallinan

Music and Movement
"Friendship March" from *Kidding Around with Steve and Greg* by Steve and Greg

Learning Centers

Art

Friends at the Easel
Encourage the children to choose a friend to create a collaborative painting at the easel.

Math

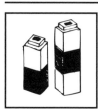

Copy Patterns
Provide color tiles for each pair of the children. Encourage the children to take turns creating and copying patterns.

Blocks

Tower Building
Invite the children to work in pairs building towers. Which pair can build the tallest tower?

Outdoors

Three-Legged Race
Help the children run three-legged races. Use soft cloths to tie their legs together.

Games

Tic-Tac-Toe
Provide chalk and a chalkboard. Encourage the children to play Tic-Tac-Toe with a friend.

Science

Identify by Touch
Provide a blindfold and several unique objects. Encourage the children to work in pairs, taking turns identifying the objects by touch only.

Friends Come in All Sizes

Day 7

Materials
pictures of people of different ages doing things together

Morning Circle
1. Tell the children about friends you have: some older, some younger, maybe even some from the animal kingdom.
2. Show pictures of people doing things together, such as walking, riding bicycles, picnicking and so on.
3. Lead the children to discuss activities they share with friends of different ages (sizes).

Story Circle
The Lion and the Mouse by Aesop

Music and Movement
Do a partner dance such as "Paw Paw Patch" from *One Elephant, Deux Elephant* by Sharon, Lois and Bram.

Learning Centers

Art

Friendly Fun Pictures
Invite the children to draw pictures of themselves having fun with a friend (younger or older).

Construction

Friendship Mobile
Provide paper circles. Invite the children to name a friend for each circle, then draw a picture of that friend inside. String the circles to make Friendship Mobiles.

Dramatic Play

Friends Dress-Up
Provide dress-up clothes in a variety of sizes. Invite the children to help dress each other.

Fine Motor

Body Tracing
Encourage the children to trace around each other's bodies on butcher paper and then color in the details.

Games

Find a Friend
Play Find a Friend. Photocopy two sets of class photos. Glue one set inside a colored folder. Let the children use the other set as cards for matching.

Math

People Sort
Provide magazine pictures of people of different sizes. Invite the children to sort the pictures into groups.

Friends Have Fun Together   Day 8

Materials
none

Morning Circle
Help the children brainstorm a list of fun activities friends can do together, such as play games, dance, sing, ride bikes, have picnics and so on.

Story Circle
Chester's Way by Kevin Henkes

Music and Movement
Invite the children to lie on the floor with their heads on each other's stomachs. Encourage giggling and laughing. Ask them to describe what giggling and laughing feels like.

Learning Centers

Art

Fingerpaints
Provide fingerpaints and paper. Invite the children to work together if they want.

Language

Puppet Show
Provide puppets for the children to put on a friendly puppet show.

Fine Motor

Playdough
Provide clay or playdough for the children to work with. Suggest that they work with a friend.

Language

Friends Book
Encourage the children to make books of fun things they can do with their friends.

Games

Table Games
Provide a table game, such as Candyland or Ants in the Pants, for the children to play.

Music

Dance
Play some favorite tunes and encourage the children to dance. Invite them to mimic each other's movements.

Friends Can Live Far Away

Materials
letter from a friend or relative

Morning Circle
1. Read a note or letter from a friend who lives in another town.
2. Ask the children about friends they've had who moved away or who live across town or out of town.
3. Talk about ways we communicate with our friends we can't see every day (letters, visits, phone calls).

Story Circle
Arthur's Pen Pal by Lillian Hoban

Music and Movement
Invite the children to play Red Light, Green Light.

Learning Centers

Art

Red and Green
Put out red and green art materials (paper, glitter, sticky dots, markers, crayons, chalk, etc.) and encourage the children to create just red or just green or red and green creations.

Fine Motor

Magnetic Maze
Draw a maze of roads and streets on a cookie sheet. Provide metal cars or glue small magnets to plastic cars. Invite the children to hold a second magnet on the backside of the cookie sheet and use it to move the cars through the maze.

Blocks

Auto Transport
Invite the children to build two houses a distance apart and use cars to transport friends from one house to the other.

Language

Pen Pals
Ask the children to dictate letters to pen pals or to the children in another school.

Dramatic Play

Pack for a Trip
Provide clothing, personal items and luggage. Invite the children to pack for a trip or a sleepover at a friend's house.

Science

Can Telephones
Make can telephones by removing the tops from two soup cans, then punching a hole in the bottoms. Thread a string through each hole; tie a knot on the ends inside each can. Stretch the string and talk to a friend.

Friends Share Things

Day 10

Materials
Stone Soup by Marcia Brown, vegetables, tray

Morning Circle
1. Ask the children to bring a vegetable to school.
2. Read *Stone Soup*.
3. Invite the children to place their vegetables one at a time on a tray. Lead them to see how the vegetable supply grows with each contribution. How different does the whole supply look from one vegetable?

Story Circle
Amos and Boris by William Steig

Music and Movement
Play Cooperative Musical Chairs. Instead of eliminating players, the children find ways to share seats and keep everyone in the game even as chairs are removed.

Learning Centers

Art

Community Crayons
Provide paper and one of each color crayon. Encourage the children to draw a picture that requires sharing the crayons.

Language

Friendly Stories
Invite the children to dictate a story about sharing with a friend.

Cooking and Snack

Friendship Soup
Show the children how to wash, peel and slice their vegetables for the Friendship Soup.

Outdoors

Tricycle Timer
Encourage the children to use a three-minute timer to measure the time each child can spend on the tricycle before sharing with the next rider.

Fine Motor

Friendship Bracelets
Encourage the children to make friendship bracelets by weaving strips of yarn together and tying the ends.

Science

Bubbles for Two
Provide bubble soap and wands. Invite the children to take turns with a friend.

Additional Books for The More We Get Together

Alfie Gives a Hand by Shirley Hughes

All Kinds of Families by Norma Simon

Are You My Mother? by P. D. Eastman

Arthur's Baby by Marc Brown

Best Friends by Miriam Cohen

Black Is Brown Is Tan by Arnold Adoff

Chicken Sunday by Patricia Polacco

Daddy Makes the Best Spaghetti by Anna Grossnickle Hines

Friends by Helme Heine

George and Martha, One Fine Day by James Marshall

Grandfather and I by Helen Buckley

Grandmother and I by Helen Buckley

A Home by Nola Langner Malone

A House Is a House for Me by Mary Hoberman

Jessica by Kevin Henkes

Let's Be Friends Again! by Hans Wilhelm

Loving by Ann Morris

Mama, Do You Love Me? by Barbara M. Joose

Nana Upstairs, Nana Downstairs by Tomie dePaola

Too Many Tamales by Gary Soto

We Are Best Friends by Aliki

Who's in a Family? By Robert Skutch

William and the Good Old Days by Eloise Greenfield

Workers, Tools & Uniforms

It takes lots of people doing lots of jobs to keep our communities going. This unit takes a nonsexist look at a variety of workers, their tools and, when applicable, their uniforms.

Unit at a Glance

Day	Focus	Centers	Story Circle	Music/Movement
1	**Office Workers**	Which Works Best At the Office Tool Match Business Letters Filing Typing	Guess Who	Keyboard Pop-Ups
2	**Grocery Workers**	Container Construction Grocery Store Coupon Clipping Cereal Match-Up Paper-Tube Knock-Down Label Matching	We Keep a Store	Sammy
3	**Hairdressers**	Hairbrush Painting Hair Curling Hair Salon Yarn Braids Haircut Race Watch the Hair Grow	Mop Top	Rapunzel Tug-of-War
4	**Firefighters**	Fiery Art Firefighter's Hat Station House Spot on the Dalmatian Worker Concentration Water Play	The Fire Station	Fire Dance
5	**Carpenters and Painters**	Paint the Town Block Construction Workbench Homebuilders Wallpaper Collage Pulley and Bucket	Building a House	Johnny Works with One Hammer

Day	Focus	Centers	Story Circle	Music/Movement
6	Police Officers	Squad Car Worker Concentration What We Know Lock and Key Match Directing Traffic Fingerprints	A Day in the Life of a Police Officer	Red Light, Green Light
7	Doctors and Dentists	Medical Paintings Toothpaste Doctor's Office Water Transfer Weigh-In Heartbeats	Going to the Doctor	Doctor
8	Teachers	Apple Snacks Classroom Ruler Lines Ring the Bell Magnetic Letters Chalk and Chalkboard	Miss Nelson Is Missing	Teacher, May I?
9	Mail Carriers	Greeting Cards Mailbags and Boxes Post Office Letter Dictation Envelope Sort Weighing Boxes	My Mother the Mail Carrier (Mi Mama la Cartera)	Drop the Letter
10	Bakers	Rolling Pin Press Donuts Bakery Kneading Dough Muffin-Tin Toss Cookie Patterns	Walter the Baker	Muffin Man

Office Workers

Day 1

Materials
office supplies: folders, pens, pencils, paper clips, stapler; pictures of office workers (optional)

Morning Circle
1. Display an assortment of office supplies. Encourage the children to talk about the purpose of each item.
2. Show pictures of office workers, if available.
3. Visit the office workers in your school.

Story Circle
Guess Who by Margaret Miller

Music and Movement
Play Keyboard Pop-Ups. Invite the children to stand together, pretending to be keys on a typewriter or computer keyboard. Call out letters. The children squat when you call out the first letter of their names and stand again when you call out the next letter.

Learning Centers

Discovery

Which Works Best?
Provide an assortment of paper clips, staplers, binder clips, etc. and pieces of paper. The children determine which one holds papers together best. What are other ways to hold papers together?

Dramatic Play

At the Office
Provide materials and help the children set up an office area with typewriter, paper, markers, paper clips, copier (made from box), computer (made from box), phone and dress-up clothes.

Games

Tool Match
Invite the children to play Shadow Tool Match-Up. Lay several office items (e.g., stapler, tape dispenser, paper clip) on black paper, then trace and cut out. Invite the children to match cutouts to materials.

Language

Business Letters
Provide writing paper, carbon paper and pens and pencils. Invite the children to make copies of their business letters.

Math

Filing
Provide file folders and geometric shapes cut from colored index cards. Glue one shape to each file folder. Invite the children to file the cutouts in the folders.

Writing

Typing
Provide a typewriter and paper for the children to explore.

Grocery Workers Day 2

Materials
grocery items: cash register, play money, apron

Morning Circle
1. Encourage the children to talk about trips they've made to the grocery store.
2. Ask the children to name and describe the tools a grocer uses.

Story Circle
We Keep a Store by Anne Shelby

Music and Movement
"Sammy" from *Getting to Know Myself* by Hap Palmer

Learning Centers

Construction

Container Construction
Provide grocery items (e.g., toilet paper tubes, empty boxes and cans, berry baskets), glue and pipe cleaners. Invite the children to create a sculpture.

Dramatic Play

Grocery Store
Provide carts, bags, empty food containers, plastic fruits and vegetables, cash register, play money and aprons. Invite the children to set up a grocery store.

Fine Motor

Coupon Clipping
Provide old magazines, newspapers, coupon booklets and scissors. Encourage the children to clip coupons.

Games

Cereal Match-Up
Cut the front and back panels from several cereal boxes. Encourage the children to match the fronts and backs.

Gross Motor

Paper-Tube Knock-Down
Invite the children to set up empty toilet paper tubes in stacks of three or in rows like bowling pins. Provide foam balls for tossing.

Language

Label Matching
Provide labels from food boxes and cans for the children to match.

Hairdressers Day 3

Materials
hair care items: shampoo, conditioner, comb, brush, curlers, hair dryer, spray bottles; pictures of hairdressers (optional)

Morning Circle
1. If possible, wear your hair in a different style.
2. Display the hair care items.
3. Solicit stories from the children about haircuts and salon visits.
4. Show pictures of hairdressers, if available.

Story Circle
Mop Top by Don Freeman

Music and Movement
Invite the children to play Rapunzel Tug-of-War. Braid or twist three lengths of rope together to make Rapunzel's hair.

Learning Centers

Art

Hairbrush Painting
Invite the children to paint with tempera paint and hairbrushes.

Fine Motor

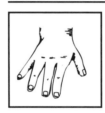
Yarn Braids
Provide strips of yarn for braiding. Provide hair clips and accessories. Encourage the children to pick up the accessories with the clips.

Construction

Hair Curling
Encourage the children to create paper-plate puppets using yarn and ribbon for the hair. Teach the children how to curl ribbon by wrapping it around a pencil.

Games

Haircut Race
Provide yarn ponytails for the children to trim. Make sure they understand they are to cut only one "hair" at a time. Encourage them to choose partners to have a race.

Dramatic Play

Hair Salon
Provide a hair dryer, hair clips, curlers, brushes, combs, mirrors and empty shampoo bottles. Invite the children to set up a hair salon or barber shop.

Science

Watch the Hair Grow
Invite the children to draw faces on Styrofoam cups, then fill them with potting soil and plant rye grass. How long until their "clients" need haircuts?

Firefighters

Materials
firefighter tools: hose, hat, gloves, coat, boots; pictures of firefighters (optional); "Firefighter" from *Songs for the Whole Day* by Thomas Moore

Morning Circle
1. Display firefighter equipment.
2. If possible, invite local firefighters to visit your class.
3. Teach the "Stop, Drop and Roll" safety procedure.
4. Play the song "Firefighter." Discuss some of the responsibilities mentioned.

Story Circle
The Fire Station by Robert Munsch

Music and Movement
Do a Fire Dance. Provide orange, yellow and red streamers. Put on "fiery" music and let the children dance.

Learning Centers

Art

Fiery Art
Provide red, orange and yellow paints for the children to create pictures of fire. Encourage the children to roll marbles or golf balls across the wet paint to add interesting textures and patterns.

Construction

Firefighter's Hat
Invite the children to make firefighter hats (see the directions in the appendix, page 432).

Dramatic Play

Station House
Provide hoses, hats, coats, gloves, boots and a stuffed Dalmatian. Invite the children to set up a fire station. A large box makes a great fire truck.

Games

Pin the Spot on the Dalmatian
Invite the children to play Pin the Spot on the Dalmatian.

Games

Worker Concentration
Make a set of cards for the children to play Worker Concentration (see the appendix, page 408).

Sand and Water Table

Water Play
Provide clear plastic tubing and a variety of containers for water play.

Carpenters and Painters   Day 5

Materials
small object made from wood; carpenter and painter tools: apron, pencil, tape measure, hammer, nails, screwdriver, screws, saw, paintbrushes and rollers; pictures of carpenters and painters (optional)

Morning Circle
1. Bring in a small object made from wood, such as a birdhouse or toy.
2. Display the carpenter apron and tools.
3. Invite the children to talk about how each tool is used.
4. Show pictures of carpenters and painters, if available.

Story Circle
Building a House by Byron Barton

Music and Movement
Sing "Johnny Works with One Hammer" (see the appendix, page 395).

Learning Centers

Art

Paint the Town
Invite the children to use the same tools as house painters (i.e., paintbrushes and rollers with rolling tray) to paint a mural.

Dramatic Play

Homebuilders
Provide a washing machine box for the children to make into a house. Glue bricks (red construction paper) to the outside. Decorate inside with wallpaper.

Blocks

Block Construction
Provide pictures of several different types of buildings. Encourage the children to experiment with blocks to build similar buildings.

Fine Motor

Wallpaper Collage
Provide wallpaper samples, scissors and glue. Invite the children to create a wallpaper collage.

Construction

Workbench
Provide a table, small pieces of wood, a hammer and nails. Encourage the children to build something.

Science

Pulley and Bucket
Provide a pulley, rope and bucket for the children to explore.

Police Officers

Materials
badge, flashlight, whistle, ticket book; pictures of police officers (optional)

Morning Circle
1. Encourage the children to tell what they know about police officers.
2. Show pictures of police officers, if available.

Story Circle
A Day in the Life of a Police Officer by Mary Bowman-Kruhm

Music and Movement
Use whistles to play a familiar song such as "Row, Row, Row Your Boat." Whistle the tune loudly, then softly.

Learning Centers

Dramatic Play

Squad Car
Invite the children to help create a squad car from a large cardboard box. Provide badges, radio, ticket books and flashlights for dramatic play.

Math

Lock and Key Match
Provide an assortment of locks and keys. Invite the children to find the matching sets.

Games

Worker Concentration
Invite the children to play Worker Concentration (see the appendix, page 408).

Outside

Directing Traffic
Set up a tricycle biking path. Suggest that the children take turns directing "traffic."

Listening

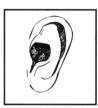

What We Know
Make a tape of what the children know about police officers. Let the children listen to the tape.

Science

Fingerprints
Invite the children to dip their fingertips into tempera paint on a paper towel or a stamp pad, print their fingerprints on paper and examine them with magnifying glasses.

Doctors and Dentists

Day 7

Materials
medical tools and supplies: stethoscope, tongue depressors, medicine bottles, reflex hammer, thermometer, bandages, syringe, toothbrush, toothpaste; pictures of doctors and dentists (optional)

Morning Circle
1. Display a few of the medical tools and supplies.
2. Encourage the children to discuss their visits to doctors and dentists.
3. Show pictures of doctors and dentists, if available.

Story Circle
Going to the Doctor by Fred Rogers

Music and Movement
"Doctor" from *Singing, Moving, and Learning* by Thomas Moore

Learning Centers

Art

Medical Paintings
Fill a hanging IV bag with tempera paint. Encourage the children to paint with drips from the tube. Provide empty syringes and thin paint. Hang paper outside on a wall or fence. Invite the children to squirt paint onto the paper.

Fine Motor

Water Transfer
Provide one empty cup, one cup of water and an eyedropper. Invite the children to transfer the water from one cup to the other using the eyedropper.

Discovery

Toothpaste
Provide old toothbrushes, toothpaste and coins. Invite the children to clean coins with toothpaste, then rinse them.

Math

Weigh-In
Encourage the children to weigh and measure each other. Record measurements on a chart.

Dramatic Play

Doctor's Office
Provide stethoscope, tongue depressors, bandages, syringe (without a needle) and other medical supplies for the children to set up a doctor's office.

Science

Heartbeats
Provide a stethoscope for the children to listen to each other's heartbeats.

Teachers

Day 8

Materials
teaching tools: books, paper, pencils, rulers, charts, posters; pictures of teachers (optional)

Morning Circle
1. Show the teacher's tools.
2. Encourage the children to brainstorm a list of items that remind them of a teacher or a classroom. Find out what they know about older siblings and their school experiences.

Story Circle
Miss Nelson Is Missing by Harry Allard

Music and Movement
Invite the children to play Teacher, May I? as they would Mother, May I? (see the appendix, page 404).

Learning Centers

Cooking and Snack

Apple Snacks
Invite the children to mix 1 cup (250 ml) of sour cream with ½ cup (125 ml) of brown sugar. Provide apple slices for dipping.

Gross Motor

Ring the Bell
Invite the children to play Ring the School Bell. Provide small beanbags for the children to toss at service bells (placed on the floor).

Dramatic Play

Classroom
Provide chalkboard, chalk, chairs, paper, pencil and books. Invite the children to set up a classroom.

Language

Magnetic Letters
Provide metal cookie sheets and magnetic letters for the children to play with.

Fine Motor

Ruler Lines
Provide rulers and crayons for the children to create designs on paper.

Writing

Chalk and Chalkboard
Provide small chalkboards and chalk for the children to practice writing.

Mail Carriers Day 9

Materials
mail box, mail bag, assorted pieces of mail; pictures of postal workers (optional); "Mail Carrier" from *Songs for the Whole Day* by Thomas Moore

Morning Circle
1. Show the stack of mail.
2. Discuss how mail gets from one place to another.
3. Show pictures of mail carriers, if available. Talk about a mail carrier's clothing. Why do all mail carriers dress alike?
4. Encourage the children to talk about the equipment mail carriers need to do their job.
5. Listen to the song "Mail Carrier." Discuss some of the responsibilities mentioned.

Story Circle
My Mother the Mail Carrier (Mi Mama la Cartera) by Inez Maury

Music and Movement
Invite the children to play Drop the Letter as they would Drop the Handkerchief (see the appendix, page 402).

Learning Centers

Art

Greeting Cards
Invite the children to design greeting cards. Provide paper, markers, scissors, glue and other materials.

Language

Letter Dictation
Encourage the children to dictate letters to friends.

Construction

Mailbags and Boxes
Encourage the children to make postal bags from paper bags or mail boxes from shoe boxes.

Math

Envelope Sort
Provide a variety of junk mail envelopes. Invite the children to sort the envelopes into shoe boxes according to size, color or other criteria they come up with.

Dramatic Play

Post Office
Provide shoe boxes, stamps, envelopes, scales, packages and large bags for the children to set up a post office.

Math

Weighing Boxes
Provide a scale and several boxes. Invite the children to weigh the boxes and prepare them for mailing.

Bakers

Materials
small pastries or muffins; bakery supplies: muffin tins, cookie sheets, cake and bread pans, rolling pin, bowls, mixers, spoons, measuring cups, apron, hat; pictures of bakers (optional); bread machine (optional)

Morning Circle
1. If available, have bread-making machine baking bread when the children arrive. You can share the bread later on in the day.
2. Serve small pastries or muffins from a bakery.
3. Ask the children who they think made the treats.
4. Show pictures of a baker, if available. Talk about the baker's hat and apron. Why do bakers wear these?
5. Show tools from the bakery. Encourage the children to talk about uses for each tool.

Story Circle
Walter the Baker by Eric Carle

Music and Movement
Invite the children to sing "Muffin Man" (see the appendix, page 396).

Learning Centers

Art

Rolling Pin Press
Invite the children to fingerpaint on the table top. Encourage them to lay a sheet of paper over their design and then roll over it with a rolling pin to make a print.

Fine Motor

Kneading Dough
Provide flour dough for the children to knead, roll, shape and cut.

Cooking and Snack

Donuts
Invite the children to make donuts. Punch or cut holes in prepared refrigerator biscuits, then deep fry them. Dust with powdered sugar.

Games

Muffin-Tin Toss
Provide small pompoms or balls of playdough for the children to toss into muffin tins.

Dramatic Play

Bakery
Provide aprons, hats, bakery tools and playdough for the children to set up a bakery.

Math

Cookie Patterns
Provide two or three different kinds of construction paper cookies with magnets on the back. Encourage the children to create and copy cookie patterns on metal cookie sheets.

Additional Books for Workers, Tools & Uniforms

An Auto Mechanic by Douglas Florian
At the Supermarket by David Hautzig
The Checkup by Helen Oxenbury
Daddies at Work by Eve Merriam
Garage Song by Sarah Wilson
The Jolly Postman by Janet and Allan Ahlberg
A Letter to Amy by Ezra Jack Keats
Mommies at Work by Eve Merriam
My Doctor by Harlow Rockwell
My Father's Luncheonette by M. Greenberg
My First Doctor Visit by Julia Allen
Storekeeper by Tracey Campbell Pearson
What's It Like to Be a Chef by Susan Poskazer
What's It Like to Be a Doctor by Judith Bauer
What's It Like to Be a Grocer by Shelley Wilks
What's It Like to Be a Nurse by Judith Bauer
What's It Like to Be a Police Officer by Michael J. Pellowski

How Much Is That Doggie?

Most children love animals, and family pets often play a big part in their lives. This unit explores a variety of pets, their special characteristics and what it takes to be a responsible pet owner.

Unit at a Glance

Day	Focus	Centers	Story Circle	Music/Movement
1	Dogs	Puppy Paw Prints Puppy Paw Biscuits Veterinarian Dog Food Pick-Up Biscuits in the Bowl Dog Sort	The Puppy Who Wanted a Boy	Dog and Bone
2	Rabbits	Modeling Clay Rabbits Carrot Snacks Bunny Tail Pick-Up Bunny Hopping Bunny Tales Carrot Tops	The Tale of Peter Rabbit	Bunny Hop
3	Cats	Whisker Paintings Cat Walk Cat Toys Pin the Tail on the Cat Cat Cartoons Cat's Eye Marbles	Millions of Cats	My Kitty Cat
4	Turtles	Crayon Rubbings Turtle Shell Boxes Name That Turtle Turtle Shell Count Hidden Turtles Turtle Observation	Turtle Take Their Time	Turtle Rock
5	Birds	Feather Painting Bird Cages Birdseed Sweep Drop the Feather Bird Watching Birdseed Designs	Pete the Parakeet	Fly Like a Bird

Day	Focus	Centers	Story Circle	Music/Movement
6	Fish	Fish Stencil Cracker Pick-Up Beanbag Toss Fish Story Starters Order by Size Fish Observation	Rainbow Fish	How Does It Feel to Be a Fish?
7	Frog	Painted Frogs Frog Legs Feed the Frog Lily Pad Toss Lily Pad Match Frog Watch	A Boy, a Dog and a Frog	Leap Frog
8	Exotic Pets	My Own Snake Lizard Delight Clay Snakes Ordering Snakes Hide-n-Seek Snakes Exotic Pets Observation	The Mixed-Up Chameleon	Move like Snakes and Lizards
9	Temporary Pets	Grasshopper Hop Pet Concentration Insect Hunt Pet Stories Pet Sort Insect Cages	Can I Keep Him?	Caterpillar, Caterpillar, Butterfly
10	Pet Show	Prize Ribbons Cages and Stages Pet Collars Animal Puppets My Favorite Pet Animal Graph	Pet Show	Animal Antics

Dogs

Day 1

Materials
a real dog if available, pictures of dogs

Morning Circle
1. Bring in pictures of dogs or a real dog, accompanied by its owner. Note: dogs sometimes get nervous around large groups of small children.
2. Talk about dogs as pets. Where do they live? What do they eat?

Story Circle
The Puppy Who Wanted a Boy by Jane Thayer

Music and Movement
Play Dog and Bone. The children sit in a circle. Choose a child to be IT. IT goes to another part of the room while the others choose one child to hold a construction-paper bone. IT returns and tries to guess who has the bone.

Learning Centers

Art

Puppy Paw Prints
Let the children make puppy paw prints by pressing a fist in fingerpaint and then on a piece of paper.

Fine Motor

Dog Food Pick-Up
Provide dog biscuits, dry dog food, tongs, tweezers and two dog bowls. Encourage the children to use tongs and tweezers to move the bones and food from one bowl to the other. (Leftover dog food and biscuits can be given to the animal shelter.)

Cooking and Snack

Puppy Paw Biscuits
Give each child an uncooked refrigerator biscuit. Have them press their folded fists with fingers bent into the biscuits. Brown and serve.

Games

Biscuits in the Bowl
Provide dog biscuits and a large bowl. Invite the children to drop or toss the dog biscuits into the dog bowl. (Leftover dog food and biscuits can be given to the animal shelter.)

Dramatic Play

Veterinarian
Fill the center with stuffed animals, stethoscopes and lab coats. Let the children play veterinarian.

Math

Dog Sort
Give the children stuffed dogs in three sizes or more and ask them to sort them by size.

Rabbits

Materials
a rabbit if available, pictures of rabbits

Morning Circle
1. Show the children the live rabbit or pictures of rabbits.
2. Talk about what it would be like to have a rabbit for a pet. Where would it live? What would it eat?

Story Circle
The Tale of Peter Rabbit by Beatrix Potter

Music and Movement
"Bunny Hop" from *Hokey Pokey* by Sharron Lucky

Learning Centers

Art

Modeling Clay Rabbits
Provide the children with modeling clay or playdough and encourage them to create rabbits.

Gross Motor

Bunny Hopping
Place a strip of masking tape on the floor as a starting line. Encourage the children to see how far they can squat and hop. Let the children use blocks to measure their hops.

Cooking and Snack

Carrot Snacks
Invite the children to peel and cut carrots for snacks. Provide sour cream and a dip mix for the children to make dip.

Listening

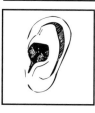

Bunny Tales
Let the children dictate bunny tales into a cassette recorder and then use their "bunny ears" to listen to their stories.

Fine Motor

Bunny Tail Pick-Up
Provide tongs, cotton balls and two containers. Encourage the children to use the tongs to move bunny tails from one container to the other.

Science

Carrot Tops
Provide carrot tops, plastic containers, potting soil, spoons and a watering can. Invite the children to plant the carrot tops.

Cats

Materials

a cat if possible, pictures of cats, chart paper and marker

Morning Circle

1. Show the children pictures of cats.
2. Ask the children to tell you what they know about cats.
3. Let the children demonstrate walking, stretching, slinking, stalking and sleeping like a cat.
4. Make a list of "cat words" such as catnip, cat's eye marble, cattails, cat nap.

Story Circle

Millions of Cats by Wanda Gag

Music and Movement

"My Kitty Cat," from *Animal Antics* by Hap Palmer

Learning Centers

Art

Whisker Paintings
Give the children broom straws or pine needles to use as cat-whisker paintbrushes.

Games

Pin the Tail on the Cat
Draw a cat without a tail on a piece of butcher paper. Make tails out of yarn. Let the children play Pin the Tail on the Cat.

Blocks

Cat Walk
Make a few sets of cat whiskers the children can wear. Have the children build a walled pathway with blocks. Encourage them to crawl along the path without letting their whiskers touch a wall.

Language

Cat Cartoons
White-out the words on cartoons with cat characters. Let the children make up new lines.

Fine Motor

Cat Toys
Encourage the children to make cat toys by winding yarn into balls. Let the children bring them home.

Science

Cat's Eye Marbles
Look at cat's eye marbles with a magnifying glass. Do they really look like cat's eyes?

Turtles

Materials

a turtle if possible, pictures of turtles

Morning Circle

1. Bring a turtle for the children to observe, if possible. Show pictures of turtles.
2. Ask the children, "If you had a pet turtle, where would it live? What would it eat?"
3. Explain that turtles that live in water have webbed feet and land turtles (tortoises) do not.

Story Circle

Turtles Take Their Time by Allan Fowler

Music and Movement

Encourage the children to lie on their backs, pull their knees and heads toward their tummies and rock to music. It isn't easy.

Learning Centers

Art

Crayon Rubbings
Invite the children to make crayon rubbings on floor tiles. Do they look like turtle shells?

Math

Turtle Shell Count
Write the numerals one to five on five paper plates. Have the children count the correct number of turtle shells (walnut shells) into each plate.

Gross Motor

Turtle Shell Boxes
Paint small boxes green. Encourage the children to move like turtles as they wear them on their backs like turtle shells.

Sand and Water Table

Hidden Turtles
Provide plastic turtles for the children to hide and find in the sand.

Language

Name That Turtle
Encourage the children to draw a picture of a turtle and choose a name for you to transcribe underneath.

Science

Turtle Observation
Place a turtle in an aquarium for the children to observe. Provide a magnifying glass for close-up looks at the shell and the skin.

Birds

Materials
live bird in a cage (if possible), pictures of parakeets, parrots, doves, etc.

Morning Circle
1. Ask the children if any of them have a pet bird.
2. Show pictures of pet birds or show a real bird if available.
3. Discuss what pet birds eat, how they bathe and where they live.

Story Circle
Pete the Parakeet by Sharon Gordon

Music and Movement
Give the children paper or plastic plates to use as wings. Play music and encourage the children to use their "wings" to soar like birds.

Learning Centers

Art

Feather Painting
Provide tempera paints or watercolors and a variety of feathers for the children to use as brushes. (Feather dusters are a good source of feathers.)

Games

Drop the Feather
Play Drop the Feather. Provide a bowl or bucket and several feathers. Encourage the children to drop the feathers into the bowl. What makes this difficult?

Construction

Bird Cages
Provide wooden or plastic straw connecting toys, such as Tinker Toys or Connecto-Straws, for the children to build bird cages with.

Science

Bird Watching
Provide pictures of several different birds for the children to examine. If possible, bring in a live bird for the children to observe.

Fine Motor

Birdseed Sweep
Provide birdseed, scoops, pastry brushes and margarine tubs. Encourage the children to scoop birdseed from the margarine tub onto a large piece of construction paper, then brush it back into a scoop and pour it into the tub.

Writing

Birdseed Designs
Pour birdseed onto a cookie sheet. Invite the children to "write" in the seed with their fingers.

Fish

Materials

a fish in a fish bowl

Morning Circle

1. Bring a fish in a fish bowl to the circle. Let the children take turns describing the fish. How does it move? How does it breathe?
2. Have the children move around the room pretending to be fish in a fish bowl, then a fish in the ocean.

Story Circle

Rainbow Fish by Marcus Pfister

Music and Movement

"How Does It Feel to Be a Fish?" from *We've Got to Come Full Circle* by Tom Wisner and Teresa Whitaker

Learning Centers

Art

Fish Stencil

Provide the children with a cardboard fish stencil. Encourage them to make fish and glue sequins on for scales. Always supervise the children when they use sequins. [Use caution.]

Language

Fish Story Starters

Fill a fish bowl with story starters. Let the children draw one each and dictate a story. Story starters are phrases or sentences used to begin a story. (e.g., "My Aunt Pam caught the biggest fish one day when…").

Fine Motor

Cracker Pick-Up

Give the children fish-shaped crackers, tweezers and two containers. Encourage them to use the tweezers to move the crackers from one container to the other.

Math

Order by Size

Cut out eight fish shapes of graduated sizes. Encourage the children to order the shapes from smallest to largest.

Gross Motor

Beanbag Toss

Encourage the children to toss beanbags into a fish bowl.

Science

Fish Observation

Let the children observe the fish in the fish bowl with a magnifying glass, or get fish scales from a supermarket and let the children examine them.

Frogs

Materials

a live frog if possible, or pictures of frogs

Morning Circle

1. Show the children a live frog or pictures of several different kinds of frogs (tree frogs, toads, bullfrogs, etc.).
2. Ask the children to talk about frogs they have seen.
3. Discuss where frogs live and what they eat. Do frogs make good pets?
4. Teach the children "Five Little Speckled Frogs."

Story Circle

A Boy, a Dog, and a Frog by Mercer Mayer

Music and Movement

Invite the children to play Leap Frog (see the directions in the appendix, page 404).

Learning Centers

Art

Painted Frogs

Provide several shades of green paint and let the children paint frogs at the easel.

Cooking and Snack

Frog Logs

Invite the children to enjoy Frog Logs (breadsticks) and Lily Pad Dip (spinach dip) for snack.

Fine Motor

Feed the Frog

Spray the ball of a meatball press with green paint. Add two wiggle eyes to create a frog face. Encourage the children to use the frog face to pick up pompoms.

Gross Motor

Lily Pad Toss

Glue two pieces of lily-pad-shaped felt three-fourths of the way around. Slip a service bell inside. Encourage the children to toss beanbags at the lily pad to ring the bell.

Math

Lily Pad Match

Make five frogs out of brown construction paper. Cut five lily pads from construction paper. Place one to five dots on each one. Encourage the children to match frogs to dots on each pad.

Science

Frog Watch

Provide several pictures of frogs for the children to examine. If possible, bring in a live frog for the children to observe.

Exotic Pets (Iguanas, Lizards and Snakes) Day 8

Materials
pictures of iguanas, lizards and snakes

Morning Circle
1. Show the pictures to the children. How are snakes and lizards the same? How are they different?
2. Talk about why these pets are called "exotic."
3. Why might these pets be difficult to keep and take care of?
4. What do these animals eat? Where and how do they sleep? What do they do with their time?

Story Circle
The Mixed-Up Chameleon by Eric Carle

Music and Movement
Encourage the children to move like a snake, then a lizard. Which movement is easier? Why?

Learning Centers

Construction

My Own Snake
Cut sections of bicycle tires for the children to use in printmaking. When the prints are dry, cut them in the shape of snakes and add eyes.

Math

Ordering Snakes
Cut out several snakes of varying lengths. Invite the children to arrange the snakes in order from shortest to longest.

Cooking and Snack

Lizard Delight
Provide raw, washed vegetables (broccoli, carrots, squash, zucchini), a cutting board and a plastic knife. Encourage the children to cut and taste each vegetable.

Sand and Water Table

Hide-n-Seek Snakes
Hide plastic snakes in the dry sand and invite the children to find them.

Fine Motor

Clay Snakes
Provide salt dough, clay or play-dough and challenge the children to make snakes and lizards.

Science

Exotic Pets Observation
Provide pictures of snakes and lizards for the children to examine. If possible, bring in a live snake or lizard for the children to observe.

Temporary Pets

Day 9

Materials
pictures of insects and other small critters that children often catch and keep for a day or two

Morning Circle
1. Show the children pictures of temporary pets.
2. Solicit stories from the children about times they've caught a temporary pet.
3. Discuss why we don't keep insects and other small critters for a long time.

Story Circle
Can I Keep Him? by Steven Kellogg

Music and Movement
Invite the children to play Caterpillar, Caterpillar, Butterfly like they would Duck, Duck, Goose (see the directions in the appendix, page 402).

Learning Centers

Fine Motor

Grasshopper Hop
Play Grasshopper Hop like Tiddly Winks. Provide chips with pictures of grasshoppers glued on top.

Language

Pet Stories
Encourage the children to dictate stories about temporary pets they have had.

Games

Pet Concentration
Create a concentration game and invite the children to play (make two copies of page 424 in the appendix).

Math

Pet Sort
Provide plastic fishing worms, flies and other insects for the children to sort.

Games

Insect Hunt
Hide plastic insects and other small critters in the dramatic play center. Invite the children to find the temporary pets.

Science

Insect Cages
Help the children make a bug cage by cutting out the side of an oatmeal box and covering it with netting.

Pet Show

Materials
stuffed animals from home (Be sure to bring extras for children who forget or who may not have a stuffed animal.)

Morning Circle
1. Send a note home the day before asking the children to bring in a stuffed toy animal the next day.
2. Let the children describe their "pets."

Story Circle
Pet Show by Ezra Jack Keats

Music and Movement
Animal Antics by Hap Palmer

Learning Centers

Art

Prize Ribbons
Let the children make and decorate pet show prize ribbons made from construction paper.

Blocks

Cages and Stages
Encourage the children to build a stage for the pet show or cages for the animals.

Construction

Pet Collars
Provide construction paper, scissors, glue and Velcro. Encourage the children to make collars for their pets. Provide sequins and trinkets for decoration. Supervise the children when using sequins.

Dramatic Play

Animal Puppets
Encourage the children to use animal puppets to put on a pet show.

Language

"My picture is about . . ."

My Favorite Pet
Invite the children to draw a picture of their favorite pet and dictate a sentence telling why it is their favorite.

Math

Animal Graph
Make a graph of the kinds of animals the children brought to school.

Additional Books for How Much Is That Doggie?

Carl Goes Shopping by Alexandra Day

Cats Do, Dogs Don't by Norma Simon

Charlie Anderson by Barbara Abercrombie

The Day Jimmy's Boa Ate the Wash by Trinka Hakes Noble

Emma's Pet by David McPhail

Every Buddy Counts by Stuart Murphy

Hop Jump Ellen Stoll Walsh

I Can't Get My Turtle to Move by Elizabeth O'Donnell

Jump Frog Jump by Robert Kalan

The Last Puppy by Frank Asch

Lost in the Storm by Carol Carrick

My Dog Never Says Please by Suzanne Williams

Pretend You're a Cat by Jean Marzollo

Surprise by Sally Noll

These Are My Pets by Mercer Mayer

It's Raining, It's Pouring

Weather is like magic to children. This unit explores rain, sunshine, snow storms and more.

Unit at a Glance

Day	Focus	Centers	Story Circle	Music/Movement
1	Weather	Weather Art Weather Wheel Weather Station Weather Books Temperatures Weather Words	I Like Weather	Musical Clouds
2	Sunshine	Sunny Pictures Sunglasses Solar Art Weather Concentration Sundial Prisms	Let's Find Out About the Sun	You Are My Sunshine
3	More Sunshine	Sun Hats Sunshine Puppets Sunny Dress-Up Tracing Shadows Summer Clothes Windowsill Garden	What Is the Sun?	Shadow Chase
4	Cloudy Day	Cloud Pictures Cloud Bites Tearing Cloud Match Cloud Songs Water Science	It Looked Like Spilt Milk	Rain, Rain, Go Away
5	Rain	Rainy Day Pictures Rainsticks Thirsty Plants Raindrop Ordering Making Rain Water Path	Rain	Rain Dance

Day	Focus	Centers	Story Circle	Music/Movement
6	More Rain	Rainy Day Art Umbrella Toss Percussion Rainy Day Activities Water Drop Count Terrarium Mud Writing	Listen to the Rain	Rainstick
7	Snow	Snow Cones Freezing Snowflakes Snowflake Match Packaged Snow Float or Drop	The Snowy Day	Snowflake Dance
8	Snow Again	Snow Art Ice Painting Dress the Bear Snow Dough Mitten Match Ice Melt	Frosty the Snowman	The Freeze
9	Wind	Straw Blowing Kites and Windsocks Ping-Pong Race Blow Bubbles Sailboats Paper Planes	Gilberto and the Wind	Scarf Dancing
10	Storms	Storm Paintings Wind Power Hurricane Safety Weather Concentration Hail Sort Tornado	Thundercakes	Storm Dance

Weather

Day 1

Materials
videotape of weather report or photographs showing different weather conditions

Morning Circle
1. Show the video of a weather report or photographs of different weather conditions to the children.
2. Talk about "good" weather and "bad" weather. How does weather affect our clothing choices and activities?
3. Explain that a person who studies the weather is called a meteorologist.

Story Circle
I Like Weather by Aileen Fisher

Music and Movement
Invite the children to play Musical Clouds (like Musical Chairs). Cut out cloud shapes from white bulletin board paper and use them instead of chairs.

Learning Centers

Art

Weather Art
Invite the children to draw pictures of their favorite weather days.

Library

Weather Books
Fill the library with books about weather.

Dramatic Play

Weather Station
Provide maps, graphs, charts, pointers, cameras (small boxes) and other equipment for the children to set up a weather station.

Science

Temperatures
Invite the children to place thermometers around the room (sunny window, dark closet or cubby, under a table, on top of a table) and check them for differences.

Construction

Weather Wheel
Encourage the children to make a weather wheel by dividing a paper plate into four sections. In each section, draw sun, wind, rain or snow (see the appendix on page 426 for patterns). Use a paper clip to indicate each day's weather conditions.

Writing

Weather Words
Write weather words on cards. Provide tracing paper and pencils for the children to trace the words.

80 • • • *IT'S RAINING, IT'S POURING*

Sunshine

Materials

chart paper or poster board with large sun drawn on it, sun hat and sunglasses

Morning Circle

1. Wear the sun hat and sunglasses.
2. Show the picture of the sun.
3. Encourage the children to brainstorm a list of activities they enjoy when the sun shines.

Story Circle

Let's Find Out About the Sun by Martha Charles Shapp

Music and Movement

Invite the children to sing "You Are My Sunshine."

Learning Centers

Art

Sunny Pictures
Invite the children to use tempera paints and yellow-colored glue to create pictures of a sunny day.

Games

Weather Concentration
Invite the children to play Weather Concentration (make two copies of page 409 in the appendix).

Construction

Sunglasses
Provide poster board frames, crayons, colored cellophane and glue or tape for the children to make and decorate sunglasses.

Outdoors

Sundial
Invite the children to make and use a sundial. Hammer a 6' (2 m) pole into an open area. Place twelve rocks around the perimeter. Check the shadow several times during the day. Adjust the rocks to show each hour.

Discovery

Solar Art
Encourage the children to arrange items (keys, leaves, shape blocks, stones, etc.) on sheets of dark blue paper and leave them outside for several hours. What happens?

Science

Prisms
Provide several prisms for the children to explore.

More Sunshine

Day 3

Materials
summer clothes

Morning Circle
Encourage the children to talk about appropriate clothes for warm, sunny weather. Use the props (summer clothes) to add to their understanding.

Story Circle
What is the Sun? by Reeve Lindbergh

Music and Movement
Invite the children to chase their shadows outside.

Learning Centers

Art

Sun Hats
Invite the children to design sun hats. Provide paper plates and tissue paper, ribbon, markers and flowers for decoration.

Fine Motor

Tracing Shadows
Hang large sheets of butcher paper on a wall. Place a lamp nearby. Invite the children to take turns standing between the light and the paper while another child traces the first child's shadow.

Construction

Sunshine Puppet
Provide paper plates, markers, tongue depressors and glue for the children to make sunshine puppets.

Language

Summer Clothes
Provide paper dolls and summer clothes (see the appendix, pages 433-434). Encourage the children to describe the outfits they put on the dolls.

Dramatic Play

Sunny Dress-Up
Provide sunny weather clothes (e.g., hats, sunglasses, sundresses, swimsuits, tank tops) for dress-up play.

Science

Windowsill Garden
Invite the children to plant seeds in small planters (milk cartons, coffee cans, etc.) and place them in the window.

Cloudy Days

Materials
photographs of clouds

Morning Circle
1. Encourage the children to describe what they think clouds are made of.
2. Explain that clouds are formed when tiny drops of water vapor rise into the air.
3. Show photographs of different clouds (cirrus—wispy, white; stratus—layered looking; cumulus—puffy).

Story Circle
It Looked Like Spilt Milk by Charles Shaw

Music and Movement
Invite the children to sing "Rain, Rain, Go Away" (see the appendix, page 398).

Learning Centers

Art

Cloud Pictures
Provide white tempera paint and blue construction paper for the children to paint cloud pictures.

Cooking and Snack

Cloud Bites
Give each child a slice of bread. Invite the children to bite the edges to make a cloud shape.

Discovery

Tearing
Encourage the children to tear white paper into cloud shapes. Do the cloud shapes resemble other things?

Games

Cloud Match
Cut sets of cloud shapes from white and black construction paper. Encourage the children to match clouds with their shadows.

Music

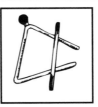

Cloud Songs
Sing songs about clouds, rain, thunderstorms, lightening, etc. Ask the children to suggest songs they like.

Science

Water Science
Provide glasses of ice water to show condensation (drops forming on the outside of the glass). Chill a mirror. Demonstrate blowing warm breath across it to create a cloud.

Rain

Day 5

Materials
rain stick

Morning Circle
1. Talk about rainy days. Ask questions like, "What does rain feel like? What do you wear on rainy days? What activities do you enjoy on rainy days?"
2. Show the rain stick. If you don't have a rain stick, make one following the instructions below. The children can see what they will be making in the Construction Center.
3. Sing "The Raindrop Song."

Story Circle
Rain by Peter Spier

Music and Movement
Lead the children in a rain dance.

Learning Centers

Art

Rainy Day Pictures
Invite the children to draw pictures of a rainy day.

Math

Raindrop Ordering
Cut different sizes of raindrops from blue construction paper. Encourage the children to arrange the raindrops from smallest to largest and largest to smallest.

Discovery

Thirsty Plants
Provide stalks of celery, glasses of water and food coloring. Invite the children to color the water and place a celery stalk in each glass. What happens?

Sand and Water Table

Making Rain
Place several sieves, strainers and colanders at the water table so the children can make rain.

Construction

Rain Sticks
Invite the children to use small nails or push pins to poke holes in paper towel tubes (supervise closely). Dip toothpicks in glue and slide them through the holes. Let dry. Close one end of the tube with tape. Pour ½ cup (125 ml) of fine gravel inside. Tape the other end closed. [Use caution.]

Science

Water Path
Encourage the children to drop water through an eyedropper onto an inclined cookie sheet. Watch the paths the water takes.

More Rain

Day 6

Materials
pictures of rainstorms and rainbows

Morning Circle
1. Show the children pictures of rainstorms and rainbows.
2. If the day is sunny, go outside with a water hose and demonstrate how a rainbow occurs.
3. Talk about rainbows. Demonstrate with a prism and a bright light (an overhead projector works great).

Story Circle
Listen to the Rain by Bill Martin Jr.

Music and Movement
Use rain sticks as percussion instruments to accompany slow "rain" music.

Learning Centers

Art

Rainy Day Art
Provide light blue tempera for the children to paint rainy day pictures. You might add red, orange, yellow, green, blue and violet for rainbow pictures.

Math

Water Drop Count
Invite the children to count water drops into pill bottles or film canisters. How does the water level change as they add drops?

Games

Umbrella Toss
Prop up an umbrella turned upside down. Provide crunched-up paper balls. Who can toss the paper balls inside?

Science

Terrarium
Encourage the children to build a terrarium by adding soil, rocks, charcoal, green plants and water to a 2-liter soda bottle.

Language

Rainy Day Activities
Invite the children to dictate a list of activities they enjoy on rainy days.

Writing

Mud Writing
Provide a tray of wet dirt for the children to write on with various tools, such as a pencil, a stick, a straw, a finger.

Snow

Materials
pictures of snow

Morning Circle
1. Show pictures of snow. Ask the children if they know what snow is. Explain that snow is frozen rain.
2. Talk about the differences between snow and rain. Point out how rain falls hard while snow seems to float down.

Story Circle
The Snowy Day by Ezra Jack Keats

Music and Movement
Encourage the children to move like snowflakes. Provide white scarves and slow music for dancing.

Learning Centers

Cooking and Snack

Snow Cones
Provide shaved or chipped ice and flavored syrups for the children to make snow cones.

Games

Snowflake Match
Cut two each of several different snowflake shapes. Encourage the children to match identical snowflakes.

Discovery

Freezing
Encourage the children to fill resealable plastic bags halfway with water and then put the bags in the freezer. What happens?

Sand and Water Table

Packaged Snow
Fill the table with snow or blocks of ice (freeze water in different-sized plastic containers) if snow is not available. Remove from containers and put in the sand and water table. Use mittens so hands stay warm.

Fine Motor

Snowflakes
Provide white paper or coffee filters and scissors for the children to cut out snowflakes.

Science

Float or Drop
Provide several lightweight objects such as cotton balls, feathers and small balls. Invite the children to experiment with the objects to see which ones float and which ones drop.

Snow Again

Materials
none

Morning Circle
1. Talk about snowy days. What kinds of clothes do we wear when it's snowing? What activities do people enjoy on snowy days?
2. Encourage the children to raise their hand to vote for their favorite kind of day—snowy or sunny.

Story Circle
Frosty the Snowman retold by Annie North Bedford

Music and Movement
"The Freeze" from *We All Live Together, Volume II* by Steve and Greg

Learning Centers

Art

Snow Art
Provide white tempera and blue paper for the children to paint snowy pictures.

Fine Motor

Snow Dough
Invite the children to add rock salt to playdough for more textured sculpting.

Discovery

Ice Painting
Invite the children to sprinkle dry tempera on blue paper. Let them hold ice cubes (use tongs) over the paper so that they drip into the dry paint.

Games

Mitten Match
Provide several pairs of gloves and mittens for the children to try on and then put in pairs.

Dramatic Play

Dress the Bear
Provide paper bears for the children to dress (see the appendix, pages 433–434). How are winter clothes different from summer clothes?

Science

Ice Melt
Invite the children to watch the ice melt in resealable plastic bags. You may want to freeze small toys inside the ice cubes and let the children discover different ways to get the toys out of the ice.

Wind

Materials
pinwheel, fan, streamers

Morning Circle
1. Have a fan with streamers attached blowing when the children arrive.
2. Blow on the pinwheel to show the children the effect of wind.
3. Encourage the children to look outside for clues that wind is blowing or not blowing.
4. Ask the children to tell about things people do on windy days.

Story Circle
Gilberto and the Wind by Mary Ets

Music and Movement
Invite the children to dance outside with scarves on a windy day.

Learning Centers

Art

Straw Blowing
Provide art paper, tempera paint, spoons and straws. Spoon paint onto paper. Encourage the children to blow (out only!) through the straws to move paint around the paper.

Construction

Kites and Wind Socks
Provide tissue paper, thin dowel rods, scissors, glue and tape. Invite the children to make kites or wind socks.

Discovery

Ping-Pong Race
Mark two lines 6' (2 m) apart with masking tape on the floor. Provide paper towel tube, turkey baster, eyedropper, paper fan, straw and piece of cardboard. Invite the children to blow and fan the Ping-Pong balls from one line to the other. Which way is fastest?

Outdoors

Blow Bubbles
Provide bubble soap and an assortment of wands for the children to blow bubbles (see recipe in the appendix, page 388).

Sand and Water Table

Sailboats
Provide a variety of sailboats for the children to experiment with.

Science

Paper Planes
Provide paper and invite the children to make paper airplanes. Which models fly fastest? Farthest? What is the best launch method?

Storms

Materials
pictures of storms

Morning Circle
1. Ask the children, "What makes a storm? Wind? Lightning? Thunder? Rain? Hail?"
2. Show pictures of storms.
3. Talk about hurricanes, typhoons and tornadoes. What safety precautions can people take in these storms? If you are in an area where any of these storms occur, go over the safety precautions with the children.

Story Circle
Thundercakes by Patricia Polacco

Music and Movement
Invite the children to pretend to be a tornado or a hurricane. Encourage them to pretend to walk in a rainstorm or through a hail storm.

Learning Centers

Art

Storm Paintings
Invite the children to paint pictures of storms using yellow tempera paint to create lightning. While paint is wet, they can blow on it through straws to make jagged lightning.

Games

Weather Concentration
Invite the children to play Weather Concentration (see the appendix, page 409).

Discovery

Wind Power
Place a fan in the area and encourage the children to experiment with different objects, testing how the wind blows objects of different weights.

Math

Hail Sort
Make hail (ice balls of different sizes). Provide the children with tongs to use in sorting the hail according to size.

Dramatic Play

Hurricane Safety
Encourage the children to practice for severe weather. Provide flashlights, water bottles, food cans, etc.

Science

Tornado
Fill one 2-liter bottle with water (you might color it just a little). Attach a second bottle with a tornado maker. Invite the children to experiment and explore with it.

Additional Books for It's Raining, It's Pouring

Caps, Hats, Socks, and Mittens by Louise Bordon
The Cloud Book by Tomie dePaola
Cloudy With a Chance of Meatballs by Judith Barrett
First Snow by Emily Arnold McCully
The First Snowfall by Anne and Harlow Rockwell
Little Cloud by Eric Carle
Look! Snow! By Kathryn O. Galbraith
The Mitten by Alvin Tresselt
Rabbits and Raindrops by Jim Arnosky
Rain by Robert Kalan
Rain Drop Splash by Alvin Tresselt
Sadie and the Snowman by Allen Morgan
The Snowman by Raymond Briggs
Snowsong Whistling by Karen Lotz
Something Is Going to Happen by Charlotte Zolotow
Splash! by Ann Jonas
Thunderstorm by Mary Szilagyi
Weather by Pasquale De Bourgoing
What Will the Weather Be by Lynda De Witt
When the Wind Stops by Charlotte Zolotow
White Snow, Bright Snow by Alvin Tresselt
Wild Wild Sunflower Child Anna by Nancy White Carlstrom
The Wind Blew by Pat Hutchins

Under the Rainbow

Color is an important part of every child's world. This unit focuses on a different color each day and presents some interesting "what if" questions. You may want to send home a schedule of colors and encourage parents to help children wear something in the corresponding color each day.

Unit at a Glance

Day	Focus	Centers	Story Circle	Music/Movement
1	Colors of the Rainbow	Crayon Melt Hand Print Rainbows Color Pick-Up Rainbow Toss Rainbow Patterns Prisms	Is It Red, Is It Yellow, Is It Blue?	Rainbow Dance
2	Red	Painting Red Colorglass Strawberry Delights Red Patterns Red Water Writing Red	The Red Balloon	Red Light, Green Light
3	Orange	Painting Orange Colorglass Orange Sodas Orange Patterns Color Mixing Writing Orange	The Mystery of the Flying Orange Pumpkin	Fruit Basket Turnover
4	Yellow	Painting Yellow Colorglass Pineapple Chunks Happy Face Puzzles Yellow Patterns Writing Yellow	Yellow and You	Yellow Streamer Dance
5	Green	Painting Green Colorglass Green Eggs and Ham Green Gobbler Beanbag Color Writing Green	Green Eggs and Ham	Leap Frog

Day	Focus	Centers	Story Circle	Music/Movement
6	Blue	Painting Blue Colorglass Blueberries on a Stick Writing Blue Blue Necklaces Blue Patterns	Blueberries for Sal	Blues and Bluegrass
7	Purple	Painting Purple Colorglass Grapes Purple Objects Purple Crayon Drawings Color Mixing	Harold and the Purple Crayon	Red, Red, Purple
8	Black	Painting Black Oreos Black Sand Etchings Black and White Sort Writing Black	Ten Black Dots	Miss Mary Mack
9	White	Painting White Marshmallow Strings White as Snow Chalkboard Drawing Black and White Patterns Writing White	Look! Snow!	White Parachute Play
10	Kaleidoscope	Multicolored Painting Kaleidoscopes Kaleidoscope Cookies Rainbow Falling Down Outdoor Kaleidoscopes Rainbow Crayons	Color, Color, Color, Color	The World Is a Rainbow

Colors of the Rainbow   Day 1

Materials
prism, water hose (optional)

Morning Circle
1. Use a prism to create rainbows for the children to observe. Shine them onto the walls, floor or ceiling.
2. Make a rainbow outside if the day is sunny and a water hose is available.
3. Talk about how rainbows are created. If you discussed this during the weather unit, ask the children what they remember.

Story Circle
Is It Red, Is It Yellow, Is It Blue? by Tana Hoban

Music and Movement
Invite the children to perform a Rainbow Streamer Dance using plates they made in the math center.

Learning Centers

Art

Crayon Melt
Provide a warming tray, drawing paper and crayons. Invite the children to explore coloring with warm crayons. Supervise closely. [safety icon]

Construction

Hand Print Rainbows
Provide a large piece of blue bulletin-board paper (labeled in six sections, one for each rainbow color) and red, orange, yellow, green, blue and purple paints. Invite the children to stamp their hand prints in a rainbow arc pattern.

Fine Motor

Color Pick-Up
Provide large beads in a variety of colors. Encourage the children to use tweezers to sort the beads by color. Supervise closely.

Games

Rainbow Toss
Paint a large rainbow about 3' (1 m) long on a piece of butcher paper. Make each color section about 6" (15 cm) wide. Invite the children to call out a color name, then toss a beanbag on that color.

Math

Rainbow Patterns
Provide paper plates and colored crepe-paper streamers in 8" (20 cm) strips. Invite the children to tape colored streamers to the plates. Attach a tongue depressor to make a rainbow kite.

Science

Prisms
Provide a light source and a collection of prisms for the children to explore.

Red

Day 2

Materials
red marker, chart paper

Morning Circle
1. Wear red. (Send a note home at the beginning of the unit that provides a color-of-the-day schedule. Encourage the children to dress accordingly.)
2. Invite the children to brainstorm a list of red things. Write their responses in red. Post the list somewhere in the classroom.
3. Ask, "What does it mean when someone says that something is red hot?"

Story Circle
The Red Balloon by A. Lamorisse

Music and Movement
Invite the children to play Red Light, Green Light (see the directions in the appendix, page 404).

Learning Centers

Art

Painting Red
Provide red tempera paint, red crayons, red glitter and red construction paper for the children to create red art.

Math

Red Patterns
Provide several sets of red objects (e.g., red crayons, red buttons, red blocks). Encourage the children to create patterns.

Construction

Colorglass
Make a red colorglass for the children to explore with. Cut a magnifying glass shape from cardboard and cover the hole with red cellophane.

Sand and Water Table

Red Water
Color the water red. Provide clear tubing, cups and funnels for the children to play with.

Cooking and Snack

Strawberry Delights
Invite the children to make a dip by mixing 1 cup (250 ml) sour cream and 1/4 cup (60 ml) brown sugar. Serve with strawberries for snack.

Writing

Writing Red
Write the word RED on several index cards. Provide tracing paper and red crayons for the children to trace the word.

Orange Day 3

Materials
orange marker, chart paper

Morning Circle
1. Wear orange. (Send a note home at the beginning of the unit that provides a color-of-the-day schedule. Encourage the children to dress accordingly.)
2. Invite the children to brainstorm a list of orange things. Write their responses in orange. Post the list somewhere in the classroom.

Story Circle
The Mystery of the Flying Orange Pumpkin by Steven Kellogg

Music and Movement
Invite children to play Fruit Basket Turnover (see the directions in the appendix, page 402).

Learning Centers

Art

Painting Orange
Provide red and yellow tempera paint and encourage the children to create orange art.

Math

Orange Patterns
Provide several sets of orange objects (e.g., orange crayons, orange buttons, orange blocks). Encourage the children to create patterns.

Construction

Colorglass
Make an orange colorglass for the children to explore with. Cut a magnifying glass shape from cardboard and cover the hole with orange cellophane.

Science

Color Mixing
Provide paper and red and yellow fingerpaints. What happens when the two colors mix?

Cooking and Snack

Orange Sodas
Serve oranges with peppermint sticks stuck in the top to look like straws.

Writing

Writing Orange
Write the word ORANGE on several index cards. Provide tracing paper and orange crayons for the children to trace the word.

Yellow

Materials
yellow marker, chart paper

Morning Circle
1. Wear yellow. (Send a note home at the beginning of the unit that provides a color-of-the-day schedule. Encourage the children to dress accordingly.)
2. Invite the children to brainstorm a list of yellow things. Write their responses in yellow. Post the list somewhere in the classroom.

Story Circle
Yellow and You by Candace Whitman

Music and Movement
Invite the children to dance with yellow streamers.

Learning Centers

Art

Painting Yellow
Provide yellow tempera paint and yellow crayons for the children to create yellow art.

Fine Motor

Happy Face Puzzles
Cut yellow happy faces into puzzle pieces for the children to put back together. You may want to use the pattern from Feelings Concentration (see the appendix, page 406).

Construction

Colorglass
Make a yellow colorglass for the children to explore with. Cut a magnifying glass shape from cardboard and cover the hole with yellow cellophane.

Math

Yellow Patterns
Provide several sets of yellow objects (e.g., yellow crayons, yellow buttons, yellow blocks). Encourage the children to create patterns.

Cooking and Snack

Pineapple Chunks
Provide pineapple rings and plastic knives for the children to make pineapple chunks for snack.

Writing

Writing Yellow
Write the word YELLOW on several index cards. Provide tracing paper and yellow crayons for the children to trace the word.

Green

Materials
green marker, chart paper

Morning Circle
1. Wear green. (Send a note home at the beginning of the unit that provides a color-of-the-day schedule. Encourage the children to dress accordingly.)
2. Invite the children to brainstorm a list of green things. Write their responses in green. Post the list somewhere in the classroom.

Story Circle
Green Eggs and Ham by Dr. Seuss

Music and Movement
Invite the children to play Leap Frog (see the directions in the appendix, page 404).

Learning Centers

Art

Painting Green
Provide green tempera paint and green crayons for the children to create green art.

Fine Motor

Green Gobbler
Spray paint a meatball press green. Glue on wiggle eyes. Invite the children to use the "green gobbler" to pick up green pompoms.

Construction

Colorglass
Make a green colorglass for the children to explore with. Cut a magnifying glass shape from cardboard and cover the hole with green cellophane.

Games

Beanbag Color
Lay out 8" (20 cm) circles of green, red, blue and yellow. Invite the children to call out one of the color names, then toss a beanbag on that color.

Cooking and Snack

Green Eggs and Ham
Add green food coloring to ham and eggs to make Green Eggs and Ham.

Writing

Writing Green
Write the word GREEN on several index cards. Provide tracing paper and green crayons for the children to trace the word.

Blue

Day 6

Materials
blue marker, chart paper

Morning Circle
1. Wear blue. (Send a note home at the beginning of the unit that provides a color-of-the-day schedule. Encourage the children to dress accordingly.)
2. Invite the children to brainstorm a list of blue things. Write their responses in blue. Post the list somewhere in the classroom.

Story Circle
Blueberries for Sal by Robert McCloskey

Music and Movement
Listen to bluegrass music and the blues. Ask children how they think the music got its name.

Learning Centers

Art

Painting Blue
Provide blue tempera paint and blue crayons for the children to create blue art.

Discovery

Writing Blue
Provide white paper, pencils and blue carbon paper for the children to explore. How does carbon paper work?

Construction

Colorglass
Make a blue colorglass for the children to explore with. Cut a magnifying glass shape from cardboard and cover the hole with blue cellophane.

Fine Motor

Blue Necklaces
Encourage the children to string blue straws and blue beads on blue yarn to make blue necklaces.

Cooking and Snack

Blueberries on a Stick
Invite the children to pick up and eat blueberries with a toothpick.

Math

Blue Patterns
Provide several sets of blue objects (e.g., blue crayons, blue buttons, blue blocks). Encourage the children to create patterns.

Purple

Materials
purple marker, chart paper

Morning Circle
1. Wear purple. (Send a note home at the beginning of the unit that provides a color-of-the-day schedule. Encourage the children to dress accordingly.)
2. Invite the children to brainstorm a list of purple things. Write their responses in purple. Post the list somewhere in the classroom.

Story Circle
Harold and the Purple Crayon by Crockett Johnson

Music and Movement
Invite the children to play Red, Red, Purple, which is a game similar to Duck, Duck, Goose (see the directions in the appendix, page 402).

Learning Centers

Art

Painting Purple
Provide red and blue tempera paint and encourage the children to mix the colors to create purple.

Discovery

Purple Objects
Ask the children to find classroom objects that are purple. Do they look like the same color or do they look different?

Construction

Colorglass
Make a purple colorglass for the children to explore with. Cut a magnifying glass shape from cardboard and cover the hole with purple cellophane.

Fine Motor

Purple Crayon Drawings
Encourage the children to draw with purple crayons on a warming tray. Supervise closely. [Use caution]

Cooking and Snack

Grapes
Invite the children to wash and eat purple grapes.

Science

Color Mixing
Provide bowls of red and yellow food coloring, eyedroppers and an egg carton. Invite the children to squeeze drops of both colors onto the carton. What happens?

Black

Materials
black marker, chart paper

Morning Circle
1. Wear black. (Send a note home at the beginning of the unit that provides a color-of-the-day schedule. Encourage the children to dress accordingly.)
2. Invite the children to brainstorm a list of black things. Write their responses in black. Post the list somewhere in the classroom.

Story Circle
Ten Black Dots by Donald Crews

Music and Movement
"Miss Mary Mack" from *You'll Sing a Song and I'll Sing a Song* by Ella Jenkins

Learning Centers

Art

Painting Black
Provide black tempera paint and black crayons for the children to create black art.

Fine Motor

Etchings
Encourage the children to color over a watercolor picture with a black crayon and then scratch off a design.

Cooking and Snack

Oreos
Invite the children to eat Oreo cookies for snack.

Math

Black and White Sort
Provide several black and white objects (e.g., buttons, blocks, crayons, shoes) for the children to sort according to color.

Discovery

Black Sand
Encourage the children to add black dry tempera paint to sand to make black sand. Does the sand change to black sand quickly? Why do you think it happens that way?

Writing

Writing Black
Write the word BLACK on several index cards. Provide tracing paper and black crayons for the children to trace the word.

White

Materials
white chalk, black paper

Morning Circle
1. Wear white. (Send a note home at the beginning of the unit that provides a color-of-the-day schedule. Encourage the children to dress accordingly.)
2. Invite the children to brainstorm a list of white things. Write their responses in white chalk on black paper. Post the list somewhere in the classroom.

Story Circle
Look! Snow! by Kathryn O. Galbraith

Music and Movement
White Parachute Play. Provide a king-sized white sheet and invite the children to play with it outside. Encourage them to bounce a ball on it, run under it and toss it.

Learning Centers

Art

Painting White
Provide colored paper, white tempera paint and white crayons for the children to create white art.

Fine Motor

Chalkboard Drawing
Provide a small chalkboard and white chalk for the children.

Cooking and Snack

Marshmallow Strings
Invite the children to string large white marshmallows on licorice laces for snack.

Math

Black and White Patterns
Provide several sets of black and white objects (e.g., crayons, buttons, blocks). Encourage the children to create patterns.

Fine Motor

White as Snow
Squirt shaving cream on the table top for the children to fingerpaint with. Clean up with sponges and water.

Writing

Writing White
Write the word WHITE on a piece of black paper. Provide white crayons and chalk for the children to practice copying the word.

Kaleidoscopes   Day 10

Materials
jar of jelly beans

Morning Circle
1. Talk about how color adds pizzazz to our world.
2. Encourage the children to brainstorm a list of reasons why we can be thankful for colors.

Story Circle
Color, Color, Color, Color by Ruth Heller

Music and Movement
"The World Is a Rainbow" from *We All Live Together* by Steve and Greg

Learning Centers

Art

Multicolored Painting
Provide many colors for the children to paint with. Encourage them to use as many colors as possible.

Cooking and Snack

Kaleidoscope Cookies
Invite the children to decorate butter cookies with icing and multicolored sprinkles.

Construction

Kaleidoscopes
Place wax paper on a warming tray and invite the children to color on it with crayons. Wrap the colored paper around one end of a toilet paper tube and secure with a rubber band. Encourage the children to point their tubes at a light and look through the open end. Supervise closely. [Use caution]

Discovery

Rainbow Falling Down
Encourage the children to put crayon shavings in an empty soda bottle along with a half-and-half mixture of white corn syrup and water. Turn the bottle upside down for a multi-colored show. How does this work?

Outdoors

Outdoor Kaleidoscopes
Provide sheets of colored cellophane (or the red, orange, yellow, green, blue and purple colorglasses made for this unit) for the children to experiment with outside in the sun.

Science

Rainbow Crayons
Invite the children to make rainbow crayons. Melt crayons in a can on a warming tray. Pour the melted wax (one color at a time) into a plastic cup. Let cool. Color! Supervise closely. [Use caution]

Additional Books Under the Rainbow

The Big Orange Splot by Daniel Pinkwater
Brown Bear, Brown Bear, What Do You See? by Bill Martin, Jr.
Chidi Only Likes Blue by Ifeoma Onyefulu
Color by Ruth Heller
Color Dance by Ann Jonas
A Color of His Own by Leo Lionni
A Color Sampler by Kathleen Westray
Color Zoo by Lois Ehlert
Colors by Tana Hoban
Colors Everywhere by Tana Hoban
Do You Know Colors? By Katherine Howard
Green Bear by Alan Rogers
Growing Colors by Bruce McMillan
Little Blue and Little Yellow by Leo Lionni
Mary Wore Her Red Dress and Henry Wore His Green Sneakers by Merle Peek
Mouse Paint by Ellen Stoll Walsh
My Many Colored Days by Dr. Suess
Of Colors and Things by Tana Hoban
Planting a Rainbow by Lois Ehlert
Purple, Green, and Yellow by Robert Munsch
Rainbow of My Own by Don Freeman
Red Day, Green Day by Edith Kunhardt
Red, Blue, Yellow Shoe by Tanan Hoban
The Mixed-up Chameleon by Eric Carle
White Rabbit's Color Book by Alan Baker
Who Said Red? by Mary Serfozo

Funny Farm

Many children have never seen a farm, yet they are fascinated by farm animals and activities. This unit develops children's concepts of the family farm and farm life. It includes everything from the farmer and tractor to the horses and chickens.

Unit at a Glance

Day	Focus	Centers	Story Circle	Music/Movement
1	What Is a Farm?	Paint a Farm Old MacDonald's Farm Farm Kitchen Seed Transfer Farm Concentration Plant Beans	Farm Morning	The Farmer in the Dell
2	Farmers	Old MacDonald's Farm Sculpt a Farmer Farmer Dress-Up Scarecrow Farm Puzzles Digging	This Is the Farmer	Old McDonald Had a Farm
3	Farm Animals	Old MacDonald's Farm Farm Animal Puppets Farm Animal Concentration Act Like Animals Farm Animal Puzzles Animal Sound Match	Once Upon MacDonald's Farm	Down on the Farm
4	Cows and Horses	Horse Tails Better Butter Horseshoes Ring the Bell Horse Tales Clop Clop	What a Wonderful Day to Be a Cow	Did You Feed My Cow?
5	Chickens and Ducks	Deviled Eggs Egg Roll Drop the Feather Duck Walk Patterns Duck Match	Quack and Honk	Chicken

Day	Focus	Centers	Story Circle	Music/Movement
6	Pigs	Pretty in Pink Paper Plate Pigs Nice and Warm Pig Tails Pin the Tail on the Pig Pig Talk	Oink	Pig Jig
7	Sheep, Lambs & Goats	Yarn Painting Hand Print Sheep Feed the Sheep Lost Sheep Tales Counting Sheep Wool Sort	The Shepherd Boy (El Niño Pastor)	Nursery Rhymes
8	Farm Tools	Butter Churns Farm Baking Tractor Tracks Apple Toss Patterns in the Dirt Digging and Plowing	Big Red Barn	I Like the Way They Stack the Hay
9	Vegetable	Carrot Snacks Corn Shucking Seed Sorting Fruit/Vegetable Sort Corny Counting A Closer Look	Three Stalks of Corn	Corn on the Cob
10	Fruits	Fruit/Vegetable Painting Fruit Salad Pumpkin Patch Harvest Fruit/Vegetable Stand Lemon-Lime Sort Sweet and Sour	The Biggest Pumpkin Ever	Apples and Bananas

What Is a Farm?

Materials
photographs of farms

Morning Circle
1. Ask the children to tell what they know about farms.
2. Talk about the photographs of farms.
3. Help the children understand that there are different kinds of farms (e.g., dairy farms, chicken farms, crop farms, tree farms).

Story Circle
Farm Morning by David McPhail

Music and Movement
Sing and play The Farmer in the Dell (see the directions in the appendix, page 402).

Learning Centers

Art

Paint a Farm
Provide tempera paints and paper. Encourage the children to paint farm scenes at the easel.

Fine Motor

Seed Transfer
Provide a variety of seeds and containers. Encourage the children to use tweezers to move seeds from one container to another.

Construction

Old MacDonald's Farm
Invite the children to build a farm. Paint a sheet brown (dirt), green (grass and fields) and blue (pond). Provide blocks, boxes, toy trucks and tractors. Cover a round container with red paper to make a silo.

Games

Farm Concentration
Invite the children to play Farm Concentration (see the appendix, page 411).

Dramatic Play

Farm Kitchen
Provide materials for the children to set up a farmhouse kitchen (playdough, pie tins, pots and pans).

Science

Plant Beans
Provide paper cups, soil, watering can and lima beans for planting.

Farmers

Materials
farm clothes, chart paper and marker; *Farmer Duck* by Martin Waddell

Morning Circle
1. Dress like a farmer (jeans, work boots, straw hat).
2. Help the children brainstorm a list of jobs a farmer does.
3. Write their responses on the chart tablet paper.
4. Read and discuss the book *Farmer Duck*.

Story Circle
This Is the Farmer by Nancy Tafuri

Music and Movement
"Old MacDonald Had a Farm" from *Bert and Ernie's Sing Along*

Learning Centers

Construction

Old MacDonald's Farm
Add people to the farm the children are building.

Construction

Sculpt a Farmer
Provide salt dough, clay or play-dough and invite the children to sculpt a farmer and farm animals.

Dramatic Play

Farmer Dress-Up
Provide overalls, jeans, straw hats, gloves and boots for dress-up play.

Fine Motor

Scarecrow
Invite the children to stuff hay and old newspapers into a shirt and jeans to make a scarecrow.

Games

Farm Puzzles
Make enlargements of illustrations on page 411 in the appendix and glue them to poster board. Cut each in four or five pieces for the children to put together.

Sand and Water Table

Digging
Provide digging tools (spoons, small trowels, scoops, etc.) in the sand table.

Farm Animals

Materials
photographs of farm animals, plastic farm animals

Morning Circle
1. Sing "Old MacDonald Had a Farm" (see the appendix, page 397). Invite the children to add verses for as many animals as they can.
2. Show the pictures and/or plastic farm animals.
3. Talk about animals you don't usually see on a farm.

Story Circle
Once Upon MacDonald's Farm by Stephen Gammell

Music and Movement
"Down on the Farm" from *One Light, One Sun* by Raffi

Learning Centers

Construction

Old MacDonald's Farm
Add plastic farm animals to the farm the children are building.

Gross Motor

Act like Animals
Invite the children to move like the animals in Old MacDonald's Farm.

Dramatic Play

Farm Animal Puppets
Encourage the children to make farm animal puppets from paper plates or use patterns from Farm Animal Concentration (see the appendix, page 410). Invite them to act out "Old MacDonald Had a Farm."

Language

"My picture is about..."

Farm Animal Puzzles
Cut out magazine pictures of farm animals and glue them onto poster board. Cut each picture into three or four pieces for the children to put together.

Games

Farm Animal Concentration
Invite the children to play Farm Animal Concentration (see the appendix, page 410).

Listening

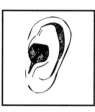

Animal Sound Match
Provide pictures of farm animals (see the appendix, page 410) and an audio tape including each animal's sound. Encourage the children to match pictures to sounds.

Cows and Horses

Day 4

Materials
photographs of cows and horses, cowbell

Morning Circle
1. Let the children take turns ringing the cowbell. Talk about the purpose of the bell.
2. Discuss the work and purpose of cows and horses on a farm.
3. Show the pictures. Ask the children to tell how cows and horses are alike and different.

Story Circle
What a Wonderful Day to Be a Cow by Carolyn Lesser

Music and Movement
"Did You Feed My Cow?" from *You'll Sing a Song and I'll Sing a Song* by Ella Jenkins

Learning Centers

Art

Horse Tails
Tie several strands of coarse hair (horse hair if you can get it) onto a craft stick. Encourage the children to experiment with this as a paintbrush.

Cooking and Snack

Better Butter
Let the children make butter. Give each child a baby food jar. Measure 2 tablespoons (30 ml) of whipping cream (room temperature) into each jar. Shake. Add a pinch of salt. Enjoy on crackers.

Games

Horseshoes
Invite the children to play Horseshoes. Use a plastic commercial set of horseshoes or cut a set from plastic lids and throw them around weighted plastic bottles.

Gross Motor

Ring the Bell
Hang cowbells from the ceiling in an out-of-the way place. Provide bean-bags for the children to toss and ring the bells.

Language

"My picture is about . . ."

Horse Tales
Invite the children to dictate stories about meeting, riding and/or owning a horse. Write on horse-shaped paper (see the appendix, page 435). Encourage the children to attach clothespins for legs.

Music

Clop Clop
Provide several different types of blocks and a plank of wood. Invite the children to experiment with the blocks to get the best "clopping" sound.

Chickens and Ducks

Materials
photographs of chickens and ducks, plastic chickens and ducks, feathers

Morning Circle
1. Spread feathers around the circle before the children arrive.
2. Sing "Two Little Ducks" (see the appendix, page 400).
3. Invite the children to describe chickens and ducks they have seen.
4. Show the photographs.
5. Invite the children to point out ways chickens and ducks are alike and different.
6. Have the children demonstrate a duck walk and a chicken walk.

Story Circle
Quack and Honk by Allen Fowler

Music and Movement
"Chicken" from *All Time Favorite Dances*

Learning Centers

Cooking and Snack

Deviled Eggs
Make deviled eggs. Invite the children to peel hard-boiled eggs and slice them in half. Remove and mash the yolks, adding 1 teaspoon (5 ml) mayonnaise and 1 teaspoon (5 ml) relish. Spoon the mixture into the white halves.

Gross Motor

Duck Walk
Provide flippers and let the children explore walking with webbed feet like ducks.

Discovery

Egg Roll
Fill plastic eggs with objects of different weights. Encourage the children to match eggs that roll the same. What makes the eggs roll differently?

Math

Patterns
Draw footprints of chickens and ducks on several index cards. Invite the children to create patterns with the cards.

Games

Drop the Feather
Encourage the children to drop feathers (from shoulder or waist height) into bowls on the floor.

Sand and Water Table

Duck Match
Use a permanent marker to put colored dots on the bottoms of six rubber ducks (two red, two blue, two green). Place ducks in the water table. Invite the children to find matching pairs.

Pigs

Materials
photographs of pigs, plastic pigs

Morning Circle
1. Recite the nursery rhyme "This Little Piggy Went to Market."
2. Talk about what pigs eat and how they act.
3. Show the photographs. Encourage the children to talk about characteristics of pigs.
4. Add plastic pigs to the farm in the Block Center.

Story Circle
Oink by Arthur Geisert

Music and Movement
Make curly pig tails from pipe cleaners. Attach one to each child's clothing and then dance a pig jig together.

Learning Centers

Art

Pretty in Pink
Put drops of red and drops of white fingerpaint on fingerpaint paper. Encourage the children to make pink fingerpaint and then paint with it.

Fine Motor

Pig Tails
Provide pipe cleaners and invite the children to shape pig tails by rolling the pipe cleaners around pencils or dowel rods.

Construction

Paper Plate Pigs
Encourage the children to make pig masks from paper plates. Use small paper cups or sections of toilet paper tubes for snouts. Provide markers, tape, paint, brushes and yarn.

Games

Pin the Tail on the Pig
Cut a large pig from poster board. Provide curly paper tails and invite the children to play Pin the Tail on the Pig.

Cooking and Snack

Nice and Warm
Invite the children to make Pigs in a Blanket. Wrap canned biscuits around breakfast sausages and bake in a toaster oven for twelve minutes.

Listening

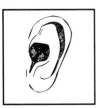

Pig Talk
Invite the children to make pig sounds and record them on audio tape. They can play them back again and again.

Sheep, Lambs and Goats   Day 7

Materials
photographs of sheep, lambs and goats

Morning Circle
1. Sing "Mary Had a Little Lamb" and "Little Boy Blue" (see the appendix, page 396).
2. Show the photographs. Ask the children to look for likenesses and differences.
3. Discuss the role of sheep and goats on a farm.
4. Recite "Little Bo Peep."
5. Add plastic animals to the farm in the Block Center.

Story Circle
The Shepherd Boy (El Niño Pastor) by Kristine L. Franklin

Music and Movement
Encourage the children to act out "Little Bo Peep" and "Little Boy Blue."

Learning Centers

Art

Yarn Painting
Provide art paper (creased down the middle), yarn and tempera paints. Invite the children to dip yarn in paint, then arrange it in a design on one side of the paper. Fold the paper along the crease and press. Unfold.

Construction

Hand Print Sheep
Invite the children to make hand print sheep. Make black prints on white paper (fingers make legs, thumb makes neck and face), then cover the "body" and "head" with cotton balls.

Fine Motor

Feed the Sheep
Glue a picture of a sheep onto a paper plate. Provide tweezers and grass. Encourage the children to pick up the grass with tweezers and feed the sheep.

Language

Lost Sheep Tales
Encourage the children to dictate a story about where Little Bo Peep's sheep might be and what they might be doing.

Math

Counting Sheep
Place one to five dots on sheets of green construction paper. Encourage the children to take the sheep to pasture by matching plastic or cutout sheep to the dots on each sheet.

Science

Wool Sort
Place woolen socks, placemats and scraps of yarn and fabrics in a box. Invite the children to sort the materials by color and/or texture.

Farm Tools Day 8

Materials
photographs of farms and farmland, photographs of working farm equipment (milking machines, tractors, etc.) and tools (rakes, hoes, shovels, curry combs, etc.)

Morning Circle
1. Show the photographs. Talk about tools and equipment used on different farms and different parts of a farm.
2. Ask, "How would you plow a field without a tractor? Dig a garden without a shovel? Gather eggs without a bucket or basket?"

Story Circle
Big Red Barn by Margaret Wise Brown

Music and Movement
"I Like the Way That They Stack the Hay" from *Cheerful Songs and Chants* with Ella Jenkins and Children from Tennessee

Learning Centers

Construction

Butter Churns
Provide Tinker Toys and coffee cans for the children to build butter churns.

Games

Apple Toss
Provide pails and bushel baskets. Invite the children to toss apples (crumpled red construction paper) into the containers.

Dramatic Play

Farm Baking
Provide baking utensils and play-dough for pie making.

Math

Patterns in the Dirt
Provide rakes (forks) and shovels (spoons) for the children to use in creating patterns in a tray of sand.

Fine Motor

Tractor Tracks
Attach markers to the backs of toy tractorsor wagons. Provide butcher paper and encourage the children to make tracks.

Sand and Water Table

Digging and Plowing
Provide tractors, hand shovels, small rakes and buckets for play in the sand and water table.

Vegetables

Materials
corn on the cob, chart paper and marker

Morning Circle
1. Let the children watch you shuck an ear of corn.
2. Discuss the many kinds of corn (popcorn, sweet corn for humans, feed corn for other animals).
3. Make a list of other vegetables that grow on a farm.

Story Circle
Three Stalks of Corn by Leo Politi

Music and Movement
"Corn on the Cob" from *I Am Special* by Thomas Moore

Learning Centers

Cooking and Snack

Carrot Snacks
Invite the children to peel raw carrots and eat them for snack.

Math

Fruit and Vegetable Sort
Encourage the children to sort pictures of fruits and vegetables.

Discovery

Corn Shucking
Provide ears of corn for the children to shuck. What does each layer feel like? Why does corn grow this way?

Math

Corny Counting
Provide margarine tubs with one to five stick-on dots on each lid and a hole cut in the center. Invite the children to count the corresponding number of corn kernels into each tub.

Fine Motor

Seed Sorting
Provide several types of seeds for the children to sort.

Science

A Closer Look
Provide a magnifying glass and several vegetables (peeled and unpeeled) for the children to examine.

Fruits

Materials

slices of apples and/or oranges, chart paper and marker

Morning Circle

1. Pass out slices of the fruit.
2. Encourage the children to describe the fruit.
3. Talk about how fruits are different from vegetables (where they grow, location of seeds, etc.).
4. Make a list of as many fruits as the children can think of that might grow on a farm.

Story Circle

The Biggest Pumpkin Ever by Steven Kroll

Music and Movement

"Apples and Bananas" from *Where Is Thumbkin?* by The Learning Station

Learning Centers

Art

Fruit and Vegetable Painting
Provide easel paints and paper for the children to paint fruits and vegetables.

Dramatic Play

Fruit and Vegetable Stand
Provide bushel baskets, berry baskets, small paper sacks and plastic fruits and vegetables for the children to set up a fruit and vegetable stand.

Cooking and Snack

Fruit Salad
Provide fruits for the children to peel, cut and mix into a fruit salad.

Fine Motor

Lemon-Lime Sort
Provide two bowls and a pail of lemons and limes. Encourage the children to use tongs to sort the fruits.

Dramatic Play

Pumpkin Patch Harvest
Create a pumpkin patch by making orange paper balls (pumpkins) and attaching them to strips of green paper (vines). Encourage the children to harvest the pumpkins.

Science

Sweet and Sour
Provide a couple of sweet fruits (peaches, melons) and a couple of sour fruits (grapefruit, lemons) for the children to taste and classify.

Additional Books for Funny Farm

Apples and Pumpkins by Anne Rockwell
Baby Animals by Margaret Wise Brown
Barn Dance! by Bill Martin, Jr. and John Archambault
The Carrot Seed by Ruth Krauss
The Cow That Went Oink by Bernard Most
Early Morning in the Barn by Nancy Tafuri
Eating the Alphabet: Fruits and Vegetables from A to Z by Lois Ehlert
Egg to Chick by Millicent Selsam
Farming by Gail Gibbons
From Seed to Pear by Ali Mitgutsch
Good Morning, Chick by Mirra Ginsburg
Grandpa's Garden Lunch by Judith Casely
Growing Vegetable Soup by Lois Ehlert
Moo, Moo, Brown Cow by Jakki Wood
The Mouse and the Potato retold by Thomas Berger
Old MacDonald Had a Farm by Carol Jones
The Scarebird by Sid Fleischman
This Year's Garden by Cynthia Rylant
Vegetable Garden by Douglas Florian

Way Out West

Cowpokes, horses, cows, cattle drives and ranch fun make this unit appealing to the children. It's everything from cowboy stew to rodeos.

Unit at a Glance

Day	Focus	Centers	Story Circle	Music/Movement
1	Cowpokes	Draw a Cowpoke Tie-Dye Bandannas Cowpoke Dress-Up Beanbag Toss Hat Prints Western Music	Cowboys	Home on the Range
2	More Cowpokes	Squirt-Bottle Painting Cowpoke Role-Play Yarn Braiding Target Practice Build a Cowpoke Ordering Ropes	Pecos Bill	Get Along, Little Dogies
3	At the Ranch	Cowpoke Vests Ranch Building Haystacks Bunkhouse Longhorn Roping Cattle Brand Match	Yipee-Yah: A Book About Cowboys and Cowgirls	I'm an Old Cowhand
4	On the Trail	Trail Mix Chuck Wagon Covered Wagon Golf Bedrolls Bean Counting Shoe Box Guitars	Zebra-Riding Cowboy	She'll Be Comin' 'Round the Mountain
5	Continuing Trail Ride	Dust Storm Campfire Thistle Pick-Up Card Game Western Music Western Words	Cowboys of the West	Oh, Susanna

Day	Focus	Centers	Story Circle	Music/Movement
6	Horses	Horse-Tail Painting Horseshoe Prints Feed the Horses Horseshoes Hands High Making Hay	Pony Rider	Saddle Up Your Pony
7	Cows	Cow Puppets Rope Tying Ring the Longhorn Cattle Drive Brand Concentration Cattle Drive II	The Zebra-Riding Cowboy	Cow, Cow, Bull
8	Around the Campfire	Campfire Painting Harmonicas S'Mores Campfire Fun Fire Collage Charcoal Writing	Rosie and the Rustlers	Harmonica Happiness
9	Getting Ready for the Rodeo	Rodeo Posters Western Hats Buckaroo Cookies Clown Face Paints Barrel-Racing Barrels Ropes and Roping	Rodeo	Home on the Range
10	Rodeo Day	Hot Dogs Announcer Barrel Racing Stick Horse Race Horseshoes Sack Race	Rodeo	Ol' Texas

Cowpokes   Day 1

Materials
western wear, pictures of cowpokes

Morning Circle
1. Dress in western wear (at least a hat and bandanna).
2. Let the children name each article of clothing you are wearing.
3. Discuss the purpose of large-brimmed hats (weather protection), bandannas (dust protection), chaps, boots, ponchos, etc.

Story Circle
Cowboys by Teri Martini

Music and Movement
Sing "Home on the Range."

Learning Centers

Art

Draw a Cowpoke
Invite the children to use crayons to draw pictures of cowpokes.

Gross Motor

Beanbag Toss
Encourage the children to toss small beanbags into a cowboy hat.

Discovery

Tie-Dye Bandanna
Provide 16" (40 cm) squares of fabric (cut-up old sheets), rubber bands and red dye. Show the children how to tie-dye a bandanna. Why does the dye go on some places and not others?

Math

Hat Prints
Provide sponges cut into western hat shapes and two or three colors of tempera paints. Invite the children to create hat print patterns.

Dramatic Play

Cowpoke Dress-Up
Provide chaps, vests, hats, boots and other cowpoke dress-up clothes for pretend play.

Music

Western Music
Place a guitar, banjo or harmonica in the music center for the children to explore.

More Cowpokes

Materials
pictures of cowpokes

Morning Circle
1. Talk about all the special clothing cowpokes wear. If you have pictures, show them.
2. Discuss the way cowpokes use ropes, such as roping and tying.

Story Circle
Pecos Bill by Steven Kellogg

Music and Movement
Sing "Get Along, Little Dogies."

Learning Centers

Art

Squirt-Bottle Painting
Hang large sheets of butcher paper on the wall. Put a drop cloth on the floor underneath. Give the children paint-filled squirt guns and let them create paintings.

Dramatic Play

Cowpoke Role-Play
Add ropes, tin cups and blankets to the center for dramatic play.

Fine Motor

Yarn Braiding
Provide yarn and show the children how to braid it into a rope.

Games

Target Practice
Hang a felt target on the wall. Wrap two strips of Velcro around Ping-Pong balls. Encourage the children to throw the balls at the target.

Games

Build a Cowpoke
Number each piece of a cowpoke's outfit. For example, hat-1, chaps-2, vest-3, rope-4, boots-5 and bandanna-6. Let the children roll a die until they hit all six numbers and build a cowpoke.

Math

Ordering Ropes
Provide ropes of several different lengths and ask the children to place them in order from the shortest to longest.

At the Ranch

Materials

Lincoln logs, plastic ranch animals, green poster paper, blue and brown construction paper

Morning Circle

1. Bring Lincoln logs and plastic ranch animals to the circle.
2. Build a ranch on green poster paper. Add a blue construction-paper lake and some brown construction-paper corral areas.
3. Discuss aspects of ranch life as you build.

Story Circle

Yipee Yah: A Book About Cowboys and Cowgirls by Gail Gibbons

Music and Movement

Sing "I'm an Old Cowhand."

Learning Centers

Art

Cowpoke Vests
Cut vests from grocery sacks and invite the children to decorate them with crayons or tempera paints.

Dramatic Play

Bunkhouse
Provide materials for a bunkhouse, such as sleeping bags, cooking utensils and playing cards.

Blocks

Ranch Building
Provide Lincoln logs, plastic ranch animals and construction paper for the children to build a ranch.

Games

Longhorn Roping
Cut an old tire in half and stand it so that the cut ends are up, like horns. Give the children a rope and let them rope the longhorn.

Cooking and Snack

Haystacks
In an electric skillet, melt one package of butterscotch morsels. Stir in one can of Chinese noodles. Drop by spoonfuls onto wax paper to look like haystacks.

Language

Cattle Brand Match
Let the children match cattle brands. Maybe they'd like to design their own.

On the Trail   Day 4

Materials
blanket, two 24" (60 cm) lengths of rope or yarn

Morning Circle
1. Talk about items cowpokes might need on the trail, like matches, frying pans, cups and plates.
2. Show the children how to fold and roll the blanket into a bedroll and tie it with rope or yarn.

Story Circle
The Zebra-Riding Cowboy by Angela Shelf Medearis

Music and Movement
"She'll Be Comin' 'Round the Mountain" from *Where Is Thumbkin?* by The Learning Station

Learning Centers

Cooking and Snack

Trail Mix
Let the children combine dry cereal such as Wheat Chex and Rice Chex, raisins, peanuts, pretzel sticks and pumpkin seeds to make Trail Mix.

Dramatic Play

Chuck Wagon
Fill the center with items you might find in a chuck wagon, such as frying pans, cups, plates, coffee pot, empty match boxes and cans of beans. Let the children pack their wagon.

Games

Chuck Wagon Golf
Invite the children to play Chuck Wagon Golf. Curve 9" x 12" (23 cm x 30 cm) sheets of paper into wagon covers and tape them to the floor in a croquet-like pattern. Give the children Ping-Pong balls and clubs made from wrapping-paper tubes.

Gross Motor

Bed Rolls
Provide blankets and lengths of rope for the children to practice making bedrolls.

Math

Bean Counting
Provide bags of beans, several containers, scoops, strainers and balance scales. Encourage the children to scoop, measure and count beans.

Music

Shoe Box Guitars
Provide shoe boxes and large rubber bands for the children to make shoe box guitars. Empty paper towel or wrapping paper tubes make good guitar necks.

Continuing Trail Ride

Day 5

Materials
none

Morning Circle
1. Discuss things cowpokes do on a trail ride, like protect cattle, cook meals, sing around the campfire, play games and so on.
2. Sing a campfire song, such as "Streets of Laredo," "Red River Valley" or "You Are My Sunshine."

Story Circle
Cowboys of the West by Russell Freedman

Music and Movement
"Oh, Susanna" from *The Hokey Pokey* by Melody House

Learning Centers

Art

Dust Storm
Provide sand, paper and glue. Invite the children to create a dust storm.

Language

Card Game
Provide playing cards and teach the children a simple card game like the cowpokes might play.

Dramatic Play

Campfire
Leave campfire materials in the center. Add musical instruments for the children to play.

Music

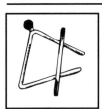

Western Music
Invite the children to play their guitars to western music.

Fine Motor

Thistle Pick-Up
Cut monofilament or broom straws into 2" (5 cm) lengths. Provide tweezers for picking up the thistles and moving them from the table top to a box.

Writing

Western Words
Write western words like cowpoke, cow, horse, boots and hat on index cards. Provide tracing paper and pens for tracing.

Horses

Materials
Pony Rider by Edna Walker Chandler

Morning Circle
1. Discuss the many uses of horses on a ranch.
2. Use the pictures in Pony Rider to get some ideas of how horses are used on a ranch.
3. Talk about how to take care of horses. Explain that they need to be exercised and groomed daily. Mention that they are measured in hands.

Story Circle
Pony Rider by Edna Walker Chandler

Music and Movement
"Saddle Up Your Pony" from *Saddle Up Your Pony* by Andrew Gunsberg

Learning Centers

Art

Horse-Tail Painting
Unravel pieces of rope to make horse-tail paintbrushes. Encourage the children to paint with the horse tails.

Games

Horseshoes
Provide horseshoes and stakes. Encourage the children to toss the horseshoes "around" the stakes.

Fine Motor

Horseshoe Prints
Provide clay and some horseshoes. Urge the children to make horseshoe prints.

Math

Hands High
Invite the children to mark their height on the wall with chalk. Encourage them to count how many hands high they are.

Fine Motor

Feed the Horses
Tie small pieces of hay or straw together with yarn. Invite the children to use tongs to pick up the bales and move them from one section of the table to another.

Science

Making Hay
Invite the children to plant rye grass seeds. After it grows tall, they can cut and dry it to make hay.

Cows

Materials
cowpoke hat, bandanna

Morning Circle
1. Dress in hat and bandanna.
2. Ask, "Who remembers why cowpokes wear big hats (sun and rain protection) and bandannas (dust protection)?"
3. Ask, "Does anyone know why cowpokes moved cows from one place to another?"
4. Ask, "How do we move cattle today?"

Story Circle
The Zebra-Riding Cowboy by Angela Shelf Medearis

Music and Movement
Invite the children to play Cow, Cow, Bull like Duck, Duck, Goose (see the appendix, page 402).

Learning Centers

Construction

Cow Puppets
Provide brown construction paper cut in the shape of cow faces (peanut shapes). Provide more paper for the children to cut ears and crayons for drawing eyes and nostrils. Attach to tongue depressors.

Fine Motor

Rope Tying
Provide pieces of rope for the children to practice tying knots.

Games

Ring the Longhorn
Cut a pair of horns from poster board and mount them to the back of a chair. Provide rings (plastic lids with centers cut out) for the children to toss.

Games

Cattle Drive
Make a game board. Decorate it to look like a western prairie (cactus, sand, rocks, etc.). Use plastic cows as game markers. Provide a spinner or number cube.

Language

Brand Concentration
Make two sets of branding symbol cards (see blank concentration form in the appendix, page 424). Invite the children to match the cards or play Brand Concentration.

Sand and Water Table

Cattle Drive II
Provide plastic cows, horses and cowpokes. Invite the children to stage a cattle drive.

Around the Campfire

Materials
logs, pots and pans, orange and yellow tissue paper, guitar (if available)

Morning Circle
1. Use the logs and tissue paper to build a make-believe campfire in the middle of the circle area.
2. As the children come to the circle, strum on the guitar (you can make one with a shoe box and rubber bands).
3. Talk about campfires. Explain that this is where cowpokes eat dinner and entertain themselves. Fires keep wild animals away and they keep cowpokes warm on cool nights. Teach the children a campfire song.

Story Circle
Rosie and the Rustlers by Roy Gerrard

Music and Movement
"Harmonica Happiness" from *Play Your Instruments and Make a Pretty Sound* by Ella Jenkins

Learning Centers

Art

Campfire Painting
Provide orange and yellow paints. Invite the children to paint a campfire.

Dramatic Play

Campfire Fun
Encourage the children to build their own make-believe fire. Provide pots and pans, cups and plates.

Construction

Harmonicas
Provide plastic combs and wax paper for the children to make harmonicas by wrapping the wax paper around the comb (attach with a rubber band, if needed), then humming through the wax paper.

Fine Motor

Fire Collage
Provide yellow, red and orange tissue paper for the children to use in a collage. Does it look like a fire?

Cooking and Snack

S'Mores
Provide a hot plate for the children to toast marshmallows. Place toasted marshmallows, along with squares of chocolate, between two graham crackers. Supervise closely. [Use caution.]

Writing

Charcoal Writing
Explain that burned logs (charcoal) can be used for marking and drawing. Provide black chalk for the children to practice writing.

Getting Ready for the Rodeo   Day 9

Materials
photographs or pictures of rodeos

Morning Circle
1. Show pictures of rodeos.
2. Encourage the children to talk about what they know about rodeos.

Story Circle
Rodeo by James Fain

Music and Movement
Sing "Home on the Range."

Learning Centers

Art

Rodeo Posters
Provide poster board, paints, markers, magazine pictures, etc. Invite the children to make posters that tell about a rodeo.

Construction

Western Hats
Follow the directions on page 432 in the appendix to make cowboy hats from 12" x 18" (30 cm x 45 cm) sheets of brown construction paper. Invite the children to decorate their hats.

Cooking and Snack

Buckaroo Cookies
Invite the children to make Buckaroo Cookies (see recipe in the appendix, page 389).

Discovery

Clown Face Paints
Provide face paint (see recipe in the appendix, page 388). Invite the children to create their own rodeo clown faces. Why do clowns use face paint?

Fine Motor

Barrel-Racing Barrels
Decorate large coffee cans to represent barrels for barrel racing. Invite the children to glue on collage materials.

Gross Motor

Ropes and Roping
Invite the children to practice roping and rope twirling.

Rodeo Day

Materials
none

Morning Circle
1. Send a note home in advance letting parents know that the children can wear their western "duds" to school. If they don't have special clothing at home, they can wear the hat and vest they made during the unit.
2. Introduce the centers as if you were a rodeo announcer. Encourage the children to "mosey on over to the arenas" (learning centers).

Story Circle
Rodeo by Cheryl Walsh Bellville

Music and Movement
Sing "Ol' Texas."

Learning Centers

Cooking and Snack

Hot Dogs
Cut buns and wieners in half. Serve the mini hot dogs for snack.

Math

Horseshoes
Invite the children to toss plastic rings around potato chip cans (such as Pringles) and use tally marks to keep score.

Dramatic Play

Announcer
Invite the children to take turns being the rodeo announcer. Provide a microphone (decorated toilet paper tube) or megaphone (paper rolled into a cone).

Outdoors

Sack Race
Provide burlap feed sacks or old pillow cases and invite the children to have sack races.

Games

Barrel Racing
Lay twenty 2" (5 cm) squares of paper around the coffee can barrels. Provide plastic horses and a number cube. Invite the children to roll and move the number of squares indicated. The first horse around wins.

Gross Motor

Stick Horse Race
Provide paper sacks, newspaper, yarn and markers. Invite the children to stuff a paper sack with old newspaper and shape it into a horse's head. Draw on nose, eyes and mouth. Glue on paper ears and a yarn mane. Attach the head to a wrapping paper tube.

Additional Books for Way Out West

Black Cowboy, Wild Horses: A True Story by Julius Lester

Boss of the Plains: The Hat That Won the West by Laurie Carlson

Buffalo Bill and the Pony Express by Eleanor Coerr

Cowboy Baby by Sue Heap

Cowboys by Glen Rounds

The Girl Who Loved Wild Horses by Paul Goble

Matthew the Cowboy by Ruth Hooker

One Good Horse by Ann Herbert Scott

Tales of the American West by Neil and Ting Morris

Tyrannosaurus Tex by Betty Birney

White Dynamite and Curly Kidd by Bill Martin, Jr.

Zoo Crew

This unit is as good as a trip to the zoo. It's a study of zoo animals and their homes and habits.

Unit at a Glance

Day	Focus	Centers	Story Circle	Music/Movement
1	Who Lives in the Zoo?	Zoo Portraits Zoo Architects Animal Cages Zoo Puppets Zoo Collage Closer Look	At the Zoo	Animal Movements
2	Who Works at the Zoo?	Zoo Visitors Zoo Worker Dress-Up Feed the Animals Feeding Pail Toss Animal Sort Wash the Animals	I Can Be a Zoo Keeper	Mulberry Bush
3	Lions and Tigers	Lion Faces Tiger by the Tail Cat Walk Tiger Patterns Lion and Tiger Sort Tiger Stories	Brave as a Tiger	Cat Movements
4	Monkeys and Gorillas	Bananas on a Stick Fleas Barrel of Monkeys Monkey See, Monkey Do Swinging Monkey Finger Spelling	The Day the Teacher Went Bananas	Five Little Monkeys
5	Zebras and Giraffes	Spots on a Giraffe Animal Camouflage Footprint Match Black and White Long Necks Animals are Coming	My First Visit to the Zoo	Animal Movements

Day	Focus	Centers	Story Circle	Music/Movement
6	Bears	Bear Cave Bear Claws Three Bears Play Bear Race Feed the Bear Bear Patterns	We're Going on a Bear Hunt	Going on a Bear Hunt
7	Seals, Otters & Penguins	Building Dams Animal Coverings Feed the Seal Animal Concentration Water Animals Animal Shapes	Sammy the Seal	Seals, Otters and Penguins
8	Birds	Feather Painting Bird Feeders Water Repellent Sort Birdseed Sweep Feather Race Feather Pens	About Birds	Waddle, Hop, Prance
9	Elephants	Elephant Creations Haystacks Elephant Pretend Shelling Peanuts Elephant Feet Feed the Elephant	Sam Who Never Forgets	One Elephant
10	Reptile	Snake Skins Spiral Snakes Frogs on Lily Pads Frog Feet Up-Close Look Snake Trails	Outside and Inside Snakes	Leap Frog

Who Lives in the Zoo?

Day 1

Materials
plastic animals, fences and trees

Morning Circle
1. Build a zoo in the circle area.
2. Ask, "Do you know what this is?"
3. Invite the children to come up one at a time and choose an animal.
4. Go around the circle, inviting the children to tell all they know about the animals they are holding. Add to their knowledge when you can.

Story Circle
At the Zoo by Paul Simon

Music and Movement
Move like the animals in your zoo.

Learning Centers

Art

Zoo Portraits
Encourage the children to paint their favorite zoo animals.

Dramatic Play

Zoo Puppets
Provide animal puppets or paper-plate animal faces for a puppet show.

Blocks

Zoo Architects
Provide plastic animals, fences and construction paper (blue, green and brown) for landscapes. Invite the children to build a zoo.

Fine Motor

Zoo Collage
Invite the children to cut animal pictures from magazines and make a collage.

Construction

Animal Cages
Provide popsicle sticks, toothpicks and glue. Invite the children to create animal cages.

Science

Closer Look
Provide pictures of zoo animals and magnifying glasses. Encourage the children to examine the animals up close.

Who Works at the Zoo? Day 2

Materials

apron, baseball cap, push broom, pail, brush, chart paper, pen

Morning Circle

1. Be dressed in apron and ball cap when the children arrive.
2. Explain that you are dressed like a zoo worker.
3. Encourage the children to name all the jobs they think a zoo worker might do (feed the animals, clean the pens, sell tickets and souvenirs, etc.). Write their responses on the chart paper.

Story Circle

I Can Be a Zoo Keeper by James P. Rowan

Music and Movement

Sing "Mulberry Bush" to reflect tasks of a zoo worker ("this is the way we feed the seals, clean the cage…").

Learning Centers

Blocks

Zoo Visitors
Provide plastic people to visit the zoo built earlier. Encourage the children to make zoo signs.

Games

Feeding Pail Toss
Invite the children to toss paper balls into feeding pails.

Dramatic Play

Zoo Worker Dress-Up
Provide dress-up clothes and props for zoo workers (aprons, rubber boots, brooms, pails, brushes, shovels, etc.).

Math

Animal Sort
Encourage the children to sort plastic animals into cages (berry baskets).

Fine Motor

Feed the Animals
Provide tweezers and seeds, dried grass (hay) and corn kernels to feed the animals. Provide plastic birds and elephants (or pictures) and invite the children to feed each the appropriate food.

Sand and Water Table

Wash the Animals
Provide plastic animals and small brushes. Encourage the children to give the animals a bath.

Lions and Tigers

Materials
photographs of lions and tigers

Morning Circle
1. Show the children the photographs.
2. Encourage the children to describe how the animals are alike and different. How is each different from a house cat?
3. Invite the children to tell what they know about lions and tigers. Ask, "What do they eat? Where do they sleep? What are their babies called?"

Story Circle
Brave as a Tiger by Libuse Palecek

Music and Movement
Invite the children to sneak, run, leap and stretch like a cat.

Learning Centers

Construction

Lion Faces
Invite the children to make lion masks from paper plates. Curl yellow paper strips (1" x 10" or 3 cm x 25 cm) around a pencil to make curly hair. Glue the curly strips around the plate for the lion's mane.

Games

Tiger by the Tail
Make three tiger shapes (or use stuffed tigers). Glue a yarn tail on each. Place tigers in a box with their tails hanging out. Add two more pieces of yarn (with no tigers). Invite pairs to take turns "catching the tigers."

Gross Motor

Cat Walk
Provide a balance beam for the children to walk across like cats.

Math

Tiger Patterns
Provide orange and black crayons for the children to create patterns.

Science

Lion and Tiger Sort
Provide plastic lions and tigers for the children to sort.

Writing

Tiger Stories
Invite the children to write a story about a tiger.

Monkeys and Gorillas   Day 4

Materials
photographs of monkeys and gorillas

Morning Circle
1. Start circle time by reciting "Five Little Monkeys Jumping on the Bed" (see the appendix, page 392).
2. Ask the children to tell what they know about monkeys and gorillas.
3. Show photographs of both animals and discuss their similarities and differences.
4. Explain that some gorillas have learned to "talk" to people using sign language.

Story Circle
The Day the Teacher Went Bananas by James Howe

Music and Movement
"Five Little Monkeys" from *One Elephant, Deux Elephants* by Sharon, Lois and Bram

Learning Centers

Cooking and Snack

Bananas on a Stick
Invite the children to peel bananas, stick them on popsicle sticks and dip them in chocolate or caramel.

Gross Motor

Monkey See, Monkey Do
Encourage the children to work in pairs. One child makes funny faces and does silly things while the other imitates the actions.

Discovery

Fleas
Explain that monkeys are often bothered by fleas. Provide a large picture of a flea (available from a vet's office) and a magnifying glass. Encourage the children to examine the flea up close.

Science

Swinging Monkey
Hang a heavy string from the ceiling or door jamb. Tie on a stuffed monkey by the hand. Invite the children to swing the monkey. Can they make it go in a circle? Side to side? Front to back? How do they change the movement?

Games

Barrel of Monkeys
Invite the children to play with a commercial or teacher-made game of Barrel of Monkeys.

Writing

Finger Spelling
Invite the children to learn to finger spell their names or teach them a few simple words in sign language.

Zebras and Giraffes   Day 5

Materials
photographs of zebras and giraffes

Morning Circle
1. Show the children the photographs.
2. Discuss similarities (four legs, patterns in coverings, diet, etc.) and differences (size, color, footprints, etc.). Be sure to discuss the fact that no two zebras and no two giraffes are marked exactly alike.
3. Talk about being able to put your ear to the ground to hear a herd of zebras or giraffes coming.
4. Discuss animal camouflage. Explain that the skin patterns of zebras and giraffes make it difficult to see only one when it's in a crowd.

Story Circle
My First Visit to the Zoo by J. M. Parramon and G. Sales

Music and Movement
Move like zebras and giraffes. On your hands and knees, you might graze like a zebra, run from a lion or spread your arms to drink like a giraffe.

Learning Centers

Art

Spots on a Giraffe
Provide yellow and brown paint and invite the children to paint giraffes.

Math

Black and White
Provide strips of black and white paper for the children to create patterns.

Discovery

Animal Camouflage
Spray paint two old sheets or towels—one brown and yellow spots, one black and white stripes. Invite the children to place giraffes and zebras on the backgrounds. Are they easy or difficult to see?

Math

Long Necks
Explain that a giraffe's neck is about 6' (2 m) long. Place a 6' strip of masking tape on the floor. Invite the children to find out how many blocks it takes to match the line.

Games

Footprint Match
Make a set of cards showing six giraffe footprints and six zebra footprints. Invite the children to turn the cards over to find matching pairs.

Science

Animals are Coming
Invite the children to put their ears to a table top and lightly tap with their fingers. What do they hear? What does it sound like?

Bears

Materials
photographs of polar bears, grizzly bears, brown bears; chart paper and marker

Morning Circle
1. In advance, invite the children to bring stuffed bears from home. Have extras on hand for the children who don't have one or who forget.
2. Show the photographs. Talk about similarities and differences among the different bears. What do they look like? What do they eat? Where do they live?
3. Invite the children to introduce their stuffed bears to the class.
4. Make a list of famous bears (Yogi, Smoky, etc.).

Story Circle
We're Going on a Bear Hunt by Michael Rosen

Music and Movement
Play "Going on a Bear Hunt" (see the appendix, page 393).

Learning Centers

Blocks

Bear Cave
Provide a large box and invite the children to create a bear cave.

Cooking and Snack

Bear Claws
Give each child a refrigerator biscuit. Show them how to make a fist and press it into the dough. Brown and serve.

Dramatic Play

Three Bears Play
Provide props (dishes, chairs, etc.) and the bears that the children brought from home to dramatize the story of *The Three Bears*.

Games

Bear Race
Make a game board and number cards (numerals or dots 1-3) from poster board. Provide bear counters for game pieces. Encourage the children to draw a card and move that number of spaces. Who can get to the end first?

Games

Feed the Bear
Invite the children to feed the bear. Paint a bear's face on the side of a box. Cut a hole for the mouth. Encourage the children to toss beanbags into the bear's mouth.

Math

Bear Patterns
Invite the children to create and copy patterns using bear counters or the bears that children brought from home.

Seals, Otters & Penguins   Day 7

Materials
photographs of seals, otters and penguins

Morning Circle
1. Encourage the children to walk like penguins.
2. Show the photographs. Talk about what the animals have in common.
3. Encourage the children to think of a well-known characteristic for each animal (e.g., penguin's walk, otter's swimming, seal's bark or balance). Encourage them to demonstrate each characteristic.

Story Circle
Sammy the Seal by Syd Hoff

Music and Movement
Play Seals, Otters and Penguins. Designate an area for each animal. As you call out each animal's name, have the children run to the appropriate area.

Learning Centers

Blocks

Building Dams
Provide several branches and twigs. Encourage the children to build a dam like otters. Provide blue paper for water.

Games

Animal Concentration
Invite the children to play Animal Concentration (use the patterns from the appendix, page 417, to make cards).

Discovery

Animal Coverings
Provide samples of feathers, seal skin and fur for the children to explore.

Sand and Water Table

Water Animals
Provide plastic seals, otters and penguins along with ice cubes. Encourage dramatic play.

Fine Motor

Feed the Seal
Glue a picture of a seal to the lid of a small box. Cut a hole around the mouth. Invite the children to use tweezers to pick up and feed Goldfish crackers to the seal. Eat the crackers for snack.

Writing

Animal Shapes
Provide tracing paper and crayons. Invite the children to trace animal shapes from an enlarged copy of appendix page 417.

Birds

Materials
live bird (if possible), photographs of birds, bird feather, tempera paint, chart paper

Morning Circle
1. Show the bird and/or the photographs of birds.
2. Invite the children to brainstorm a list of ways birds are different from other animals (feathers, nests, feet, flying ability, etc.).
3. Record responses on chart paper. Use the feather dipped in tempera as your marker.

Story Circle
About Birds by Cathryn Sill

Music and Movement
Invite the children to waddle like ducks, walk like chickens, hop like sandpipers, stand like flamingoes, prance like peacocks and so on.

Learning Centers

Art

Feather Painting
Provide single feathers and feather dusters to use as paintbrushes for easel painting.

Fine Motor

Birdseed Sweep
Provide a scoop, whisk broom and large can or cookie sheet. Invite the children to sweep up birdseed and dump it in the can.

Construction

Bird Feeders
Invite the children to make a bird feeder. Cut a section from a plastic bottle. Pour birdseed into the bottle and hang it outside.

Games

Feather Race
Mark Start and Finish lines with strips of masking tape 6' (2 m) apart. Provide two feathers. Invite pairs of children to race to the Finish, moving their feathers without touching them. Provide basters, paper fans, straws and other "helpers."

Discovery

Water Repellent Sort
Provide several kinds of feathers, various small objects and a bowl of water. Encourage the children to test and sort the items according to which repel and which absorb water.
Why do some bird feathers repel water?

Writing

Feather Pens
Provide tempera paints and bird feathers. Invite the children to write and draw with the feathers.

Elephants

Materials
chalk, photographs of elephants

Morning Circle
1. Make a mark on the wall 7½' (2 m) above the floor.
2. Show the pictures. Discuss an elephant's size, skin texture and trunk. Point out the mark on the wall, telling the children it shows how tall an elephant can be.
3. Tell the children that when elephants live in captivity, their toenails must be filed every two weeks. In the wild, the elephants' toenails are trimmed naturally while they walk.

Story Circle
Sam Who Never Forgets by Eve Rice

Music and Movement
"One Elephant" from *Where Is Thumbkin?* by The Learning Station

Learning Centers

Construction

Elephant Creations
Encourage the children to paint elephants. Fold 2" x 18" (3 cm x 45 cm) strips of gray construction paper accordion style to make elephant trunks. Attach them to the paintings.

Fine Motor

Shelling Peanuts
Provide peanuts for the children to shell and eat.

Cooking and Snack

Haystacks
Invite the children to make Haystacks (see the recipe in the appendix, page 389).

Math

Elephant Feet
An elephant's foot is about 8" (20 cm) in diameter. Provide 8" paper plates for the children to cover with blocks. How many blocks does it take?

Dramatic Play

Elephant Pretend
Provide long socks and headbands with elephant ears glued on so the children can pretend to be elephants. Dryer and vacuum hoses make good trunks.

Math

Feed the Elephant
Glue a picture of an elephant to the side of a cardboard box. Cut a hole for the mouth. Invite the children to roll a number cube and feed that many peanuts to the elephant.

Reptiles

Materials
photographs of snakes, lizards, turtles and frogs

Morning Circle
1. Show the photographs.
2. Encourage the children to move like each animal pictured.
3. Invite the children to help make a list of things common to all the animals (e.g., rough skin, egg laying, skin shedding, etc.).

Story Circle
Outside and Inside Snakes by Sandra Markle

Music and Movement
Invite the children to play Leap Frog (see the appendix, page 404).

Learning Centers

Fine Motor

Snake Skins
Provide 2" x 18" (3 cm x 45 cm) strips of newsprint, an old bicycle tire and crayons. Encourage the children to make crayon rubbings and create "snake skins."

Fine Motor

Spiral Snakes
Provide copies of page 429 in the appendix. Encourage the children to cut out the circle, then cut along the dotted line. What happens when you pick up one end?

Math

Frogs on Lily Pads
Make frog counters by spray painting small stones green. Add eyes with a marker. Make five paper lily pads, with 1-5 dots on each one. Encourage the children to match frogs to dots.

Sand and Water Table

Frog Feet
Provide suction cups (like frogs' feet) and small flat objects. Invite the children to pick up the objects with the suction cups.

Science

Up-Close Look
Provide a live frog, lizard and/or turtle for the children to observe. Provide magnifying glasses. If live animals aren't available, provide photographs.

Writing

Snake Trails
Provide popsicle sticks or twigs for the children to make snake trails in a tray of sand.

Additional Books for Zoo Crew

1, 2, 3 to the Zoo by Eric Carle
Annie and the Wild Animals by Jan Brett
At the Zoo by H. Amery
At the Zoo by Paul Simon
A Book About Pandas by Ruth Belov Gross
Curious George Visits the Zoo by Margaret Rey
Endangered Animals by John Wexo
Gorilla by Anthony Brown
If I Ran the Zoo by Dr. Seuss
Jumbo by Rhoda Blumberg
Kangaroos Have Joeys by Philippa-Alys Browne
Little Elephant by Miela Ford
Monkey See, Monkey Do by Helen Oxenbury
Roar and More by Karla Kuskin
Sammy the Seal by Syd Hoff
When the Elephant Walks by Keiko Kasza
When We Went to the Zoo by Jan Ormerod
Zoo by Gail Gibbons
Zoo Day by John Brennan

Under the Big Top

Everyone loves the circus. This unit is filled with colors, shapes and sizes. Circus animals and performers surface in every lesson. It will delight both the children and teachers.

Unit at a Glance

Day	Focus	Centers	Story Circle	Music/Movement
1	Here Comes the Circus	Circus Posters Painted Boxes Circus Circus Tickets Stage Names Circus Books	Circus	Circus Parade
2	The Giant Big Top	Circus Colors Tent Construction Hula Hoops Mini Circus Tent Building Tent Patterns	If I Ran the Circus	The Calliope Song
3	Elephants at Work	Elephant Mask Pulleys and Pails Peanut Shelling Drop the Peanut Jumbo Comparisons Water Spray	Little Elephant	Elephant Walk
4	Clowns Are Funny	Clown Costumes Clown Cones Clown Faces Clown Beanbag Toss Clown Shoes Ordering Clown Hats	You Think It's Fun to Be a Clown!	The Clown
5	Tightrope Walkers, Bareback Riders & Trapeze Artists	Rope Painting Heel to Toe Another Balance Pick-Up Sticks Balance Beam Walk Balance Scale	Mirette on the High Wire	Tightrope Walking

Day	Focus	Centers	Story Circle	Music/Movement
6	**Lion Tamers**	Whisker Painting Lion Cages Lion Face Cookies Taming Lions Cat Paws Counting Lions	Big Top Circus	Streamer Dance
7	**Jugglers, Musicians, Acrobats & Strong Men**	Ball Paintings Magic Wands Magic Tricks Acrobats How Strong Are You? Rhythm Instruments	Circus	Juggling
8	**Dogs, Seals & Dancing Bears**	Doggie Hats Animal Treats Balance Seal and Dog Act Dancing Bears Ball Patterns	Grusha	Ring Master, May I?
9	**Traveling Town**	Circus Highlights Circus Train Wheels Tiny Circus Circus Tent Which Animals?	Night Ride	Human Train
10	**Circus Finale**	Face Paints Popcorn and Lemonade Now I Know Tightrope Walking My Favorite Balancing	See the Circus	Circus Parade

Here Comes the Circus   Day 1

Materials
photographs of circus performers, the big top and the animals; four 12" (30 cm) wide strips of fabric

Morning Circle
1. Hang fabric strips from the ceiling to create a "big top" effect.
2. Sit under the "Big Top" and show the children photographs of the circus.
3. Ask the children, "Who has seen the circus?" Let those who have seen a circus describe what they remember about it.

Story Circle
Circus by Peter Spier

Music and Movement
Play circus music and invite the children to parade around the room. When the music stops, the children stop; when the music starts again, the children continue their parade.

Learning Centers

Art

Circus Posters
Write *Here Comes the Circus* on sheets of butcher paper. Let the children decorate the announcement posters and put them on the walls around the classroom.

Art

Painted Boxes
Let the children paint boxes to put under the Big Top in the Dramatic Play Center.

Dramatic Play

Circus
Move the center beneath the tent. Fill with costumes, a mirror, stuffed animals and a small stool for animal performers. Encourage pretend play. Add or change props daily.

Fine Motor

Circus Tickets
Let the children use a hole puncher to punch holes in construction-paper tickets.

Language

Stage Names
Encourage the children to create stage names for circus acts, like "The Magnificent Bears," "The Flying Trio" or "The Dynamic Duo."

Library

Circus Books
Fill the library with books about the circus.

The Giant Big Top Day 2

Materials
pictures of circus tents or Dr. Seuss's book about the circus (see Story Circle below)

Morning Circle
1. Show the children pictures of the circus tent and tell them that many people call it "the big top." Explain that circus tents are among the biggest tents in the world.
2. Talk about the bright colors on circus tents. You may want to ask the children how circus tents are different from camping tents.

Story Circle
If I Ran the Circus by Dr. Seuss

Music and Movement
Sing "The Calliope Song" (see the appendix, page 392).

Learning Centers

Art

Circus Colors
Provide red and white easel paint and let the children make red and white striped paintings.

Fine Motor

Mini Circus
Drop a sheet over the dramatic play table and provide small plastic animals for the children to play circus.

Construction

Tent Construction
Provide paper, markers, tape, scissors and half-circle patterns. Show the children how to roll a half circle into a tent (cone). Encourage the children to decorate their tents.

Gross Motor

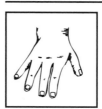

Tent Building
Provide a couple of large sheets and three or four chairs. Encourage the children to build circus tents.

Dramatic Play

Hula Hoops
Add hula hoops to the circus tent. Encourage the children to learn tricks with them.

Math

Tent Patterns
Provide two colors of tempera paint, drawing paper and tent-shaped sponges. Encourage the children to sponge-paint tent patterns.

Elephants at Work

Materials

"The Circus Elephant" (poem by John Foster, *Another Poetry Book*), photographs of circus elephants, song "One Elephant" (see the appendix, page 397), 18' (5 m) length of yarn

Morning Circle

1. Read "The Circus Elephant" if available.
2. Teach the children "One Elephant." Ask the children why it's funny to think of an elephant in a spider web.
3. Tell the children that Jumbo, a famous circus elephant, was 18' (5 m) around. Show the piece of yarn.
4. Describe things elephants do, such as put up the tent, pull heavy loads, perform and spray water from their trunks for washing.

Story Circle

Little Elephant by Miela Ford

Music and Movement

"Elephant Walk" from *Elephants Aloft* by Kathi Appelt

Learning Centers

Art

Elephant Mask
Provide 8" (20 cm) paper plates and let the children color or paint them gray. Give each child two ears cut from gray construction paper and a 2" x 9" (5 cm x 23 cm) strip to fold accordion-style for a nose. Cut out eyes or glue on wiggle eyes.

Games

Drop the Peanut
Invite the children to play Drop the Peanut in the Pail.

Discovery

Pulleys and Pails
Hang a pulley and provide a rope and a pail. Let the children experiment picking up the bucket with their own power, then with a pulley.

Math

Jumbo Comparisons
Arrange an 18' (5 m) piece of yarn in a circle on the floor. Experiment with how many children it takes to stand around it. How many children will fit inside the circle?

Fine Motor

Peanut Shelling
Provide roasted peanuts for the elephants (children) to shell.

Outside

Water Spray
Provide some plastic spray bottles and let the children spray water like elephants.

Clowns Are Funny

Day 4

Materials
clown costume for you (if possible), chart paper and marker

Morning Circle
1. If you can put a clown costume together, do it and wear it to class. (Perhaps a parent would dress up and come for a visit.)
2. Invite the children to tell everything they know about clowns. Create a word web on the chart.
3. Encourage the children to use words from the word web to describe the clown's job at the circus.
4. Let the children demonstrate things a clown might do.

Story Circle
You Think It's Fun to Be a Clown! by David Adler

Music and Movement
"The Clown" from *Let's Pretend* by Hap Palmer

Learning Centers

Art

Clown Costumes
Provide colored tissue paper streamers and construction paper or butcher paper for the children to create clown hats and collars.

Cooking and Snack

Clown Cones
Give each child a scoop of ice cream and a cone. Let the children make clowns by placing the cones on top of the ice cream like a hat. Decorate with raisins, red hots and chocolate chips.

Dramatic Play

Clown Faces
Add face paint (see the recipe in the appendix, page 388), gloves and big shoes to the other materials under "the big top."

Games

Clown Beanbag Toss
Draw a clown face with an open mouth and tape it to the side of a box. Cut out the mouth and provide beanbags for the children to toss through.

Math

Clown Shoes
Provide several pairs of big shoes in different colors, styles and sizes. Let the children match the pairs.

Math

Ordering Clown Hats
Place several sizes of clown hats (made from construction paper) in the center and encourage the children to order them from smallest to largest.

Tightrope Walkers, Bareback Riders & Trapeze Artists   Day 5

Materials
12′ (4 m) piece of rope or masking tape

Morning Circle
1. Have piece of rope or tape leading from the door to the circle area. Invite the children to walk on it to get to the circle.
2. Discuss tightrope walkers. What do they have to learn to do? Why do they carry a long pole? What do they wear on their feet?
3. Explain that bareback riders and trapeze artists need balance, too. Ask the children if they know why.

Story Circle
Mirette on the High Wire by Emily A. McCully

Music and Movement
Put masking tape tightropes on the floor.
Provide wrapping paper tubes as balance beams.
Invite the children to play Follow the Leader.

Learning Centers

Art

Rope Printing
Give each child a 12″ (30 cm) piece of rope and two sheets of construction paper. Invite the children to dip ropes into tempera paint, then arrange them on one sheet of paper. Place the other paper on top and press. Remove to find a design.

Discovery

Heel to Toe
Provide a large tray of tempera paint and a 10′ (3 m) strip of butcher paper. Invite the children to step bare-footed into the paint, then walk heel to toe down the paper.
Supervise closely. [Use caution.]

Dramatic Play

Another Balance
Place several pairs of high heels in the center. Invite the children to experiment walking in them.

Games

Pick-Up Sticks
Invite the children to play Pick-Up Sticks. What kind of balance do they need to play? How are the sticks balanced?

Gross Motor

Balance Beam Walk
Provide a balance beam (or strip of masking tape) for the children to walk. Provide a balance pole (wrapping paper tube).

Science

Balance Scale
Encourage the children to balance objects and sets of objects on a balance scale.

Lion Tamers   Day 6

Materials
crepe paper streamers, photographs of a lion tamer (optional)

Morning Circle
1. Hang crepe paper streamers from the ceiling to create a cage. Sit in the cage during circle time.
2. If you have photographs of lion tamers at work, show them.
3. Talk about lion tamers and the tools they use to do their job.

Story Circle
Big Top Circus by Neil Johnson

Music and Movement
Invite the children to perform a streamer dance.

Learning Centers

Art

Whisker Painting
Cut several 4" (10 cm) strips of monofilament. Band the pieces together in bunches of ten. Invite the children to use these "whiskers" as paintbrushes.

Construction

Lion Cages
Provide popsicle sticks and glue. Invite the children to make lion cages.

Cooking and Snack

Lion Face Cookies
Provide sugar cookies and let the children decorate them with peanut butter, yellow coconut for manes and M&M eyes.

Dramatic Play

Taming Lions
Provide berry basket cages and plastic people and lions for dramatic play.

Fine Motor

Cat Paws
Invite the children to make fist prints with tempera paints. Show them how to use crayons to draw toenails and create cat paws.

Math

Counting Lions
Provide five berry baskets with 1-5 dots on each. Encourage the children to count the corresponding number of plastic lions into each "cage."

Jugglers, Magicians, Acrobats & Strong Men   Day 7

Materials
materials to do a magic trick (deck of cards, scarf, coin, etc.)

Morning Circle
1. Start circle time with a simple magic trick or the magic trick in the appendix, page 438.
2. Encourage the children to discuss what they know about magicians, jugglers, acrobats and strong men.
   If possible, teach the children how to do front and back somersaults.

Story Circle
Circus by Lois Ehlert

Music and Movement
Provide soft balls, such as Nerf balls, and invite the children to practice juggling.

Learning Centers

Art

Ball Paintings
Place Ping-Pong or golf balls in paint. Provide small boxes with art paper laid on the bottom. Invite the children to roll the paint-covered balls around in the box to create designs on the paper.

Construction

Magic Wands
Provide jumbo straws and art materials for the children to create magic wands.

Dramatic Play

Magic Tricks
Provide playing cards, black cape, top hat, magic wand and stuffed rabbit for dramatic play.

Gross Motor

Acrobats
Provide a mat or other soft surface. Invite the children to practice front and back rolls, somersaults and cartwheels.

Gross Motor

How Strong Are You?
Provide a set of light "weights" for the children to practice lifting. Make a barbell from a dowel and two Styrofoam balls.

Music

Rhythm Instruments
Play "circus" music. Encourage the children to play rhythm instruments to accompany the music.

Dogs, Seals & Dancing Bears   Day 8

Materials
photographs of performing dogs, seals and bears

Morning Circle
1. Show the photographs.
2. Invite the children to act out seals balancing balls on their noses, dogs doing tricks and bears dancing.
3. Ask, "How do the animals end their performance?" Seals clap their flippers together, dogs wag their tails and bears take a bow.

Story Circle
Grusha by Barbara Falk

Music and Movement
Invite the children to play Ringmaster, May I? like Mother, May I? (see the appendix, page 404). Use animal tricks (roll over, dance, shake, bark, etc.).

Learning Centers

Construction

Doggie Hats
Invite the children to make doggie clown hats. Roll large half-circles into cone shapes and glue or staple. Provide markers and other art materials for the children to use in decorating the hats.

Cooking and Snack

Animal Treats
Invite the children to decide if they'd rather be seals or dogs. Serve goldfish crackers to "seals" and pretzels (bones) to "dogs."

Discovery

Balance
Provide paper balls, beanbags, Nerf balls and beach balls. Invite the children to practice balancing the balls on their noses.

Dramatic Play

Seal and Dog Act
Provide hoops and beach balls for the children to use in dramatic play.

Fine Motor

Dancing Bears
Provide bear-shaped cutouts and scraps of wallpaper. Encourage the children to cut the wallpaper to make costumes for the paper bears (see patterns in the appendix, page 433-434).

Math

Ball Patterns
Cut balls (circles) from two or three colors of felt. Encourage the children to create patterns on the flannel board.

Traveling Town

Materials
Calliope Song (see the appendix, page 392); pictures of circus trains, buses, trucks, etc.

Morning Circle
1. Sing the Calliope Song.
2. Ask the children if they know how the circus gets from one city to the next.
3. Talk about how the animals and the people live on the road.

Story Circle
Night Ride by Michael Gay

Music and Movement
Invite the children to hold on to each other's waists to form a human train. Teach them how to make the chugga chugga and choo choo sounds as they travel around the room. You might want to play "The A Train" from *Saddle Up Your Pony* by Andrew Gunsberg.

Learning Centers

Art

Circus Highlights
Invite the children to paint pictures of their favorite part of the circus.

Dramatic Play

Tiny Circus
Use small boxes, berry baskets and plastic people and animals to make a miniature circus on a tabletop. Invite the children to dramatize circus life.

Construction

Circus Train
Invite the children to create a shoe-box train. Provide art materials for adding detail and decoration.

Gross Motor

Circus Tent
Invite the children to create a circus tent using old sheets and blankets.

Discovery

Wheels
Provide a small wagon and a heavy pail of blocks. Encourage the children to explore moving the pail of blocks with and without the wagon.

Math

Which Animals?
Provide two circus animal crackers in a small plastic bag for each child. Invite the children to graph the animals in all the children's bags.

Circus Finale

Materials

circus pictures painted by the children the previous day

Morning Circle

1. Let each child talk about a favorite part of the circus.
2. Encourage the children to show the pictures they painted yesterday and tell about them.

Story Circle

See the Circus by H. A. Rey

Music and Movement

Play march music and invite the children to have a circus parade. Encourage them to wear costumes, carry props or act like circus animals.

Learning Centers

Art

Face Paints

Provide face paints, smocks and a mirror. Encourage the children to paint the backs of their hands and/or their faces. (See the appendix, page 388, for a recipe for face paints.)

Gross Motor

Tightrope Walking

Set up the balance beam and encourage the children to "walk the tightrope."

Cooking and Snack

Popcorn and Lemonade

Invite the children to prepare and eat a snack of lemonade and popcorn.

Language

My Favorite

Ask the children to make a picture of their favorite part of the circus and tell something about it. Write down their responses.

Discovery

Now I Know

Ask the children what they know now about the circus that they did not know before. Write down their responses on chart paper. Make two columns: What I Knew Before, What I Know Now.

Science

Balancing

Provide beanbags, balls, straws, rulers, yardsticks and other objects. Invite the children to practice balancing the objects on their heads, shoulders, feet and hands.

Additional Books for Under the Big Top

Chester the Worldly Pig by Bill Peet
The Circus by Brian Wildsmith
Circus Fun by Margaret Hillert
Curious George Goes to the Circus by Margaret Rey
Morris and Boris at the Circus by Bernard Wiseman
Randy's Dandy Lions by Bill Peet

The Forest Comes to Us

The forest is filled with wonders of nature. In this unit, children investigate and learn to appreciate animal life unique to the forest.

Unit at a Glance

Day	Focus	Centers	Story Circle	Music/Movement
1	Trees Everywhere	Trees, Trees, Trees Tree Rubbings Torn Trees Leaf Sort Tree Parts Tree Lines	Tree	Tree Dance
2	Trees Help Us	Tree Paintings Tree House Wooden Structures Fruit Salad Picnic Shady Favorites	A Tree Is Nice	And the Green Grass Grew All Around
3	Mushrooms and Fungi	Miniature Forest Mushroom Dip Forest Concentration Felt Forest Mushroom Match Up-Close Look	In the Forest	Mushroom Play
4	Forest Animals	Who Lives Here? Make a Bird Nest Little Workers Tracks Animal and Home Match Animal Names	In a Cabin in a Wood	Bunny Hop
5	Forest Sounds	Painted Sounds Cricket Clickers Forest Concentration Bird Whistles Forest Sounds Sound Sort	Play With Me	Nature Dance

Day	Focus	Centers	Story Circle	Music/Movement
6	Forest Artists	A Web of My Own Underground Artist Spider Puppets Web Rubbings Moving Through the Day Ant Tunnels	The Very Busy Spider	Forest Animal Dance
7	Forest Edibles	Plant Dyes Tasting Party Fishing Dandelion Stew Forest Puzzles Edible Patterns	Blueberries for Sal	Pretend Walk
8	Forest Fires	Fire Painting Fire Prevention Posters Smoky Hats Forest Concentration Water Line Smother That Fire	The Smoky Bear Story	Stop, Drop and Roll
9	Camping	Sit-Upons Trail Mix Camping Out Ropes and Knots Camp Songs Don't Get Lost	Bailey Goes Camping	Doodle-li-doo
10	Conservation	Use It Again, Sam Conservation Collage Conservation Game Conservation Posters Electricity Savers The Root of Things	The World That Jack Built	Ask the Armadillo

Trees Everywhere

Materials
small branch, leaves, bark, photographs of different trees, large tree branch (if available)

Morning Circle
1. Place the large branch in the circle and then in one of the centers. Leave it there for the duration of the unit.
2. Show the tree parts. Name each part of the branch.
3. Show the photographs. Invite the children to stand like the different trees shown.
4. Talk about the differences among the different kinds of trees.

Story Circle
Tree by Harry Behn

Music and Movement
Invite the children to pretend to be trees that are growing, reaching for the sky, swaying in the breeze, drooping when thirsty, losing their leaves.

Learning Centers

Construction

Trees, Trees, Trees
Start a mural by painting brown tree trunks and branches on a piece of butcher paper. Invite the children to add leaves by dipping sponges in green paint (or red and yellow for fall colors) and pressing on the branches.

Discovery

Tree Rubbings
Provide leaves, pieces of bark, crayons and paper for the children to make rubbings.

Fine Motor

Torn Trees
Provide brown and green construction paper. Encourage the children to tear the paper into trunks and leaves and glue the pieces to drawing paper.

Math

Leaf Sort
Encourage the children to sort leaves into two main categories, then, if the children are able, into four subcategories.

Science

Tree Parts
Invite the children to examine leaves, twigs, barks and roots with magnifying glasses.

Writing

Tree Lines
Provide simple tree shapes and tracing paper. Invite the children to trace the shapes.

Trees Help Us

Day 2

Materials

chart paper and marker

Morning Circle

1. Make a list of all the ways trees help us (e.g., they provide lumber, shade and fruit). Look around the room for things made of wood.
2. Make a second list of ways trees help animals.
3. Ask, "Has anybody ever climbed a tree? Has anyone been inside a tree house?"

Story Circle

A Tree Is Nice by Janice Udry

Music and Movement

Sing "And the Green Grass Grew All Around" (see the appendix, page 382).

Learning Centers

Art

Tree Paintings
Provide easel paints and paper. Encourage the children to paint pictures of trees.

Cooking and Snack

Fruit Salad
Invite the children to cut up apples and bananas (fruits that grow on trees) with plastic knives and make a fruit salad.

Blocks

Tree House
Encourage the children to build a tree house. Provide photos for inspiration.

Dramatic Play

Picnic
Provide a picnic basket and props for the children to dramatize a picnic under the trees.

Construction

Wooden Structures
Encourage the children to build with popsicle sticks and glue.

Language

Shady Favorites
Encourage the children to draw pictures of something they like to do in the shade of a tree. Write down what they say about their drawings.

Mushrooms and Fungi Day 3

Materials
mushrooms, fungi, photographs of mushrooms and fungi

Morning Circle
1. Show the mushrooms and fungi or the pictures of mushrooms and fungi.
2. Ask the children if they have seen these before.
3. Talk about the role of fungi and mushrooms in the forest.

Story Circle
In the Forest by Jim Arnosky

Music and Movement
Encourage the children to pretend a parachute is a giant mushroom. Invite them to run under it, raise it with one hand and bounce a ball on it.

Learning Centers

Blocks

Miniature Forest
Cut out construction-paper mushrooms, fungi and trees. Tape the cutouts to blocks. Invite the children to create a forest. Provide logs, such as Lincoln Logs, for building a cabin.

Cooking and Snack

Mushroom Dip
Invite the children to chop up mushrooms and stir the pieces into sour cream to make a dip. What do mushrooms taste like?

Games

Forest Concentration
Invite the children to play Forest Concentration (see the appendix, page 412).

Language

Felt Forest
Cut mushrooms, fungi and trees out of felt. Encourage the children to create a forest on the flannel board.

Math

Mushroom Match
Cut a set of five paper mushrooms. Place 1–5 stick-on dots on each top and each stem. Cut the mushrooms apart. Invite the children to match stems to tops according to number of dots.

Science

Up-Close Look
Provide mushrooms and fungi for the children to examine through magnifying glasses.

Forest Animals

Day 4

Materials

plastic forest animals (raccoons, birds, deer, rabbits, frogs, spiders, etc.)

Morning Circle

1. Chant "In a Cabin in a Wood" (see the book reference below).
2. Show the plastic animals one at a time. Ask the children to tell how the forest makes a good home for each animal.
3. Talk about where in the forest each animal makes it's home.

Story Circle

In a Cabin in a Wood by Darcie McNally

Music and Movement

Do the "Bunny Hop" from *Hokey Pokey*.

Learning Centers

Blocks

Who Lives Here?
Add forest animals to the Block Center for the children to play with.

Sand and Water Table

Tracks
Provide items that will make tracks in the sand (e.g., comb, fork, file, twig, etc.). Encourage the children to make tracks like forest animals do.

Construction

Make a Bird Nest
Provide small twigs, straw and pieces of yarn. Encourage the children to build bird nests.

Science

Animal and Home Match
Provide pictures of forest animals and their homes. Invite the children to match animals to homes.

Discovery

Little Workers
Place a piece of decaying wood in the aquarium. Invite the children to observe the small creatures at work there.

Writing

Animal Names
Write forest animal names on index cards. Add pictures if available. Provide tracing paper and pencils for tracing.

Forest Sounds

Materials

tape of nature sounds, chart paper and marker

Morning Circle

1. Play the tape as the children enter the room.
2. Help the children brainstorm a list of forest sounds.
3. Assign each sound to a small group. Encourage groups to practice their sound and then ask the other groups to identify it.

Story Circle

Play With Me by Marie Hall Ets

Music and Movement

Play a tape of nature music. Invite the children to dance.

Learning Centers

Art

Painted Sounds
Encourage the children to draw pictures of things that make noise in the forest.

Language

Bird Whistles
Invite the children to practice whistling. Can they communicate with each other with whistling sounds only?

Fine Motor

Cricket Clickers
Provide aluminum cans. Encourage the children to squeeze the cans gently to create a clicking sound. Does it sound like a cricket?

Listening

Forest Sounds
Place a relaxation tape of forest sounds in the center for the children to listen to.

Games

Forest Concentration
Invite the children to play Forest Concentration (see the appendix, page 412).

Science

Sound Sort
Provide several nature items (e.g., feather, pine cone, leaf, twig, rock, etc.). Invite the children to sort the items according to whether they make a sound when dropped on a tabletop.

Forest Artists

Day 6

Materials
rope or yarn, tape

Morning Circle
1. Wind rope through an open area to create a spider web or use white yarn over a classroom door.
2. Ask the children if they can think of ways forest creatures might be like artists when they create their homes (spider webs), eat (caterpillar) or travel (leave tracks).

Story Circle
The Very Busy Spider by Eric Carle

Music and Movement
Play music and encourage the children to pretend to be dancing spiders, rushing ants, jumping frogs and hungry caterpillars.

Learning Centers

Art

A Web of My Own
Provide glue and aluminum foil. Invite the children to draw webs on the foil with the glue. When the glue dries, the children can lift their webs off the foil.

Fine Motor

Web Rubbings
Draw a spider web with glue on construction paper. When the glue dries, invite the children to make crayon rubbings of the web.

Discovery

Underground Artist
Place a shovel full of dirt in a box. Provide magnifying glasses for the children to observe underground artists at work.

Gross Motor

Moving Through the Day
Encourage the children to move like frogs, caterpillars, spiders or ants all day long.

Dramatic Play

Spider Puppets
Provide clay and pipe cleaners for the children to make spider puppets.

Science

Ant Tunnels
Display an ant farm. Invite the children to observe the ants as they create their underground tunnels.

Forest Edibles

Materials
mushrooms, onions, berries, seeds

Morning Circle
1. Show the foods from the forest.
2. Ask the children if they know where the foods came from.
3. Make a graph showing the number of children who have tasted the following: berries, mushrooms, dandelions, freshwater fish.

Story Circle
Blueberries for Sal by Robert McCloskey

Music and Movement
Invite the children to take a pretend walk through the forest. Walk around mushrooms, step over fallen trees, walk a fallen tree, stop to smell a flower, pick berries and so on.

Learning Centers

Art

Plant Dyes
Create dyes from plants and plant products (blackberries, blueberries, flower petals, etc.). Invite the children to paint with the dyes.

Language

Dandelion Stew
Invite the children to dictate a recipe for dandelion stew.

Cooking and Snack

Tasting Party
Provide several types of berries for the children to taste.

Language

Forest Puzzles
Make enlarged copies of mushrooms and fungi from Forest Concentration (see the appendix, page 412). Mount on poster board and then cut each into four or five pieces for the children to put together.

Games

Fishing
Cut several construction-paper fish. Put a paper clip on the mouth of each one. Tie a 2' (60 cm) string to a dowel rod. Tie a magnet to the loose end. Invite the children to catch fish in the forest stream.

Math

Edible Patterns
Cut mushrooms, dandelions and berries from felt. Invite the children to create patterns on the flannel board.

Forest Fires

Day 8

Materials
picture of Smoky Bear

Morning Circle
1. Show the picture and tell what Smoky Bear's job is. Sing "The Smoky Bear Song" if you know it.
2. Talk about how forest fires start and what we can do to prevent them. What is the best way to put out a camp fire?

Story Circle
The Smoky Bear Story by Ellen Morrison

Music and Movement
Teach the children the "Stop, Drop and Roll" procedure for putting out a fire on their clothing.

Learning Centers

Art

Fire Painting
Provide orange and yellow paint for the children to make fire paintings.

Games

Forest Concentration
Invite the children to play Forest Concentration (see the appendix, page 412).

Construction

Fire Prevention Posters
Provide art materials for the children to create Fire Prevention Posters.

Gross Motor

Water Line
Make a pretend water line. Have four children stand between two boxes. Encourage them to move crumpled-up blue paper from one box to the other by passing it down the line in a bucket.

Fine Motor

Smoky Hats
Cut Smoky Bear hats from brown construction paper (use the pattern in the appendix, page 432). Invite the children to decorate their hats.

Sand and Water Table

Smother That Fire
Provide a shovel and small pieces of orange tissue paper (fire). Invite the children to practice putting out a campfire by shoveling sand or dirt to cover the paper.

Camping   Day 9

Materials
camping equipment: small shovel, canteen, lantern, sleeping bag, pots and pans, raincoat, compass, flashlight, etc.

Morning Circle
1. Show the children the camping equipment.
2. Solicit camping stories from those children who have been camping.
3. Encourage the children to think of reasons that people like to camp in the forest.

Story Circle
Bailey Goes Camping by Kevin Henkes

Music and Movement
Invite the children to sing "Doodle-li-doo" with the hand motions (see the appendix, page 392).

Learning Centers

Construction

Sit-Upons
Show the children how to fold sheets of newspaper into 2" (5 cm) strips, then weave the strips together to make a square mat. Tape or staple the edges.

Cooking and Snack

Trail Mix
Provide raisins, coconut, peanuts and pretzels. Invite the children to place a spoonful of each ingredient into a small plastic bag for trail food.

Dramatic Play

Camping Out
Provide old sheets for the children to make tents. Provide logs for a fire and pots and pans for cooking. Sleeping bags will really add to the fun.

Fine Motor

Ropes and Knots
Provide pieces of rope. Teach the children to tie a simple knot and encourage them to practice.

Listening

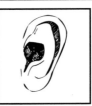

Camp Songs
Provide a tape of camp songs for the children to listen to. Wee Sing Silly Songs is a great resource for songs.

Science

Don't Get Lost
Provide a compass for the children to experiment with.

Conservation

Materials
none

Morning Circle
1. Introduce the word conservation. Explain that it means using things (resources) wisely and not wasting them.
2. Encourage the children to think about things in the forest we can take care of. How can we take care?

Story Circle
The World That Jack Built by Ruth Brown

Music and Movement
"Ask the Armadillo" from *Plant a Dream* by John Archambault and David Plummer

Learning Centers

Art

Use It Again, Sam
Provide empty paper towel tubes, fabric and wallpaper scraps and other pieces of "trash." Encourage the children to make something with the items.

Construction

Conservation Collage
Invite the children to make a collage of objects that would usually be thrown away.

Games

Conservation Game
Make a game board (use a copy of appendix page 427). Provide a spinner or number cube. After each move, players tell the others about the reminder they landed on. If they can't, they go back to start. First one through is the winner.

Language

Conservation Posters
Invite the children to draw pictures illustrating conservation rules (e.g., turn off the lights, don't waste water, recycle, etc.). Ask them to dictate the rule to you so you can write it below the drawing.

Sand and Water Table

Electricity Savers
Invite the children to bring old knee-high socks from home. Invite them to put one sock inside the other and then fill with sand. Tie off the end. Use these to stop drafts around doors and windows.

Science

The Root of Things
Provide potted plants. Encourage the children to gently spoon and brush the dirt away from the roots. Provide magnifying glasses for close examination.

Additional Books for The Forest Comes to Us

All About Ponds by Jane Rockwell

Amazing Frogs and Toads by Barry Clarke

Antler, Bear, Canoe: A Northwoods Alphabet by Betsy Bowen

The Aquarium Take-Along Book by Sheldon Gerstenfeld

Chorus of Frogs by Joni Phelps Hunt

Come to the Meadow by Anna Grossnickle Hines

Deep in the Forest by Brinton Turkle

The Fascinating World of Frogs and Toads by Maria Angels Julivert

The Fish: The Story of the Stickleback by Margaret Lane

For the Love of Our Earth by P.K. Hallinan

Frogs, Toads, Lizards and Salamanders by Joan Wright and Nancy Winslow Parker

From Tadpole to Frog by Wendy Pfeffer

Gift of the Tree by Alvin Tresselt

In the Pond by Ermanno Cristini and Luigi Puricelli

In the Small, Small Pond by Denise Fleming

In the Woods by Ermanno Cristini and Luigi Puricelli

In the Woods: Who's Been Here? by Lindsay Barrett George

Life in the Pond by Eileen Curran

Lily Pad Pond by Bianca Lavies

Nature Spy by Shelley Rotner and Ken Kreisler

Where Once There Was a Wood by Denise Fleming

Where the River Begins by Thomas Berger

Giants

Giants come in many forms. This unit explores everything from fairy tale giants to dinosaurs to tall buildings to mountains. It's a great unit for teaching perspective.

Unit at a Glance

Day	Focus	Centers	Story Circle	Music/Movement
1	**Big, Bigger, Biggest**	Big and Bigger Pictures Big Buildings Bead Patterns Concentric Circles Size Sort Does it Fit?	Is It Larger? Is It Smaller?	Mother, May I?
2	**A Matter of Perspective**	Taller Towers Fingerprint Mice Ant Watch Giant Blocks Size Arrangements Pulleys	Amos and Boris	One Elephant
3	**Giants in Nature**	Mountain Collage Mountain Changes Playdough Mountain Rock Sort Icebergs Rock in a Sock	High in the Mountains	Big Wind
4	**Tall Trees**	Tall Tree Pictures Tree Creations Tree Sculpting My Tree House How Trees Grow Seed Sort	Sky Tree	Wooden Instruments
5	**Elephants, Giraffes & Whales**	Favorite Animal Giraffe Construction Whale Spout Cupcakes Pin the Tail on the Whale What Are Elephants Like? Blowholes	The Biggest Animal Ever	Baby Beluga

Day	Focus	Centers	Story Circle	Music/Movement
6	Human-Made Giants	Skyline Mural Box Giants Empire State Building Skyscraper Toss Build with Shapes Giant Trace	Skyscrapers	Big Ship Coming
7	Ships and Airplanes	Air and Sea Pictures Block Boats Ship's Galley Miniature Golf Sink or Float Boat Float	Amazing Boats	Aerobics
8	Dinosaurs	Boxasaurus Model Dinosaurs Pin the Tail on the Dinosaur Dinosaur Concentration What Do You Know! Dinosaur Tracings	Discover Dinosaurs	Please Don't Bring a Tyrannosaurus Rex
9	More Dinosaurs	Shadow Match Giant Puzzle Dinosaur Eggs What Size Is Your Foot? Archaeological Dig I Can Spell . . .	How Big Were the Dinosaurs?	Dinosaur Course
10	Dinosaurs Again	The Pig Picture Dinosaur House Dinosaur Puppets Dinosaur Egg Hunt Dinosaur Concentration Who Ate What?	Tyrannosaurus Was a Beast	Brontosaurus, Brontosaurus, Tyrannosaurus

Big, Bigger, Biggest Day 1

Materials
sets of objects that come in three sizes

Morning Circle
1. Display objects and have the children arrange them by size, big to biggest.
2. Encourage the children to find someone in the room who is bigger and someone who is smaller.

Story Circle
Is It Larger? Is It Smaller? by Tana Hoban

Music and Movement
Play Mother, May I? using words like *big* and *little* to describe movements (see the appendix, page 404).

Learning Centers

Art

Big and Bigger Pictures
Give each child two pieces of paper (one small and one large). Invite the children to paint the same picture on both papers.

Blocks

Big Buildings
Encourage the children to build big, bigger and biggest structures.

Fine Motor

Bead Patterns
Invite the children to string beads in a big, bigger and biggest pattern.

Math

Concentric Circles
Provide three paper circles in graduated sizes. Invite the children to glue the circles together with the biggest on the bottom and the smallest on the top.

Math

Size Sort
Provide several items that come in three sizes (e.g., drinking cups, socks, shoes). Encourage the children to sort the items by size.

Science

Does It Fit?
Provide a coffee can and several items that are larger and smaller than the opening. Invite the children to sort the items according to what fits and what doesn't fit.

A Matter of Perspective   Day 2

Materials
the story "The Lion and the Mouse"

Morning Circle
1. Read or tell the story of "The Lion and the Mouse."
2. Discuss size relationships like children to ants and mosquitoes, children to adults, adults to elephants. Explain that "big" is relative to your own size.
3. Discuss the relationship of size to ability as it is portrayed in the story. Does size make you strong?
4. Challenge the children to think of a time they were able to help someone bigger. Invite discussion.

Story Circle
Amos and Boris by William Steig

Music and Movement
"One Elephant" from *Where Is Thumbkin?* by The Learning Station

Learning Centers

Blocks

Taller Towers
Invite the children to build a tower taller than they are and another smaller than they are.

Construction

Fingerprint Mice
Invite the children to make their fingerprints on paper and then draw eyes and whiskers on each one to make a mouse.

Discovery

Ant Watch
Place some large crumbs in an ant farm and let the children observe the ants lifting crumbs bigger than they are. How can ants do this?

Fine Motor

Giant Blocks
Invite the children to stuff large grocery sacks 3/4 full with crumpled newspaper. Fold the tops of the bags over and tape to make blocks. Invite the children to build with the giant blocks.

Math

Size Arrangements
Provide size-correct (proportional) pictures of various animals. Invite the children to arrange the animals from smallest to largest.

Science

Pulleys
Place a pulley in the center and invite the children to use it to pick up and pull heavy loads (e.g., blocks in a bucket).

Giants in Nature

Day 3

Materials
photographs of mountains, waterfalls, icebergs and other "natural giants"

Morning Circle
1. Tell the children that you will be learning about big things for the next two weeks. The big thing you'll learn about today is mountains.
2. Ask the children to tell what they know about mountains. Ask, "Who has seen a mountain? Did you think it was big? Tell me what you thought. Do you know that it can take weeks for mountain climbers to get to the top of some mountains?"
3. Talk about mountains being very big rocks.

Story Circle
High in the Mountains by Ruth Radin

Music and Movement
Take a parachute outside. Experiment with making big winds.

Learning Centers

Art

Mountain Collage
Encourage the children to tear pages from a magazine to make a mountain collage. The many colors from the magazine pages will resemble mountain colors.

Math

Rock Sort
Provide rocks of various sizes for the children to sort into categories of large and small.

Discovery

Mountain Changes
Encourage the children to make sand mountains and then use a straw to drop water on them. What happens? What happens when they blow on them?

Sand and Water Table

Icebergs
Place large chunks of ice in the water table. Provide small boats for the children to navigate through the icebergs.

Fine Motor

Playdough Mountain
Provide clay or playdough and invite the children to make mountains.

Science

Rock in a Sock
Provide several porous rocks for the children to examine. Then put the rocks in an old sock and hit them with a hammer to break them up. Explain that mountain rocks break down and create smaller rocks and sand. Supervise closely. [Use caution.]

Tall Trees

Materials
photographs of large trees (redwoods would be great)

Morning Circle
1. Place an 80' (24 m) length of yarn in a circle around the room. This is the size of an average redwood.
2. When the children come in, have them sit inside the circle. Explain that the yarn would fit around the trunk of a redwood tree.
3. Let the children hold hands and try to make a circle as big as the yarn circle.
4. Look at the trees outside. Are any of them giants?

Story Circle
Sky Tree by Thomas Locker

Music and Movement
Provide instruments made of wood, such as tone blocks, rhythm sticks and guitars, for the children to play.

Learning Centers

Art

Tall Tree Pictures
Provide paints for the children to paint giant trees.

Dramatic Play

My Tree House
Use a washing machine box and brown bulletin board paper to create a house inside a redwood trunk. Let the children decorate.

Construction

Tree Creations
Provide several shades of green felt cut in the shapes of pine, willow, palm and oak or maple trees. Provide several sizes of brown felt trunks. Invite the children to create trees of all sizes and shapes.

Language

How Trees Grow
Encourage the children to dictate their understanding of how a tree grows. Encourage them to illustrate their ideas.

Construction

Tree Sculpting
Build a giant tree. Use boxes or the heavy cardboard tube from a roll of carpet for the trunk. Cut the foliage from green bulletin board paper. Encourage the children to paint or color the trunk and glue on leaves.

Science

Seed Sort
Provide acorns and other tree seeds for the children to sort.

Elephants, Giraffes & Whales   Day 5

Materials
photographs of elephants, giraffes and whales

Morning Circle
1. Show the photographs.
2. Start a discussion about the size of elephants (about 8' or 2.5 m tall), giraffes (about 12' or 4 m tall), and whales (90–100' or 27–30 m long).
3. Cut a piece of yarn 90' (27 m) long and let the children stretch it out to its full length. Ask, "Is the whale a giant sea creature?"
4. Ask, "Are giraffes or elephants giants? Which one is taller? Which one is larger?"

Story Circle
The Biggest Animal Ever by Allan Fowler

Music and Movement
"Baby Beluga" from *Baby Beluga* by Raffi

Learning Centers

Art

Favorite Animal
Provide tempera paint and paper. Invite the children to paint their favorite animal giant.

Games

Pin the Tail on the Whale
Cut a large whale shape and several tail sections from poster board. Invite the children to play Pin the Tail on the Whale.

Construction

Giraffe Construction
Invite the children to build a giraffe with boxes and wrapping paper tubes.

Listening

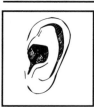

What Are Elephants Like?
Tape record the children's thoughts and ideas about elephants, giraffes and whales. Let the children listen over and over to the tape.

Cooking and Snack

Whale Spout Cupcakes
Provide cupcakes, blue icing and licorice laces. Invite the children to ice the cupcakes, then stick a few licorice sticks (streams of water) into the center into the cupcake.

Sand and Water Table

Blowholes
Provide plastic bottles and invite the children to squeeze the bottles and spray water through the "blowholes." If the weather permits, do this outside.

Human-Made Giants

Day 6

Materials

photographs of skyscrapers, bridges, trucks, ships (it's good to have people in the photos to show the size comparison); blocks

Morning Circle

1. Build a tall structure with the blocks.
2. Show the photographs. Ask, "Is this building bigger than your house? Is this structure taller than our school?"
3. Let the children brainstorm a list of big things people have created.

Story Circle

Skyscrapers by Joy Richardson

Music and Movement

"Big Ship Coming" from *We've Got to Come Full Circle* by Tom Wisner and Teresa Whitaker

Learning Centers

Art

Skyline Mural
Provide a piece of butcher paper. Encourage the children to cut buildings from construction paper and glue them on the butcher paper to create a city skyline.

Blocks

Box Giants
Fill the center with boxes and encourage children to build skyscrapers, bridges, trucks and so on.

Blocks

Empire State Building
Challenge the children to build a skyscraper taller than they are.

Games

Skyscraper Toss
Make skyscrapers from three different-sized boxes. Invite the children to toss beanbags into the boxes. Challenge them to toss their second beanbag into a skyscraper that is bigger/smaller than the first.

Math

Build with Shapes
Cut several shapes from felt and invite the children to create bridges, skyscrapers, trucks and more on the flannel board.

Writing

Giant Trace
Make several simple line drawings of skyscrapers, bridges, airplanes, trains, etc. Provide tracing paper for the children to trace them.

Ships and Airplanes

Materials
photographs of large ships and airplanes

Morning Circle
1. Show the photographs. Ask, "Who has seen a ship or an airplane? Will you tell us about it?"
2. Tell the children that cruise ships are so big that 2,000 people can sleep in them. They have swimming pools, basketball courts, tennis courts, shops and even a place to play golf.
3. Divide the class into three or four groups. Give each group a bucket of water and a lump of clay. Tell the children that ships are heavy. Ask, "How does something heavy float? Will your clay float?" Invite them to find out.
4. Talk about the need for air and the hollowness of the ship. Let the children reshape their clay and try again.

Story Circle
Amazing Boats by Margaret Lincoln

Music and Movement
Invite the children to join you in an aerobic exercise class (like you would find on a cruise ship).

Learning Centers

Art

Air and Sea Pictures
Provide blue tempera paint and have the children paint the ocean or the sky. When the paint is dry, the children can draw in boats or airplanes.

Blocks

Block Boats
Invite the children to build an ocean liner with blocks.

Dramatic Play

Ship's Galley
Provide a captain's cap and props to set up a captain's table. Invite the children to role-play dinner aboard a ship.

Games

Miniature Golf
Cut holes in the ends of several boxes and place them around the room. Provide cardboard tubes and Ping-Pong balls for the children to hit the balls through the boxes.

Sand and Water Table

Boat Float
Provide boats for the children to float in the water table.

Science

Sink or Float
Provide a variety of objects. Encourage the children to find out which sink and which float.

Dinosaurs

Materials
pictures of dinosaurs, chart paper and marker

Morning Circle
1. Show the pictures.
2. Make a list of everything the children know about dinosaurs. Check your list each day as they learn more about dinosaurs.

Story Circle
Discover Dinosaurs by Alice Jablonsky

Music and Movement
"Please Don't Bring a Tyrannosaurus Rex" from *Late Last Night* by Joe Scruggs

Learning Centers

Construction

Boxasaurus
Encourage the children to make a dinosaur out of boxes.

Language

Dinosaur Concentration
Make dinosaur cards (use page 413 in the appendix). Invite the children to play Dinosaur Concentration.

Fine Motor

Model Dinosaurs
Encourage the children to fashion dinosaurs out of clay.

Library

What Do You Know!
Put out an assortment of books about dinosaurs for the children to look at.

Games

Pin the Tail on the Dinosaur
Cut a large dinosaur and several tail sections from poster board. Invite the children to play Pin the Tail on the Dinosaur.

Writing

Dinosaur Tracings
Provide tracing paper, pencils and pictures of dinosaurs from a coloring book. Invite the children to trace the pictures.

More Dinosaurs

Materials

80' (2.5 m) length of yarn

Morning Circle

1. Ask two children to stretch out the piece of yarn. Explain that the yarn is the same length as an average brontosaurus.
2. Ask the children to lie head to toe along the yarn. Is the yarn longer or shorter than the line of children?

Story Circle

How Big Were the Dinosaurs? by Bernard Most

Music and Movement

Use a long rope, masking tape or a chalk line to make the outline of a dinosaur and invite the children to crawl, hop, walk and skip along the outline.

Learning Centers

Games

Shadow Match
Make a shadow match game (use page 413 in the appendix). Make one set of black silhouettes and one set of the line drawings. Encourage the children to match the sets.

Language

Giant Puzzle
Make a gigantic dinosaur floor puzzle and invite the children to put it together.

Math

Dinosaur Eggs
Provide several large plastic eggs filled with classroom items of different weights. Encourage the children to arrange the eggs from lightest to heaviest.

Math

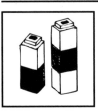

What Size Is Your Foot?
Make a dinosaur footprint (about 3' x 4' or 90 cm x 120 cm). Invite the children to see how many steps it takes to walk heel to toe across the foot print.

Sand and Water Table

Archaeological Dig
Bury several clean bones in the sand table. Invite the children to use strainers, spoons and small brushes to find and clean the bones.

Writing

I Can Spell. . .
Write names of dinosaurs on index cards. Provide tracing paper and pencils so the children can trace the names.

Dinosaurs Again

Materials
none

Morning Circle
Ask the children to talk about what it might be like to have a dinosaur as a pet.

Story Circle
Tyrannosaurus Was a Beast by Jack Prelutsky

Music and Movement
Invite the children to play Brontosaurus, Brontosaurus, Tyrannosaurus like Duck, Duck, Goose (see the appendix, page 402).

Learning Centers

Art

The Big Picture
Provide the children with a large sheet of butcher paper and invite them to paint a dinosaur.

Blocks

Dinosaur House
Invite the children to use the blocks to build a house for a pet dinosaur.

Construction

Dinosaur Puppets
Provide old socks, buttons, felt and other art materials for the children to create dinosaur sock puppets.

Dramatic Play

Dinosaur Egg Hunt
Provide several large plastic eggs. Encourage the children to take turns hiding the eggs and pretending to be a Tyrannosaurus Rex looking for them.

Games

Dinosaur Concentration
Make dinosaur cards (use page 413 in the appendix). Invite the children to play Dinosaur Concentration.

Science

Who Ate What?
Provide several pictures of dinosaurs (or plastic dinosaurs). Invite the children to sort them into meat-eaters and plant-eaters.

Additional Books for Giants

The Ant and the Elephant by Bill Peet

Big Old Bones: A Dinosaur Tale by Carol Carrick

Bones, Bones, Dinosaur Bones by Byron Barton

David Dreaming of Dinosaurs by Keith Faulkner

Digging Up Dinosaurs by Aliki

The Dinosaur Alphabet Book by Jerry Pallotta

Dinosaur Dance by Joe Noonan

Dinosaur Eggs by Francis Mosley

Dinosaur Time by Peggy Parish

Dinosaurs by Gail Gibbons

Dinosaurs Strange and Wonderful by Laurence Pringle

Dinosaurs, Dinosaurs by Byron Barton

Elephants Aloft by Kathi Appelt

Fossils Tell of Long Ago by Aliki

Giant Dinosaurs by Erna Rowe

I Can Read About Prehistoric Animals by David Eastman

If Dinosaurs Came to Town by Dom Mansell

If the Dinosaurs Came Back by Bernard Most

Little Elephant by Miela Ford

The Little Mouse, The Red Ripe Strawberry, and the Big Hungry Bear by Don and Audrey Wood

The Magic School Bus in the Time of the Dinosaurs by Joanna Cole

My Visit to the Dinosaurs by Aliki

Patrick's Dinosaurs by Carol Carrick

The Selfish Giant by Oscar Wilde

Stand Back, Said the Elephant, I'm Going to Sneeze! by Patricia Thomas

Story of Dinosaurs by David Eastman

Time Flies by Eric Rohmann

Time Train by Paul Fleischman

What Happened to Patrick's Dinosaurs? by Carol Carrick

Whatever Happened to the Dinosarus? by Bernard Most

Traditional Tales

Everyone loves a good story, and stories passed down generation to generation have a life of their own. This unit brings to life some of those old-time favorites.

Unit at a Glance

Day	Focus	Centers	Story Circle	Music/Movement
1	The Three Bears	Bear Masks Porridge Three Bears Cottage Dress Baby Bear Small, Medium, Large Hot and Cold	Deep in the Forest	Three Bears Rap
2	The Three Little Pigs	Pretty in Pink Home Building Pig Masks Pig Tails Jig Blow It Down	The Fourth Little Pig	Squeal, Pig, Squeal
3	The Three Billy Goats Gruff	Balancing Bridge Building What a Difference a Rock Makes Stone Toss The Troll Talks Size Sort	Three Cool Kids	Trip-Trap
4	Jack and the Beanstalk	Golden Art Giant's Castle Bean Dip Golden Egg Roll A Picture's Worth a Thousand Words Plant Beans	Jim and the Beanstalk	Beanstalk Ball
5	The Little Red Hen	Favorite Character Farmland Grinding Grains Making Bread Book and Tape Corny Counting	The Little Red Hen	I Had a Rooster

Day	Focus	Centers	Story Circle	Music/Movement
6	The Gingerbread Man	Gingerbread Creations It's a Maze Gingerbread People Baking Gingerbread Men Dressed to Eat Cookie Jar Fill	The Gingerbread Rabbit	Play Follow the Leader
7	Chicken Little	Acorn Roll Henny Penny's Farm Sky Puzzles Acorn Toss Rhyme Time Acorns Up Close	The Sky Is Falling	Chicken
8	The Turnip	Turnip on View Yummy Turnips Our Own Play Tell It Again Looking Beneath Largest to Smallest	The Turnip	Hot Turnip
9	This Is the House That Jack Built	Jack's House Jack's House Hammer and Nail Next, Please This Is the Story That I Told Adding On	The Napping House	Put Your Thumb in the Air
10	Little Red Riding Hood	I Like Red Build a Forest Treats for Grandma Basket for Grandma Through the Forest Friend Sort	Little Red Riding Hood	Red Riding Hood Waltz

The Three Bears

Materials

a favorite version of "Goldilocks and the Three Bears"

Morning Circle

1. Read or tell the story.
2. Talk about Goldilocks going inside when no one was home.

Story Circle

Deep in the Forest by Brinton Turkle

Music and Movement

Chant "The Three Bears Rap" (see the appendix, page 400).

Learning Centers

Construction

Bear Masks
Provide paper plates, tongue depressors, brown construction paper and other art materials for the children to make bear masks.

Cooking and Snack

Porridge
Invite the children to make oatmeal and serve it for snack. Supervise closely. [Use caution.]

Dramatic Play

Three Bears Cottage
Provide small, medium and large props for the children to use while acting out the story.

Games

Dress Baby Bear
Provide bear-shaped paper dolls and wallpaper clothes. Invite the children to dress Baby Bear.

Math

Small, Medium, Large
Provide sets of objects that come in three sizes. Encourage the children to sort them into small, medium and large groups.

Science

Hot and Cold
Provide pictures of hot and cold items for the children to sort.

The Three Little Pigs
Day 2

Materials
a favorite version of "The Three Little Pigs,"; "The Big Bad Wolf" by Steve and Greg

Morning Circle
1. Read or tell the story.
2. Encourage the children to act out the story.
3. Listen to "The Big Bad Wolf."

Story Circle
The Fourth Little Pig by Teresa Celsi

Music and Movement
Play Squeal, Pig, Squeal. IT walks around the circle blindfolded (assisted by the teacher) and eventually sits in another child's lap. That child squeals, and IT tries to guess who the squealer is. If IT is correct, the squealer becomes the new IT.

Learning Centers

Art

Pretty in Pink
Provide pink paints and encourage the children to paint pigs.

Fine Motor

Pig Tails
Encourage the children to wrap 1" x 8" (3 cm x 20 cm) strips of pink construction paper around pencils to form curly pig tails.

Blocks

Home Building
Provide straw, bricks and sticks for the children to build houses for the three pigs.

Music

Jig
Provide Irish or Gaelic music and teach the children a jig.

Construction

Pig Masks
Provide paper plates, tongue depressors, pink construction paper and other art materials for the children to create pig masks.

Science

Blow It Down
Invite the children to blow through straws to move a variety of objects (feather, ball, book, pencil, paper, etc.). Which objects move?

The Three Billy Goats Gruff Day 3

Materials
a favorite version of "The Three Billy Goats Gruff"

Morning Circle
1. Build a bridge with cardboard blocks or a balance beam. Set it up so that the children cross it when they come in the room.
2. Read or tell the story.
3. Invite the children to dramatize the story.
4. Ask the children to tell what they think about the two smaller goats passing the troll on to their bigger brother. Encourage them to explain their thinking.

Story Circle
Three Cool Kids by Rebecca Emberley

Music and Movement
Invite the children to demonstrate "trip-trap" and "tramp-tramp."

Learning Centers

Blocks

Balancing
Provide a balance beam for the children to walk across as the small, medium and big billy goat would.

Games

Stone Toss
Provide stones (large wads of paper) for the children to toss at the troll (box with picture drawn on one side).

Construction

Bridge Building
Invite the children to make bridges with popsicle sticks and clay.

Listening

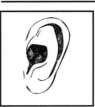

The Troll Talks
Provide a tape recorder and encourage the children to retell the story from the troll's point of view.

Discovery

What a Difference a Rock Makes
Provide three jars filled halfway with water. Invite the children to put a small pebble in one jar, a medium-sized rock in the second and a large rock in the third. How do the water levels compare?

Math

Size Sort
Provide sets of objects that come in three sizes. Invite the children to sort the items according to small, medium and large.

Jack and the Beanstalk   Day 4

Materials
a favorite version of "Jack and the Beanstalk"

Morning Circle
1. Read or tell the story.
2. Talk about the things Jack took from the giant. Ask, "How do you think the giant felt when Jack took his things? How do you think you would feel?"

Story Circle
Jim and the Beanstalk by Raymond Briggs

Music and Movement
Provide music and invite the children to dance like the giant, the goose and Jack. Ask the children to explain their movements.

Learning Centers

Art

Golden Art
Provide gold paint and egg-shaped paper. Invite the children to paint their own golden eggs.

Blocks

Giant's Castle
Invite the children to build the giant's castle.

Cooking and Snack

Bean Dip
Provide cooked beans and several spices like salt, garlic powder and Tabasco. Invite the children to mash the beans and add seasonings to make bean dip for snack. Serve with cut-up vegetables or crackers.

Discovery

Golden Egg Roll
Spray paint a Ping-Pong or golf ball and three or four plastic eggs with gold paint. Let the children place different objects in the eggs and roll them. How does the roll of the eggs compare with the roll of the ball?

Language

A Picture's Worth a Thousand Words
Invite the children to draw a picture of the giant and dictate a sentence describing him.

Science

Plant Beans
Provide beans, small plastic containers, soil and water. Invite the children to plant the beans and take care of them.

The Little Red Hen

Day 5

Materials

a favorite version of "The Little Red Hen"

Morning Circle

1. Read or tell the story.
2. Invite the children to discuss the hen's decision to keep the bread all to herself.

Story Circle

Read another version of "The Little Red Hen."

Music and Movement

"I Had a Rooster" from *Peanut Butter, Tarzan, and Roosters* by Miss Jackie

Learning Centers

Art

My Favorite Character
Provide paints and invite the children to paint a picture of their favorite character in the story.

Dramatic Play

Making Bread
Provide playdough, mixing bowls, rolling pins and bread pans for the children to role-play bread making.

Blocks

Farmland
Spray paint a sheet brown and green (yard and fields) and blue (pond). Encourage the children to build a farm on the sheet. Provide plastic animals and toy trucks and tractors.

Listening

Book and Tape
Record a reading of the story on tape. Place the tape and the book in the center for the children to enjoy.

Discovery

Grinding Grains
Provide a mortar and pestle and a variety of grains (oats, wheat, barley, etc.) for the children to grind. Compare to flour purchased in a store.

Math

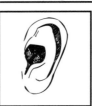

Corny Counting
Cut holes in the lids of five margarine tubs. Place one to five dots on each lid. Invite the children to count the corresponding number of corn kernels into each tub.

The Gingerbread Man

Day 6

Materials
a favorite version of "The Gingerbread Man"; chart paper and marker

Morning Circle
1. Read or tell the story.
2. Encourage the children to name all the characters who chased the Gingerbread Man. Can they remember the sequence?
3. Write down their responses on chart paper.

Story Circle
The Gingerbread Rabbit by Jarrell Randall

Music and Movement
Play Follow the Leader. Let IT be the Gingerbread Boy or Girl.

Learning Centers

Art

Gingerbread Creations
Cut paper into gingerbread man shapes. Provide paints and markers for the children to decorate them.

Dramatic Play

Baking Gingerbread Men
Provide playdough, cookie cutters and cookie sheets for the children to role-play making gingerbread people.

Blocks

It's a Maze
Invite the children to use rope and boxes to create a maze for the gingerbread man to escape through.

Language

"My picture is about...."

Dressed to Eat
Provide felt cutouts in gingerbread people shapes. Encourage the children to decorate the cutouts with lace, buttons, ribbons and rickrack.

Cooking and Snack

Gingerbread People
Provide gingerbread people for the children to decorate with icing and raisins.

Math

Cookie Jar Fill
Place one to five dots on each of five jars or boxes. Cut out several small gingerbread people. Invite the children to place the corresponding number of gingerbread cookies into each container.

Chicken Little

Materials
a favorite version of "Chicken Little"

Morning Circle
1. Read or tell the story.
2. Talk about the names of the story characters (Henny Penny, Foxy Loxy, etc.). Encourage the children to think of or make up words that rhyme with their own names.

Story Circle
The Sky Is Falling by Joseph Jacobs

Music and Movement
"Chicken" from *All Time Favorite Dances* by Melody House

Learning Centers

Art

Acorn Roll
Invite the children to dip acorns and marbles in tempera paint and roll them across paper in the bottom of a shallow box. How do they roll differently? Do they make different kinds of lines?

Blocks

Henny Penny's Farm
Provide plastic farm animals and other materials for the children to create a farm.

Fine Motor

Sky Puzzles
Paint the moon and stars on blue poster board and an orange sun on yellow poster board. Cut each into four or five pieces and invite the children to put them back together.

Games

Acorn Toss
Challenge the children to toss acorns into small bowls.

Language

Rhyme Time
Provide pictures of objects with rhyming names for the children to match.

Science

Acorns Up Close
Provide acorns for the children to examine with magnifying glasses.

The Turnip

Materials

a favorite version of "The Great Big Turnip"

Morning Circle

1. Read or tell the story.
2. Invite the children to act out the story, substituting characters from their families or a book or television show they enjoy.

Story Circle

The Turnip by Janina Domanska

Music and Movement

Play Hot Turnip like Hot Potato.

Learning Centers

Art

Turnip on View

Provide brown, purple and green paints for the children to paint pictures of turnips growing underground.

Listening

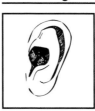

Tell It Again

Record the story so the children can listen to it in the center.

Cooking and Snack

Yummy Turnips

Provide slices of turnips for the children to taste. You might want to slice a potato or radish for comparison.

Math

Largest to Smallest

Invite the children to arrange items like carrots, turnips, blocks or beads from largest to smallest.

Dramatic Play

Our Own Play

Provide props for the children to create their own dramatic version of The Great Big Turnip.

Science

Looking Beneath

Encourage the children to plant potatoes, radishes, turnips or carrots in an aquarium so they can observe the growth of roots, food and foliage.

This Is the House That Jack Built

Materials
a favorite version of "This Is the House That Jack Built" (see one version in the appendix, page 386)

Morning Circle
1. Read or tell the story.
2. Discuss the sequence of putting the house together.

Story Circle
The Napping House by Audrey Wood

Music and Movement
"Put Your Thumb in the Air" from *Bahamas Pajamas* by Joe Scruggs

Learning Centers

Art

Jack's House
Provide crayons and paper for the children to draw pictures of Jack and his house.

Blocks

Jack's House
Encourage the children to build Jack's house.

Construction

Hammer and Nail
Provide hammers, nails and blocks of soft wood for the children to practice hammering. Supervise closely. [Use caution.]

Games

Next, Please
Make sequence cards (use copies of page 387 in the appendix). Encourage the children to place the cards in story order.

Language

This Is the Story That I Told
Challenge the children to dictate their own stories using language from the story (e.g., This Is the Cake That Austin Baked).

Math

Adding On
Provide a grid of twenty 2" (5 cm) squares. Invite the children to place graduating sets of color tiles on the grid (one tile on line 1, two tiles on line 2, etc.).

Little Red Riding Hood — Day 10

Materials
a favorite version of "Little Red Riding Hood"

Morning Circle
1. Read or tell the story.
2. Discuss talking to strangers.

Story Circle
Read another version of "Little Red Riding Hood."

Music and Movement
Provide red scarves, cellophane or streamers and ask the children to dance a Red Riding Hood Waltz.

Learning Centers

Art

I Like Red
Invite the children to create designs with red fingerpaint.

Dramatic Play

Basket for Grandma
Provide props for the children to pack a basket for Grandma.

Construction

Build a Forest
Provide green and crown construction paper, scissors, tape and small boxes. Encourage the children to cut out trees and tape them to the boxes so they stand up and become a forest.

Fine Motor

Through the Forest
Draw a forest scene with a path on the bottom of a shirt or sweater box. Glue a magnet to the back of a Red Riding Hood cutout. Encourage the children to use another magnet under the box to move her through the forest.

Cooking and Snack

Treats for Grandma
Provide raisins, dry cereal such as Rice Chex, pumpkin seeds, coconut and dried bananas for the children to make trail mix.

Math

Friend Sort
Provide pictures of class members and others. Encourage the children to sort them into stacks of friends and strangers.

Additional Books for Traditional Tales

The Bremen-Town Musicians by Ruth Gross

The Complete Tales of Peter Rabbit and Other Favorite Stories by Beatrix Potter

The Elves and the Shoemaker by Paul Galdone

The Gingerbread Boy by Paul Galdone

Goldilocks and the Three Bears by James Marshall

Henny Penny by H. Werner Zimmerman

Henny Penny by Paul Galdone

The Hungry Billy Goat by Rita Milios

The Little Red Hen by Paul Galdone

Little Red Riding Hood by David McPhail

Lon Po Po: A Red Riding Hood Story from China by Ed Young

Somebody and the Three Blairs by Marilyn Tolhurst

The Three Bears by Paul Galdone

Three Billy Goats Gruff by Ted Dewan

The Three Billy-Goats Gruff by Ellen Appleby

The Three Little Pigs by Paul Galdone

Three Little Pigs by David McPhail

Tomie dePaola's Mother Goose by Tomie dePaola

The True Story of the Three Little Pigs by Jon Scieszka

The Velveteen Rabbit by Margery Williams

Under Construction

The children love to build and create. In this unit, they will explore position vocabulary, shape, size and gravity as they construct highways, buildings and homes and create sculptures and sand castles. Animal homes are also included.

Unit at a Glance

Day	Focus	Centers	Story Circle	Music/Movement
1	Up, Down, Over, Under	Art Down Under Picture Match-Ups On the Table Weaving Classification Water in Space	Look Up, Look Down	Learning Basic Skills: Building Vocabulary
2	Shape and Size	Shape Structures Concentric Circles Balls of Clay Flannel-Board Shapes Size Sort Template Design	Circle, Triangle, Square	Shapes
3	Gravity	High Towers Do They Land at the Same Time? Stringing Up Drop the Clothespin Falling Sand What Goes Up. . .	Changes, Changes	Humpty Dumpty
4	Roads and Highways	Highway Art Building Roads Car Trails Car Tracks Divided Highway Felt Road	Road Builders	The Wheels on the Bus
5	Buildings Tall and Small	Tall and Small Art Skyscrapers Skyscraper Mural Tiny Town PVC Pipes Tall/Small Sort	Construction Zone	Hop, Skip and Jump

Day	Focus	Centers	Story Circle	Music/Movement
6	**Cardboard Construction**	Cardboard Sculpture Paper Village Small Town Home Decorating Rubbings Knock It Down	Roxaboxen	Beanbag Toss
7	**Homes**	Build a Neighborhood Pound It Graham Cracker Houses Play House Books About Homes Garages	A House Is a House for Me	Go In and Out the Windows
8	**Animal Homes**	My Honeycomb Wasp's Nest Tunnels Spider Homes Mud Homes Honeycomb	Animal Homes	Ants
9	**More Animal Homes**	Ant Pick-Ups Bird Beaks Bee Pollen Transfer Honey Making Beaver Dams Mud Daubers	Animals That Build Their Homes	Busy Animals
10	**Artistic Touches**	Clay Sculptures Bow Creations Gak Construction Construct a Story Construct a Song Sand Castles	I Can Be an Architect	Construct a Dance

Up, Down, Over, Under

Materials
none

Morning Circle
1. As the children arrive, give each one an instruction that includes a direction word. (For example: "Richele, sit *on* the carpet square *beside* the bookshelf. Tiffany, sit *beside* the chair. Alyssa, sit *under* the art table. Li stand *behind* the easel.")
2. After everyone has arrived and found their positions, call all the children to the circle. Explain that you will spend the day reviewing words that tell where things are or where they will be.

Story Circle
Look Up, Look Down by Tana Hoban

Music and Movement
Learning Basic Skills: Building Vocabulary by Hap Palmer

Learning Centers

Art

Art Down Under
Place a piece of drawing paper under the table and invite the children to draw a picture.

Fine Motor

Weaving
Stretch ¼" (6 mm) elastic strips about 1" (3 cm) apart across a piece of corrugated cardboard and staple the ends to the back. Provide ribbons, pipe cleaners, lace and rickrack for the children to weave through the elastic.

Blocks

Picture Match-Ups
Provide simple picture cards that illustrate spatial relationships using a small and a large block (e.g., small block in front, small block on top, small block beside, etc.). Invite the children to describe the placement of blocks on each card.

Math

Classification
Encourage the children to classify color tiles by placing red ones *in* a box, blue *on* the box lid, yellow *under* the box and green *beside* the box.

Dramatic Play

On the Table
Invite the children to set the table. Encourage them to verbalize the location of each piece of the place settings.

Sand and Water Table

Water in Space
Provide containers, strainers and funnels. Encourage the children to explore spatial relationships with water.

Shape and Size

Day 2

Materials
chart paper and crayon or marker

Morning Circle
1. Invite the children to look for shapes in the classroom (e.g., round clock face, square table, rectangular book, etc.). Make a list of the things they find.
2. Discuss shapes used in the building or room itself. What shapes (rectangular doors and windows, square tiles, rectangular bricks, etc.) can the children find?

Story Circle
Circle, Triangle, Square by Tana Hoban

Music and Movement
"Shapes" from *We All Live Together, Volume 3* by Steve and Greg

Learning Centers

Blocks

Shape Structures
Invite the children to build structures using only one shape of block for each (i.e., one structure from squares, one from rectangles, one from circles).

Construction

Concentric Circles
Provide five construction paper circles of graduating sizes. Invite the children to stack the circles from largest to smallest and then glue them together.

Fine Motor

Balls of Clay
Encourage the children to roll play-dough and clay into small and large balls.

Language

Flannel-Board Shapes
Provide several felt cutouts in different shapes. Invite the children to arrange the cutouts on the flannel board to create designs or shapes of familiar objects.

Math

Size Sort
Provide a box of matching small and large objects (e.g., big and little spoons, blocks, books, buttons, etc.). Invite the children to sort the objects by size.

Writing

Template Design
Provide shape templates, paper and pencils. Encourage the children to use the templates to create designs.

Gravity Day 3

Materials
beanbags, bubble soap and bubble wands

Morning Circle
1. When the children come to the circle, encourage them to pick up the beanbags, toss them into the air and watch them fall to the floor.
2. Ask, "Does anyone know why the beanbags don't stay in the air?"
3. Explain that gravity pulls things to the ground.
4. Blow bubbles. Ask, "Why do bubbles float?"

Story Circle
Changes, Changes by Pat Hutchins

Music and Movement
"Humpty Dumpty" from *I Am Special* by Thomas Moore

Learning Centers

Blocks

High Towers
Invite the children to see how tall they can build a tower before it falls.

Discovery

Do They Land at the Same Time?
Provide a variety of objects for the children to drop (e.g., feather, tissue, marble, pencil, sheet of paper, etc.). Do they hit the floor at the same time? Why?

Fine Motor

Stringing Up
Hang a long string from the ceiling and invite the children to string beads *up*. What happens? Is it more difficult to string beads up than down?

Games

Drop the Clothespin
Invite the children to drop various clothespins into a wide-mouth jar. Do wooden pins fall faster than plastic ones? What about pins with no hinges?

Sand and Water Table

Falling Sand
Hang a sand-filled water bottle upside down from the ceiling. Lay a long piece of butcher paper underneath. Invite the children to open the spout and swing the bottle back and forth over the paper. What happens to the sand? Why?

Science

What Goes Up. . .
Provide two pails, blocks and a rope and pulley. Invite the children to experiment with the pulley and one pail of blocks. Then challenge them to design a balance scale using both pails.

Roads and Highways

Day 4

Materials
none

Morning Circle
1. Talk about road construction. Most of the children have noticed it somewhere.
2. Invite sharing of stories about tractors, big trucks, bulldozers and other heavy equipment.

Story Circle
Road Builders by B. G. Hennessy

Music and Movement
"The Wheels on the Bus" from *Rise and Shine* by Raffi

Learning Centers

Art

Highway Art
Provide gray, yellow and white paints for the children to paint highways.

Blocks

Building Roads
Encourage the children to build a road. Use vinyl tiles if they are available (they will make an interesting addition to the construction).

Discovery

Car Trails
Provide bulletin board paper and a small wooden car with a marker attached to the back. Invite the children to push the car along the paper, creating a trail with the marker. What kind of trail did the car make?

Fine Motor

Car Tracks
Provide tempera paints and small cars. Invite the children to roll the cars through the paint and across the paper to create car tracks.

Math

Divided Highway
Provide a 10' (3 m) piece of butcher paper, a wide paintbrush and tempera paint. Invite the children to paint a highway divider line (line, space, line, space) down the center of the paper.

Math

Felt Road
Provide interesting felt cutouts (squares, squiggly lines, rectangles, circles, etc.) and challenge the children to create a road on the flannel board.

Buildings Tall and Small

Materials

photos of your local downtown area or of any city

Morning Circle

1. Show the photos. Talk about the sizes of the buildings.
2. Talk about the similarities and differences between a skyscraper and the children's homes.

Story Circle

Construction Zone by Tana Hoban

Music and Movement

Use chalk to draw tall buildings and invite the children to hop, skip and jump around the outlines.

Learning Centers

Art

Tall and Small Art
Invite the children to paint tall and small buildings.

Dramatic Play

Tiny Town
Provide very small boxes (like match boxes and ring boxes) for the children to use in creating a tiny town.

Blocks

Skyscrapers
Invite the children to build skyscrapers.

Fine Motor

PVC Pipes
Provide PVC pipes and connectors for construction.

Construction

Skyscraper Mural
Provide skyscraper cutouts for the children to glue to dark blue or black bulletin board paper.

Math

Tall/Small Sort
Encourage the children to sort pictures of tall and small buildings.

Cardboard Construction   Day 6

Materials
cardboard boxes

Morning Circle
1. Have a city of boxes built in the center of the circle.
2. Discuss how much fun it is to construct and reconstruct with boxes.
3. Let the children share stories about things they have made with cardboard boxes.

Story Circle
Roxaboxen by Alice McLerran

Music and Movement
Provide empty cardboard boxes and beanbags. Invite the children to toss the beanbags into the boxes from six feet (2 m), eight feet (2.5 m) and ten feet (3 m). Can anyone do it from a greater distance?

Learning Centers

Art

Cardboard Sculpture
Provide cardboard boxes, paper towel tubes, cartons and other cardboard containers. Encourage the children to create a box sculpture.

Dramatic Play

Home Decorating
Place a dryer or washer box in the center. Cut doors and windows. Provide fabric and wallpaper scraps, carpet squares, markers and paint for the children to decorate the house with.

Blocks

Paper Village
Fill the center with cardboard boxes for the children to create a village.

Fine Motor

Rubbings
Provide corrugated cardboard, paper and crayons for the children to make rubbings and create designs.

Construction

Small Town
Provide small boxes (like match boxes, ring boxes and half-pint milk cartons). Invite the children to create a small town on a tabletop. Add toy cars and other props.

Games

Knock It Down
Provide cardboard boxes and beanbags. Invite the children to stack the boxes and then toss the beanbags to knock them down.

Homes

Materials
carpenter's tools

Morning Circle
1. Show the carpenter's tools to the children.
2. Talk about the people who build homes and the tools they use.
3. Encourage the children to think of different kinds of homes (apartments, mobile homes, duplexes, condominiums, houses, townhouses, etc.).

Story Circle
A House Is a House for Me by Mary Ann Hoberman

Music and Movement
Invite the children to play Go In and Out the Windows (see the appendix, page 403).

Learning Centers

Blocks

Build a Neighborhood
Provide blocks and props for the children to create a neighborhood. Paper sacks with cut-out doors and windows add a nice touch.

Construction

Pound It
Provide a hammer, nails and a block of soft wood for the children to practice driving nails. Supervise closely. [Use caution.]

Cooking and Snack

Graham Cracker House
Make a paste from powdered sugar, butter and vanilla. Invite the children to build a house with graham crackers, using the paste. Decorate with raisins and candies.

Dramatic Play

Play House
Provide props and dress-up clothes for the children to play house.

Library

Books About Homes
Fill the center with books about homes.

Math

Garages
Make five garages out of empty pint milk cartons by cutting out one side and then painting or covering with contact paper. Glue one to five dots on each garage. Place the numerals 1 to 5 on small cars. Encourage the children to park the appropriate car in each garage.

Animal Homes

Materials
none

Morning Circle
1. Take a walk and look for animal homes (e.g., wasp's nests, bird's nests, anthills, spider webs, etc.).
2. Discuss different kinds of animal homes.

Story Circle
Animal Homes by Brian Wildsmith

Music and Movement
"Ants" from *Let's Pretend* by Hap Palmer

Learning Centers

Art

My Honeycomb
Provide bubble wrap, paper and gold tempera paint. Invite the children to use the wrap to make honeycomb prints.

Construction

Wasp's Nest
Provide watered-down glue (half water, half glue) and torn tissue paper. Invite the children to create a wasp's nest.

Fine Motor

Tunnels
Provide clay, pipe cleaners and toothpicks. Encourage the children to use the pipe cleaners and toothpicks to make tunnels in the clay like ants might make tunnels in anthills.

Gross Motor

Spider Homes
Encourage the children to string yarn around chairs and tables to make giant spider webs.

Sand and Water Table

Mud Homes
Provide clay for the children to form dirt dauber homes.

Science

Honeycomb
Provide a honeycomb, bird's nest, wasp's nest and other animal homes you find. Encourage the children to observe the homes with magnifying glasses.

More Animal Homes

Day 9

Materials
photographs of a bird, beaver, crab and bee; a saw, trowel, bucket, pliers, and tweezers

Morning Circle
1. Show the photographs.
2. Discuss the tools each animal uses (bird/beak, beaver/teeth and tail, crab/claws, bees/buckets).
3. Encourage the children to match tools to the animals that use a similar one.

Story Circle
Animals That Build Their Homes by Robert McClung

Music and Movement
Invite the children to pretend to be bees pollinating flowers, birds collecting materials for a nest and beavers building a dam.

Learning Centers

Blocks

Ant Pick-Ups
Encourage the children to use tongs to pick up and place blocks while building.

Fine Motor

Honey Making
Invite the children to use an eye-dropper to transfer water from one container to another.

Construction

Bird Beaks
Invite the children to use tweezers to move small twigs from a bowl to a sheet of paper. Can they build a nest using the tweezers?

Sand and Water Table

Beaver Dams
Provide pliers, wire cutters and small sticks for the children to build a beaver's dam. Supervise closely. [Use caution.]

Discovery

Bee Pollen Transfer
Encourage the children to use pipe cleaners to pick up powder and then run their fingers down the wire to release the powder.

Science

Mud Daubers
Encourage the children to build a mud home. Let the mud creation dry in the sun.

Artistic Touches

Materials

a sculpture, a story (book), chart paper and marker

Morning Circle

1. Explain that humans construct things all the time—not just homes, buildings and roads, but other things like stories, songs, dances and even a teacher's lesson plan.
2. Demonstrate construction of one of the things mentioned above. Talk about how you start with an idea and build on to it. Doing a thematic word web might be a good way for the children to see how this works.

Story Circle

I Can Be an Architect by Susan Clinton

Music and Movement

Invite the children to construct a dance.

Learning Centers

Art

Clay Sculptures

Encourage the children to sculpt clay into various shapes and forms.

Language

Construct a Story

Invite the children to dictate a story.

Construction

Bow Creations

Invite the children to make something from recycled gift-wrap bows.

Listening

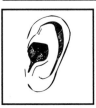

Construct a Song

Provide a tape recorder for the children to record songs they create.

Discovery

Gak Construction

Mix Gak (see the recipe in the appendix, page 388) for the children to sculpt with. What happens after their creations sit for a while?

Sand and Water Table

Sand Castles

Invite the children to dampen sand in the table and use molds and plastic containers to build sand castles.

Additional Books for Under Construction

Architecture: Shapes by Michael Crosbie and Steve Rosenthal
The Biggest House in the World by Leo Lionni
A Day in the Life of a Carpenter by John Harding Martin
Diggers and Dump Trucks by Angela Royston
Houses and Homes by Ann Morris
How a House Is Built by Gail Gibbons
The Little House by Virginia Lee Burton
Machines at Work by Byron Barton
Mike Mulligan and His Steam Shovel by Virginia Lee Burton
Tool Book by Gail Gibbons
Truck by Donald Crews
A Very Special House by Ruth Krauss

Creepy Crawlies

This unit investigates the characteristics and habits of insects and other small creatures.

Unit at a Glance

Day	Focus	Centers	Story Circle	Music/Movement
1	Bugs	Bug-Eyed Glasses Hidden Life Insect Models Insect Movements Fly, Slither, Crawl Insect Habitats	Bugs	Six-Legged Race
2	Fireflies	Glow in the Dark Art Firefly Models Bug Concentration Pin the Light Light Patterns Light Seriation	Fireflies in the Night	Find the Firefly
3	Earthworms	Colorful Worms Roll a Worm Worm Tracks Worm Works Long Worms Worm Watch	Earthworms	Earthworm Movement
4	Ants	Ants on a Log Ant Farm Picnic Time Ant Trails Sculpting Anthills Weight Lifters	Ant City	Follow the Queen Ant
5	Ladybugs	Ladybug Magnets Ladybug Play Ladybug Lace-Up Ladybug Puzzles Ladybug Dot Match Ladybug Watch	The Grouchy Ladybug	Ladybug Says

Day	Focus	Centers	Story Circle	Music/Movement
6	Caterpillars and Butterflies	Colorful Butterflies Butterfly Beauties Making Cocoons Tracing Butterflies Caterpillar Sort Caterpillar Watch	The Very Hungry Caterpillar	Butterfly Scarf Dance
7	Crickets, Grasshoppers & Locusts	Hopping Pictures Grasshopper Obstacle Course Grasshopper Shakes Sound Makers Grasshopper Puzzles Insect Sounds	The Very Quiet Cricket	Obstacle Course
8	Mosquitoes and Flies	Fly Wings Mosquitoes Insect Match-Up Old Lady and Fly Matching Flies Close-Up Look	The Bear and the Fly	Shoo Fly, Don't Bother Me
9	Bees	Build a Honeycomb Fingerprint Bees Bee Tea Honeycombs Honeycomb Puzzles One Bee, One Flower	The Bee Tree	Flight of the Bumblebees
10	Spiders	Spider Portraits Spinning Webs Spider Webs Spider Pick-Up Spider Watch Trace a Web	The Very Busy Spider	Spider

Bugs

Materials

photographs of various insects, spiders and worms; chart paper and marker

Morning Circle

1. Show the photos. Discuss the characteristics of insects: three body parts, six legs, antennae.
2. Tell the children you will be looking at things that creep and crawl for the next two weeks. They will use the "insect criteria" to determine which ones are insects and which are not.
3. Keep an Insect Chart. Record number of legs, eyes, antennae and other body parts of each bug you study.

Story Circle

Bugs by Nancy Winslow Parker

Music and Movement

Have a six-legged race. Put markers about 30' (9 m) apart. Have three children hold hands (count the legs) and race another group of three.

Learning Centers

Construction

Bug-Eyed Glasses
Provide sections of egg cartons (two cups in each), pipe cleaners and tempera paints. Poke holes in the center of each egg cup and through two outside edges. Stick pipe cleaners through outside holes, then twist to form ear pieces. Paint with tempera paints. Supervise closely.

Discovery

Hidden Life
Place a shovel full of dirt in a tub and set it in the center for the children to observe through magnifying glasses. Caution the children about touching bugs.

Fine Motor

Insect Models
Provide clay or playdough, pipe cleaners and beads (for eyes). Invite the children to create insects.

Gross Motor

Insect Movements
Challenge the children to move like insects (hop, crawl, fly, run, etc.).

Math

Fly, Slither, Crawl
Provide pictures of bugs for the children to classify according to how they move.

Science

Insect Habitats
Invite the children to make bug holders by filling a clear plastic jar with leaves and twigs and covering the top with a piece of netting or nylon stocking.

Fireflies

Materials

photographs of fireflies, light sources (candle, flashlight, lamp, matches)

Morning Circle

1. Demonstrate the light sources. Explain that an animal in nature supplies its own light. Who knows what that type of animal is called?
2. Show the photos. Count legs, antennae and so on. Is the firefly an insect? Mark your Insect Chart accordingly.
3. Explain that the firefly's light is made by a mixture of chemicals in the firefly's body. The creation of the light is called bioluminescence.

Story Circle

Fireflies in the Night by Judy Howes

Music and Movement

Play Find the Firefly. Give IT a flashlight. Turn off the lights. Have IT hide and then flash the light quickly. Whoever finds IT is the next firefly.

Learning Centers

Art

Glow in the Dark Art

Provide fluorescent paints for the children to paint firefly pictures. View the paintings under a black light.

Construction

Firefly Models

Invite the children to create fireflies out of clay. Provide diamond-like stones for tails.

Games

Bug Concentration

Invite the children to play Insect Concentration (see the appendix, page 422).

Games

Pin the Light

Make a firefly out of poster board. Cut a duplicate tail from fluorescent paper. Put Velcro on both tails. Invite the children to blindfold each other and take turns pinning the light on the firefly.

Language

Light Patterns

Encourage the children to create patterns of long and short flashes of light using a flashlight.

Math

Light Seriation

Make several fireflies with tails that range in color from white to dark yellow. Encourage the children to arrange the fireflies in order from darkest to lightest tail.

Earthworms

Day 3

Materials

photographs of earthworms, earthworms in a jar, magnifying glasses

Morning Circle

1. Show the photographs. Find out what the children know about earthworms. Is the earthworm an insect? Mark your Insect Chart accordingly.
2. Invite the children to use the magnifying glasses to examine the earthworms in the jar.
3. Explain that earthworms can range in size from $1/25''$ (1 mm) to 11" (28 cm).

Story Circle

Earthworms by Chris Henwood

Music and Movement

Invite the children to move like earthworms. Stretch out the top part of the body and pull up the bottom.

Learning Centers

Art

Colorful Worms
Invite the children to create worm art with lengths of yarn (like string art).

Language

Worm Works
Make a puzzle of a long earthworm for the children to put together.

Construction

Roll a Worm
Provide clay or playdough for the children to roll into worms.

Math

Long Worms
Cut out several yarn "earthworms" of various lengths. Encourage the children to order them from shortest to longest.

Fine Motor

Worm Tracks
Drop fingerpaints on a tabletop. Invite the children to create worms and worm tracks.

Science

Worm Watch
Encourage the children to observe the earthworms in the jar through magnifying glasses.

Ants

Day 4

Materials
photograph of an ant

Morning Circle
1. Sing "The Ants Go Marching."
2. Show the photograph. Encourage the children to count the ant's legs, body parts and antennae. Is an ant an insect? Mark your Insect Chart accordingly.
3. Explain that ants range in size from $\frac{1}{25}$" (1 mm) to 1" (3 cm). They carry things that weigh more than they do. Encourage the children to try and lift their weight.

Story Circle
Ant City by Arthur Dorros

Music and Movement
Invite the children to play Follow the Queen Ant like Follow the Leader.

Learning Centers

Cooking and Snack

Ants on a Log
Encourage the children to spread peanut butter in celery sticks and then top with raisins to make Ants on a Log for snack.

Dramatic Play

Picnic Time
Provide props for the children to role-play having a picnic. Don't forget the plastic ants.

Discovery

Ant Farm
Shovel an anthill (find nonbiting ants) into a clear jar. Drop in a cotton ball soaked in sugar water. Secure nylon hose over the top of the jar with a rubber band. Cover the jar with dark cloth until the ants have settled. Invite the children to observe the ant activity. Return the ants to their home after a few days.)

Fine Motor

Ant Trails
Provide a tray of sand or salt. Encourage the children to create ant trails using small sticks.

Fine Motor

Sculpting Anthills
Invite the children to create anthills out of clay. Provide straws and toothpicks for digging tunnels.

Science

Weight Lifters
Provide several buckets of blocks and bricks for the children to try and lift. Vary the weights from light (1 pound or 500 grams) to heavy (20 pounds or 9 kilograms).

Ladybugs

Day 5

Materials
photographs of ladybugs, real ladybugs

Morning Circle
1. Teach the children to recite the rhyme "Ladybug, Ladybug, Fly Away Home."
2. Show the photos or the live ladybugs. Find out what the children know about ladybugs. Is a ladybug an insect? Mark your Insect Chart accordingly.

Story Circle
The Grouchy Ladybug by Eric Carle

Music and Movement
Invite the children to play Ladybug Says like Simon Says (see the appendix, page 404).

Learning Centers

Construction

Ladybug Magnets
Use tempera paint to make red and black glue. Invite the children to squeeze a circle of red glue onto wax paper and small black dots onto that. Attach 1" (3 cm) lengths of black thread for antennae. Let dry.

Dramatic Play

Ladybug Play
Provide red fabric or scarves and pipe cleaner antennae for the children to wear while acting out the poem "Ladybug, Ladybug, Fly Away Home."

Fine Motor

Ladybug Lace-Up
Make construction paper ladybugs and punch holes along the outside edge. Invite the children to lace yarn through the holes.

Language

Ladybug Puzzles
Paint several paper plates to look like ladybugs. Add pipe cleaner antennae. Cut each plate into three or four pieces. Invite the children to put them together.

Math

Ladybug Dot Match
Cut red paper circles to make five ladybugs. Draw a line down the middle of each. Place one to five dots on each side of each bug. Cut in half. Invite the children to match dots to put the ladybugs back together.

Science

Ladybug Watch
Place several ladybugs (can be purchased from a nursery) in the center for the children to observe. Be sure to let them go in a garden later.

Caterpillars & Butterflies   Day 6

Materials
photographs of caterpillars, cocoons, butterflies (Provide the real thing if possible; you can order cocoons from nature stores such as The Nature Company. Be aware that some butterflies die immediately.)

Morning Circle
1. Show the photos. Find out what the children know about caterpillars and butterflies. Are caterpillars and butterflies insects? Mark your Insect Chart accordingly.
2. Encourage the children to act out crawling like a caterpillar, spinning a cocoon and emerging as a butterfly.

Story Circle
The Very Hungry Caterpillar by Eric Carle

Music and Movement
Invite the children to perform a Butterfly Scarf Dance. You might play music from Madame Butterfly for accompaniment.

Learning Centers

Art

Colorful Butterflies
Invite the children to fold sheets of construction paper in half, then open them and drop dabs of tempera paint on one side of the fold. Fold the paper and press. What's inside?

Construction

Butterfly Beauties
Invite the children to drop food coloring onto coffee filters. When the filters are dry, gather them in the middle and clip with clothespins. Attach pipe cleaner antennae.

Fine Motor

Making Cocoons
Provide plastic worms and yarn. Invite the children to wrap the worms in cocoons.

Language

Tracing Butterflies
Challenge the children to fold a sheet of paper in half, place a half-butterfly template against the fold and trace around it. Encourage them to cut around the line to make a butterfly.

Math

Caterpillar Sort
Make egg-carton caterpillars of various lengths. Invite the children to arrange them from shortest to longest.

Science

Caterpillar Watch
Place caterpillars, cocoons and butterflies (or photographs of them) in the center for the children to observe.

Crickets, Grasshoppers & Locusts

Materials
photographs of crickets, grasshoppers, and locusts; live animals if available

Morning Circle
1. Show the photos or live animals. Invite the children to count legs and other body parts. Are crickets, grasshoppers and locusts all insects? Mark your Insect Chart accordingly.
2. How are crickets, grasshoppers and locust alike? How are they different?
3. Explain that crickets are a variety of grasshopper. Grasshoppers are considered pests because they eat so many plants. In some parts of the world, people eat grasshoppers. Explain that locusts are also considered pests.

Story Circle
The Very Quiet Cricket by Eric Carle

Music and Movement
Invite the children to jump through an obstacle course made with small boxes, cans and books.

Learning Centers

Art

Hopping Pictures
Provide brown and green paints for the children to paint crickets, grasshoppers and locusts.

Blocks

Grasshopper Obstacle Course
Invite the children to build an obstacle course for grasshoppers.

Cooking and Snack

Grasshopper Shakes
Invite the children to mix ginger ale and lime sherbet in a blender to make shakes for snack.

Discovery

Sound Makers
Grasshoppers, crickets and locusts make sounds by rubbing their bristled legs together. Invite the children to experiment with making sounds by rubbing different objects together (sandpaper, combs, files, etc.).

Language

Grasshopper Puzzles
Enlarge illustrations of the grasshopper and cricket on appendix page 422. Mount on poster board and cut each in four or five pieces for the children to put together.

Listening

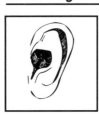

Insect Sounds
Provide a tape of insect noises for the children to listen to.

Mosquitoes & Flies

Day 8

Materials
photographs of mosquitoes and flies, Old Woman felt cutouts for flannel board story (see the appendix, pages 384–385)

Morning Circle
1. Tell the flannel board story/chant, "I Know an Old Woman Who Swallowed a Fly."
2. Show the photos. Find out what the children know about mosquitoes and flies. How many legs, wings, antennae, body parts? Are mosquitoes and flies insects? Mark your Insect Chart accordingly.
3. How are mosquitoes and flies alike? How are they different?

Story Circle
The Bear and the Fly by Paula Winter

Music and Movement
Invite the children to make up a line dance to "Shoo Fly, Don't Bother Me" (see the appendix, page 398).

Learning Centers

Construction

Fly Wings
Cut fly wings from wax paper. Invite the children to paint black "veins" on the wings. You may want to provide a photo for inspiration.

Language

Old Lady and Fly
Place the Old Lady puppet or felt cutouts in the center for the children to retell the story in order.

Fine Motor

Mosquitoes
Encourage the children to use an eyedropper to move liquid from one bowl to another.

Math

Matching Flies
Provide plastic flies and drawings of sugar cubes with dots on them. Encourage the children to match the flies to the dots.

Games

Insect Match-Up
Invite the children to play Insect Match-Up using cards from the Insect Concentration Game on appendix page 422.

Science

Close-Up Look
Provide live mosquitoes and flies for the children to observe through magnifying glasses.

Bees

Materials
photographs of bees, pieces of honeycomb

Morning Circle
1. Invite a beekeeper to discuss beekeeping with the children.
2. Show the photos and honeycomb.
3. Find out what the children know about bees. Count the legs, antennae and other body parts. Are bees insects? Mark your Insect Chart accordingly.
4. Can the children find the bee's stinger? Explain that only males have stingers. Bees don't attack unless they are disturbed.

Story Circle
The Bee Tree by Patricia Polacco

Music and Movement
Invite the children to dance around like bees as they listen to "Flight of the Bumblebee" by Rimsky-Korsakov.

Learning Centers

Construction

Build a Honeycomb
Challenge the children to build a honeycomb from individual egg-carton sections.

Discovery

Honeycombs
Provide pieces of honeycomb for the children to examine.

Construction

Fingerprint Bees
Invite the children to make finger-print bees with yellow tempera paint. When dry, the children can add black lines with markers.

Language

Honeycomb Puzzles
Provide several hexagon-shaped pieces of yellow construction paper. Challenge the children to put the pieces together to make a honey-comb.

Cooking and Snack

Bee Tea
Provide honey, crackers and juice for the children to have a Bee Tea.

Math

One Bee, One Flower
Provide paper flowers and bee cutouts for the children to match one to one.

Spiders

Materials
yarn, photos of spiders and webs

Morning Circle
1. Wrap yarn around table legs and chairs to create a giant web or make a giant web on the floor. Have the children make their way through the web as they come in. If your web is on the floor, invite the children to sit on it.
2. Show the photos. Invite the children to count legs and other body parts. Are spiders insects? Mark your Insect Chart accordingly.
3. Sing, "I Know an Old Woman Who Swallowed a Fly" (see the appendix, page 384).

Story Circle
The Very Busy Spider by Eric Carle

Music and Movement
"Spider" from *Songs for the Whole Day* by Thomas Moore

Learning Centers

Art

Spider Portraits
Invite the children to blow paint through straws to make spiders and webs.

Fine Motor

Spider Pick-Up
Encourage the children to use tweezers to move plastic spiders from one container to another.

Blocks

Spinning Webs
Provide yarn for the children to make webs.

Science

Spider Watch
Invite the children to observe a spider (in a jar) through a magnifying glass. Provide a web for observation, if possible.

Construction

Spider Webs
Encourage the children to glue white string to black construction paper to make spider webs.

Writing

Trace a Web
Provide drawings of webs for the children to trace.

Additional Books for Creepy Crawlies

Alpha Bugs by David Carter
Amazing World of Butterflies and Moths by Louis Sabin
Be Nice to Spiders by Margaret Bloy Graham
The Best Bug to Be by Dolores Johnson
Butterfly and Caterpillar by Barrie Watts
The Butterfly Hunt by Yoshi
The Caterpillar and the Polliwog by Jack Kent
A Color of His Own by Leo Lionni
Creepy Crawlies by Cathy Kilpatrick
Creepy, Crawly Caterpillars by Mary Facklam
The Fascinating World of Spiders by Maria A. Julivert
Fireflies by Julie Brincloe
From Egg to Butterfly by Ali Mitgutsch, Marlene Reidel, Annegert Fuchshuber and Franz Hogner
I Wish I Were a Butterfly by James Howe
Icky Bug Alphabet Book by Jerry Pallotta
Icky Bug Counting Book by Jerry Pallotta
In the Tall, Tall Grass by Denise Fleming
It's a Good Thing There Are Insects Big Book by Allan Fowler
The Itsy-Bitsy Spider by Iza Trapini
Look at Insects by Rena Kirkpatrick
Look—a Butterfly by David Cutts
Miss Spider's Tea Party by David Kirk
Old Black Fly by Jim Aylesworth
A Picture Book of Insects by Joanne Mattern
Quick as a Cricket by Audrey Wood
The Roly Poly Spider by Jill Sardegna
Sam and the Firefly by P.D. Eastman
Spiders by Gail Gibbons
Two Bad Ants by Chris Van Allsburg
Where Butterflies Grow by Joanne Ryder

Down by the Seashore

Ocean, sand, sun and sea life make this unit a real splash with kids. It's everything from fish and octopus to seals and turtles.

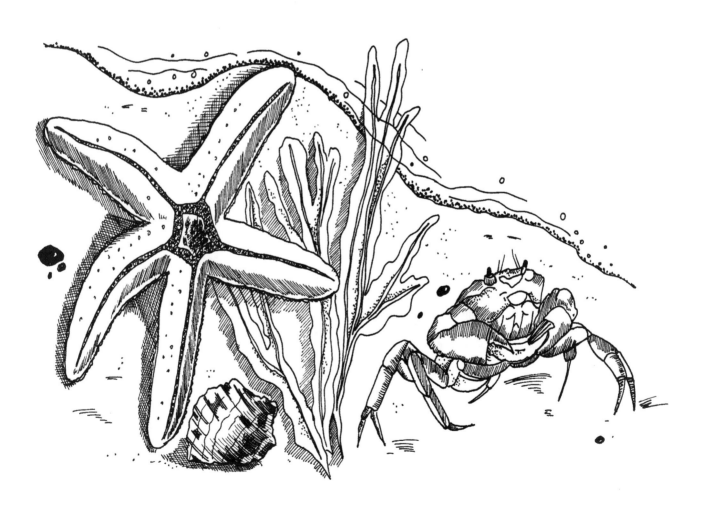

Unit at a Glance

Day	Focus	Centers	Story Circle	Music/Movement
1	Water	Salty Paintings Seashore Building Wave Machine Day at the Beach Ocean Music Letters in the Sand	Oceans	Waves
2	Seashells	Shell Sculptures Hermit Crab Shell Designs Shell Magic Seashell Patterns Close-Up Shells	What Lives in a Shell	Drop the Seashell
3	Sand	Sand Paintings Making Sand Grainy Designs Sand Castles Sandpaper Match Letters in the Sand	The Seashore Book	Rock, Paper, Scissors
4	Fish	My Aquarium Lionni Fish Fish Scale Pick-Up Giant Puzzle Fish Catch Fish to See	Rainbow Fish	Swimming Fish
5	Crabs	Crab Fest Crab Claw Concentration Crabbing Crab Claw Pick-Up Sea Life Concentration Hermit Crab	Down in the Sea: The Crab	Crab

Day	Focus	Centers	Story Circle	Music/Movement
6	Octopus	Octopus Puppets Add an Eye Making Patterns One-to-One Suction Cup Connectors Air Thrust	Octopus	One Octopus
7	Whales and Dolphins	Deep Sea Diving Reef Maze Feed the Whale Whale Tail Polo Whale Music Big, Bigger, Biggest	Whales	We're Going on a Whale Hunt
8	Seals	Whisker Pictures Sardines Balancing Act Sea Life Concentration Seal Balance Seal Training	Greyling	Duck, Duck, Seal
9	Turtles	Obstacle Course Turtle Puppets Reef Maze Letters for Help Turtle Eggs Dare to Compare	Tracks in the Sand	Turtle Races
10	Ocean Birds	Feathers Six-Pack Cut-Ups Feed the Gull Ocean Puzzles Beak Pick-Up Feather Writing	The Picture Book of Water Birds	Drop the Feather

Water

Day 1

Materials
photographs of the beaches and shorelines

Morning Circle
1. Show the photos of beaches and shorelines. If you have a globe, show the children how much water there is and how much land.
2. Invite the children to describe oceans and beaches they have seen.

Story Circle
Oceans by Seymour Simon

Music and Movement
Provide a sheet and beach ball. Invite the children to bounce the ball on the sheet as they make waves with the sheet.

Learning Centers

Art

Salty Paintings
Add salt to tempera paint and invite the children to paint. What happens to the paintings as they dry?

Dramatic Play

Day at the Beach
Provide props for the children to pretend beach play.

Blocks

Seashore Building
Provide an ocean (blue bulletin board paper). Invite the children to build houses on the beach.

Listening

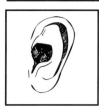

Ocean Music
Provide a tape of ocean sounds for the children to listen to.

Discovery

Wave Machine
Ask the children to bring 2-liter bottles to school. Provide cooking oil, water and blue food coloring. Children measure ½ cup (120 ml) oil into each bottle, then add blue water. Seal the tops with glue or plastic tape.

Writing

Letters in the Sand
Provide a tray of sand and a stick. Encourage the children to write notes or draw pictures in the sand.

Seashells

Day 2

Materials
conch shells, box of assorted shells

Morning Circle
1. Pass the conch shell around the circle and invite the children to listen to it. What does it sound like?
2. Pass the box of shells around the circle. Let the children choose their favorite.

Story Circle
What Lives in a Shell by Kathleen Weidner Zoehfeld

Music and Movement
Invite the children to play Drop the Seashell like Drop the Handkerchief (see the appendix, page 402).

Learning Centers

Construction

Shell Sculptures
Invite the children to design and build something with seashells.

Games

Shell Magic
Put a bean under one of three shells. Move the shells around. Invite the children to guess which shell is hiding the bean.

Discovery

Hermit Crab
Put a hermit crab in the center. Place a few empty shells with it. Does the crab change homes? Does anyone see it change homes?

Math

Seashell Patterns
Provide two or three kinds of shells for the children to arrange in patterns.

Fine Motor

Shell Designs
Invite the children to press shells into wet sand or clay to make designs.

Science

Close-Up Shells
Encourage the children to examine a variety of shells through magnifying glasses.

Sand

Materials
different grades of sand, two porous rocks, chart paper and marker

Morning Circle
1. Show the different grades of sand. Invite the children to see and feel the difference. Ask the children to describe the difference.
2. Ask, "Where does sand come from?" You'll probably get answers like the beach, the park and so on. Lead the children to understand that sand is a product of erosion. When mountains and rocks erode, we eventually get sand.
3. Demonstrate by rubbing the two rocks together to create sand.
4. Help the children make a list of ways that we use sand. Record their responses on the chart paper.

Story Circle
The Seashore Book by Charlotte Zolotow

Music and Movement
Teach the children to play Rock, Paper, Scissors.

Learning Centers

Art

Sand Paintings
Provide several salt shakers filled with fine sand and dry tempera. Invite the children to draw designs on their paper with glue and then sprinkle the colored sand over it.

Sand and Water Table

Sand Castles
Provide spoons, shovels and a variety of empty buckets and other containers for the children to make sand castles.

Discovery

Making Sand
Provide sand and magnifying glasses for examination. Invite the children to make their own sand by rubbing two porous rocks together. Is it easy to make sand?

Science

Sandpaper Match
Cut two squares from each of several grades of sandpaper. Provide a blindfold and encourage the children to match the squares by touch.

Fine Motor

Grainy Designs
Cut several shapes from sandpaper for the children to make crayon rubbings.

Writing

Letters in the Sand
Invite the children to use popsicle sticks to make designs in a tray of sand.

Fish

Materials
Swimmy by Leo Lionni; pink, red, yellow and white tissue paper; poster board; glue; scissors

Morning Circle
1. In advance, glue layers of pink, red, yellow and white tissue paper onto poster board. Cut out several fish shapes.
2. Read the story. Discuss fish, what fish eat and where fish live. What is a school of fish?
3. Show your "Lionni" fish. Show the children how you made them.

Story Circle
Rainbow Fish by Marcus Pfister

Music and Movement
Invite the children to swim to music of different tempos. Swim like happy fish, scared fish, tired fish, grumpy fish.

Learning Centers

Construction

My Aquarium
Provide a fish pattern for the children to trace onto laminating film and cut out. Add details with permanent markers. Place the fish into resealable plastic bags with 1/3 cup (80 ml) of blue-hair gel.

Fine Motor

Lionni Fish
Provide tissue paper, scissors, poster board and glue for the children to make Lionni fish.

Games

Fish Scale Pick-Up
Use buttons as fish scales. Invite the children to use tweezers to pick up the scales. How many can a child pick up before a one-minute timer goes off?

Language

Giant Puzzle
Make a giant Lionni fish and cut it into several pieces for the children to put together.

Math

Fish Catch
Provide construction-paper fish in graduating sizes. Put a paper clip on the nose of each one. Provide a fishing pole (magnet on a string tied to a wrapping paper tube). Invite the children to catch the fish and arrange them in order from smallest to largest.

Science

Fish to See
Fill the center with pictures of fish. If possible, let the children observe live fish in an aquarium (children can use the pattern and directions in the appendix, page 431, to make their own twirling fish).

Crabs

Day 5

Materials
photographs of crabs

Morning Circle
1. Show the photos. Describe different kinds of crabs (sand crabs, horseshoe crabs, hermit crabs, etc.).
2. Invite the children to discuss how crabs move, eat, see, and breathe.
3. Teach the children the Crab Walk (hands and feet on the floor, stomach toward the ceiling). Invite them to move around the room, moving only sideways and backward.

Story Circle
Down in the Sea: The Crab by Patricia Kite

Music and Movement
"Crab" from *We've Got to Come Full Circle* by Tom Wisner and Teresa Whitaker

Learning Centers

Cooking and Snack

Crab Fest
Invite the children to taste crab meat. Check in advance for allergies or religious limitations.

Discovery

Crab Claw Construction
Invite the children to build with blocks while wearing mittens. Is it harder?

Dramatic Play

Crabbing
Provide props for a pretend crabbing expedition (net, bucket, string, play-dough bait, sun hats, etc.).

Fine Motor

Crab Claw Pick-Up
Provide two pair of tongs and several pompoms or Ping-Pong balls. Encourage the children to pick up the pompoms or balls two at a time, operating both pairs of tongs simultaneously.

Games

Sea Life Concentration
Invite the children to play Sea Life Concentration (see the appendix, page 417).

Science

Hermit Crab
Invite the children to observe a hermit crab in an aquarium. If no crab is available, provide photographs.

Octopus

Materials
photograph of an octopus

Morning Circle
1. Show the photo. Invite the children to count the number of arms (tentacles) the octopus has. Explain that each tentacle has small suction cups on its underside. The Octopus uses the cups to move and to catch food.
2. Explain that most octopi have a body that is the size of a fist, but some are as long as 28' (9 m) from tip to tip.
3. Explain that an octopus moves through the water by drawing air into its body and then thrusting it out a small hole under its head.

Story Circle
Octopus by Carol Carrick

Music and Movement
Invite the children to play One Octopus like One Elephant (see the appendix, page 404).

Learning Centers

Construction

Octopus Puppets
Encourage the children to glue eight 8" (20 cm) streamers around a paper plate. Use a crayon to add an eye.

Games

Add an Eye
Lay a large poster board octopus on the floor. Invite the children to toss a beanbag on the octopus to add the eye.

Math

Making Patterns
Provide paper plates and 1" x 12" strips (3 cm x 30 cm) of construction paper (tentacles) in different colors. Invite the children to create a pattern as they place eight tentacles around the body.

Math

One-to-One
Use an octopus puppet from the Construction Center. Invite the children to match one paper fish to each tentacle.

Sand and Water Table

Suction Cup Connectors
Encourage the children to practice picking up a variety of small objects with suction cups.

Science

Air Thrust
Tie a 10' (3 m) piece of string with a straw on it between two chairs. Blow up an oblong balloon (caution for safety) and tape it to the straw. What happens when you let go of the balloon?

Whales and Dolphins Day 7

Materials
100' (30 m) of yarn, photographs of whales and dolphins

Morning Circle
1. Show the photos.
2. Tell the children that whales are the largest animals that ever lived. Dolphins are small whales, ranging in length from 4' to 30' (1 m to 10 m).
3. Outdoors, ask the children to unwind the yarn and lay it in a straight line. This is the average length of a blue whale.
4. Explain that whales are intelligent animals. They have poor eyesight and no sense of taste or smell. They have lungs like we do so they have to come above the water to breathe.

Story Circle
Whales by Seymour Simon

Music and Movement
Play "We're Going on a Whale Hunt" as you would "We're Going on a Bear Hunt" (see the appendix, page 393).

Learning Centers

Dramatic Play

Deep Sea Diving
Provide flippers, goggles and air tanks (2-liter bottles) for pretend scuba diving.

Fine Motor

Reef Maze
Draw a reef maze in the bottom of a shallow box. Glue a magnet to the back of a paper whale. Invite the children to hold a second magnet behind the box to move the whale through the maze.

Games

Feed the Whale
Cut a whale from poster board and glue it to a box. Cut a hole for the mouth. Encourage the children to toss fish-shaped beanbags into the whale's mouth.

Games

Whale Tail Polo
Glue poster board whale tails to wrapping paper tubes. Invite the children to use the tubes to putt Ping-Pong balls back and forth or into a cup.

Listening

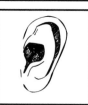

Whale Music
Provide a tape of whale sounds for the children to listen to.

Math

Big, Bigger, Biggest
Provide felt whales in several sizes. Invite the children to arrange them on the flannel board from smallest to largest.

Seals

Materials
photographs of seals

Morning Circle
1. Show the photos. Ask someone to demonstrate walking like a seal, crawling like a seal, barking like a seal.
2. Find out what the children know about seals. They may have seen them at the zoo or water park or on television.
3. Explain that seals are easy to train and are often used as show animals.
4. Explain that seals usually live in large groups. Some live for as long as forty years.

Story Circle
Greyling by Jane Yolen

Music and Movement
Invite the children to play Duck, Duck, Seal like Duck, Duck, Goose (see the appendix, page 402).

Learning Centers

Art

Whisker Pictures
Encourage the children to paint with whisker brushes (small bunches of monofilament strings).

Cooking and Snack

Sardines
Serve sardines and crackers, such as saltines, for snack. Sardines are similar to the small fish that seals enjoy.

Discovery

Balancing Act
Invite the children to try balancing a variety of lightweight objects on their noses.

Games

Sea Life Concentration
Invite the children to play Sea Life Concentration (see the appendix, page 417).

Gross Motor

Seal Balance
Place a strip of masking tape on the floor and encourage the children to move along the line like a seal, using only flippers to pull themselves. Invite them to try it again with a beanbag "fish" on their heads.

Writing

Seal Tracing
Draw the outlines of seals on poster board. Encourage the children to trace the outlines using tracing paper and crayons.

Turtles

Materials
photographs of turtles

Morning Circle
1. Show the photos.
2. Talk about how baby turtles hatch from eggs and make their way to the sea.
3. Talk about the many perils they face: crabs, birds, people.
4. Explain that turtles are an endangered species. Talk about why.

Story Circle
Tracks in the Sand by Loren Leedy

Music and Movement
Invite the children to race each other as they move like turtles, carrying boxes on their backs.

Learning Centers

Blocks

Obstacle Course
Invite the children to build an obstacle course and then pretend they are baby turtles making their way through it.

Construction

Turtle Puppets
Invite the children to paint paper bowls as turtle shells. Glue on construction-paper legs, head and tail.

Fine Motor

Reef Maze
Invite the children to maneuver a paper turtle through the reef maze.

Language

"My picture is about..."

Letters for Help
Help the children write letters to their congressional representatives or to The Center for Marine Conservation (1725 Desales St. NW, Suite 500, Washington DC 20036) asking them to help protect sea turtles.

Sand and Water Table

Turtle Eggs
Provide small plastic eggs for the children to bury like a sea turtle would.

Science

Dare to Compare
Provide photos of sea turtles and land turtles. Encourage the children to describe their differences and similarities.

Ocean Birds

Materials
photographs of ocean birds

Morning Circle
1. Show the photos.
2. Discuss an ocean bird's diet (fish, shrimp, small turtles).
3. Explain how people harm birds when they throw trash in the water. It looks like food to the birds. Sometimes birds get caught in it (especially plastic six-pack rings).
4. Talk about how oil and other chemicals in water harm birds.

Story Circle
The Picture Book of Water Birds by Grace Mabie

Music and Movement
Invite the children to play Drop the Feather like Drop the Handkerchief (see the appendix, page 402).

Learning Centers

Art

Feathers
Invite the children to use playdough and feathers to make sea birds.

Language

Ocean Puzzles
Enlarge the patterns for Sea Life Concentration (see the appendix, page 417) to make puzzles.

Fine Motor

Six-Pack Cut-Ups
Invite the children to cut up plastic six-pack rings so birds cannot get caught in them.

Sand and Water Table

Beak Pick-Up
Invite the children to be sandpipers, using their beaks (tweezers) to pick up small seeds from the sand.

Games

Feed the Gull
Invite the children to toss small fish (beanbags) into a large coffee can suspended from the ceiling (hang just out of reach for beginners and higher up for more experienced children).

Writing

Feather Writing
Encourage the children to dip feather points in tempera paint and write with them.

Additional Books for Down by the Seashore

At the Beach by Anne and Harlow Rockwell
At the Beach by Huy-Voun Lee
Baby Beluga by Raffi
Beach Day by Douglas Florian
A Day at the Beach by Mircea Vasiliu
Going on a Whale Watch by Bruce McMillan
A House for Hermit Crab by Eric Carle
Let's Take a Walk on the Beach by Karen O'Connor
Ocean Alphabet Book by Jerry Pallotta
Ocean Day by Shelley Rotner and Ken Kreisler
Oceans by Joy Palmer
One Sun: A Book of Terse Verse by Bruce McMillan
Sammy the Seal by Syd Hoff
Sea Animals by Dorling Kindersley
The Seaside by J. M. Parramon and Maria Ruis
Swimmy by Leo Lionni
Whale and Dolphin by Vincent Serventy
Whales by Laura Bour
When the Tide Is Low by Sheila Cole

Sound and Movement

The children will enjoy moving and grooving to this unit's activities, which are all about sound, music and movement.

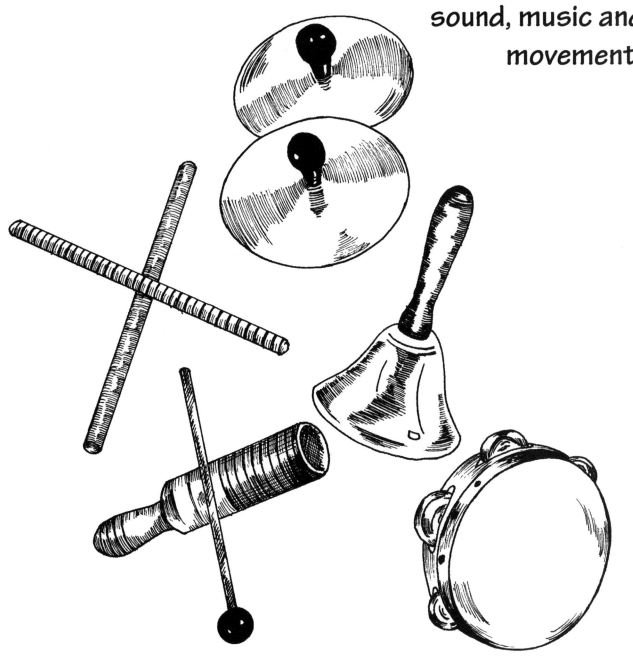

Unit at a Glance

Day	Focus	Centers	Story Circle	Music/Movement
1	**Sounds All Around**	Water Sounds Everyday Sounds Beanbag Music Sound Match Tone Bottles Jingle Seriation	Listen to the Rain	Cooperative Musical Chairs
2	**Loud and Soft**	Loud Pictures Noisy Pairs Loud-Soft Sort Lullaby Rock Clapping Sounds Sound Sort	Noisy Nora	Hot and Cold (Loud and Soft)
3	**High and Low**	Xylophone Tones Voice Variations Voices High and Low Sound Seriation Glass Sounds High and Low Sounds	The Indoor Noisy Book	Little Sir Echo
4	**Fast and Slow**	Tempo Painting Clappers Ballet Class Sculpting in Time Hot Potato Percussion	The Tortoise and the Hare	The Mulberry Bush
5	**Moving to Sound**	Musical Expression Pompoms Parade Hats Shadow Dancing Streamer Dancing Clapping Patterns	Song and Dance Man	Hey! My Name Is Joe!

Day	Focus	Centers	Story Circle	Music/Movement
6	Dancing	Dance Practice Dancing Puppets Shadow Dancing Tap Dancing Dancing a Story Dance Books	Dance, Tanya	Ballet Positions
7	Percussion Instruments	Screen Painting Wind Chimes Drumstick Differences Hammer That Nail Musical Instrument Concentration Maracas	Max Found Two Sticks	Move to the Beat
8	String Instruments	String Painting Milk Carton Guitar Can Telephones String Instrument Puzzles String Music Washtub Bass	Zin! Zin! Zin! A Violin	Scarf Dance
9	Wind Instruments	Straw Painting Kazoos Panpipes Music Store Musical Instrument Concentration Horns and Flutes	Whistle for Willie	Harmonicas, Panpipes and Kazoos
10	Sing a Song	Draw a Tune I'm a Singer Singing Stories Name That Tune Our Favorite Songs Tracing Notes	The Wheels on the Bus	Musical Mother, May I?

Sounds All Around

Materials
tape of familiar sounds, chart paper and marker

Morning Circle
1. Talk about sounds all around us. Listen to the recording.
2. Invite the children to brainstorm a list of sounds. Include pleasant and unpleasant sounds. Record the list on chart paper.
3. Invite the children to experiment making different sounds while touching their throats. Have them whisper, sing and call out. How does the vibration change?

Story Circle
Listen to the Rain by Bill Martin Jr.

Music and Movement
Invite the children to play Cooperative Musical Chairs. When the music stops, everyone must find a seat (share a seat, sit in a lap, etc.). The point is to keep as many people in the game as possible even as chairs are removed.

Learning Centers

Discovery

Water Sounds
Invite the children to drop, sprinkle, spray and pour water on different surfaces. How does the sound change?

Language

Sound Match
Encourage the children to match pictures to sounds on the tape of familiar sounds.

Dramatic Play

Everyday Sounds
Provide an assortment of familiar household objects (e.g., spoons, cans, plastic cups, coffee mugs, chopsticks, etc.). Invite the children to experiment with the different sounds they can make.

Listening

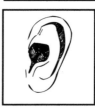

Tone Bottles
Put varying amounts of water in eight glass bottles. Invite the children to tap the bottles with a wooden spoon. Can they compose a tune?

Gross Motor

Beanbag Music
Encourage the children to toss beanbags at a service bell to ring it.

Math

Jingle Seriation
Place one to five bells in five felt bags. Invite the children to arrange the bags in order according to loudness or richness of the jingle.

Loud and Soft   Day 2

Materials
noisemakers (rattles, whistles, service bells, etc.)

Morning Circle
1. Show the noisemakers and discuss the purpose of each one.
2. Sing a favorite song, first loudly and then softly.
3. Invite the children to place their fingers on their throats as they whisper their names, speak their names and shout their names.

Story Circle
Noisy Nora by Rosemary Wells

Music and Movement
Invite the children to play Hot and Cold using their voices to indicate close (loud) and far (soft).

Learning Centers

Art

Loud Pictures
Encourage the children to draw a picture of something loud.

Listening

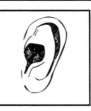

Lullaby Rock
Invite the children to listen to lullabies and Big Band music, then vote for their favorite.

Discovery

Noisy Pairs
Encourage the children to rub a pencil or small dowel across sandpaper, aluminum screen, netting and a rubber mat. Which makes the loudest noise?

Math

Clapping Sounds
Invite the children to create clapping patterns with loud and soft claps.

Language

Loud-Soft Sound Sort
Provide pictures of noisemakers for the children to sort according to loud and soft.

Science

Sound Sort
Place different objects (marble, paper clip, cotton ball, button) inside film canisters. Encourage the children to sort them according to how loud they are.

High and Low   Day 3

Materials
recording of alto or bass and soprano voices, xylophone or keyboard (if possible)

Morning Circle
1. Greet the children in high-pitched voice, then switch to a low-pitched voice.
2. Play the recording that features the soprano, then play the recording of the alto or bass.
3. If available, demonstrate the scale on the xylophone or keyboard.

Story Circle
The Inside Noisy Book by Margaret Wise Brown

Music and Movement
"Little Sir Echo" from *We All Live Together, Volume I* by Steve and Greg

Learning Centers

Discovery

Xylophone Tones
Provide a xylophone for exploration. Why are some sounds high and others low? Where does the sound come from?

Dramatic Play

Voice Variations
Invite the children to play with puppets, using high- and low-pitched voices.

Listening

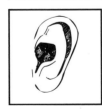

Voices High and Low
Encourage the children to listen to the recordings of soprano and alto or bass voices.

Math

Sound Seriation
Invite the children to cut straws to replicate the lengths of xylophone bars and then order them from shortest to longest.

Sand and Water Table

Glass Sounds
Provide several glasses of various thicknesses and sizes. Invite the children to experiment with tone by adding various amounts of water to each. What happens when they run a finger around the rim of a glass?

Science

High and Low Sounds
Provide pictures of things that make a sound (dog, horn, bell, telephone, etc.). Encourage the children to sort into categories of high and low sounds.

Fast and Slow

Materials
recordings of a waltz and a march tune

Morning Circle
1. Play the waltz music and invite the children to move with it. Play the marching music and invite the children to move to it.
2. Sing a song very slowly, then gradually increase the tempo until you are singing very fast. ("Row, Row, Row Your Boat" works well for this.)
3. Tell the children that the pace of a song is called the tempo.

Story Circle
"The Tortoise and the Hare" by Aesop

Music and Movement
Invite the children to sing "The Mulberry Bush" (see the appendix, page 397) or any other song slowly, then faster and faster.

Learning Centers

Art

Tempo Painting
Invite the children to paint to music of varying tempos.

Fine Motor

Sculpting in Time
Invite the children to sculpt and mold clay to music.

Construction

Clappers
Encourage the children to glue a penny to each end of a 1" x 8" (3 cm x 20 cm) strip of poster board, fold the strip in half and paper-clip it over the end of a tongue depressor. They can play their clappers to music (see the appendix, page 436).

Games

Hot Potato
Encourage the children to play Hot Potato with a beanbag (see the appendix, page 403).

Dramatic Play

Ballet Class
Provide ballet music and invite the children to pretend that they are in ballet class.

Listening

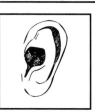

Percussion
Encourage the children to drum tongue depressors or slap tambourines to music of varying tempos.

Moving to Sound

Materials

chart paper and marker

Morning Circle

1. Sing a song that has accompanying movements (e.g., "Where is Thumbkin?" or "If You're Happy and You Know It").
2. Discuss moving to music. Invite the children to list as many music and movement activities as they can (parades, marching bands, drill teams, dancing, clapping, etc.).

Story Circle

Song and Dance Man by Karen Ackerman

Music and Movement

Invite the children to recite "Hello! My Name Is Joe!" (see the appendix, page 394).

Learning Centers

Art

Musical Expression
Invite the children to paint to music.

Gross Motor

Shadow Dancing
Invite the children to dance between a sheet hanging from the ceiling and a light source (lamp or overhead projector).

Construction

Pompoms
Invite the children to make pompoms by gluing streamers around the end of a paper towel tube.

Gross Motor

Streamer Dancing
Invite the children to glue crepe paper streamers along the curve of an 8" (20 cm) paper plate that's been cut in half. The children can dance with their streamers.

Fine Motor

Parade Hats
Provide patterns for rolling semicircles into cones and folding newspaper into hats so the children can make parade hats (see the appendix, page 437).

Listening

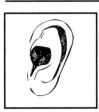

Clapping Patterns
Let the children record clapping patterns, then play them back to identify who is making the pattern.

Dancing

Day 6

Materials

music, scarves

Morning Circle

1. Play a piece of music and invite the children to dance with scarves and streamers.
2. Lead a discussion about how dancing makes us feel.
3. Let someone demonstrate dancing without music. Is it easier or more difficult than dancing with music?

Story Circle

Dance, Tanya by Patricia Gauch

Music and Movement

Teach the children the ballet positions mentioned in *Dance, Tanya*.

Learning Centers

Dramatic Play

Dance Practice
Provide tap and ballet shoes for the children to pretend they are in dance class.

Gross Motor

Tap Dancing
Invite the children to tape quarters to their shoes and try tap dancing.

Fine Motor

Dancing Puppets
Encourage the children to make finger puppets dance to music.

Language

Dancing a Story
Explain that hula dancing tells a story. Invite the children to create their own hula to tell a familiar story.

Gross Motor

Shadow Dancing
Invite the children to perform a shadow dance for their friends.

Library

Dance Books
Fill the center with books about dancing and dancers. Include everything from hula to tap to ballet to jazz.

Percussion Instruments Day 7

Materials
rhythm band instruments including a drum

Morning Circle
1. Play a drum as the children come to the circle.
2. Explain that a drum is a percussion instrument: an instrument you hit, bang or strike.
3. Encourage the children to name all the percussion instruments they know.
4. Show the instruments. Ask, "Which of these are percussion instruments?" (They all are.)

Story Circle
Max Found Two Sticks by Brian Pinkney

Music and Movement
Encourage the children to move to different drumbeats.

Learning Centers

Art

Screen Painting
Provide a shallow box, screen, paints and a toothbrush for the children to do splatter paintings.

Fine Motor

Hammer That Nail
Provide an old tree stump or a block of soft wood. Invite the children to hammer nails in the wood while trying to keep a rhythm. Supervise closely. [Use caution.]

Construction

Wind Chimes
Encourage the children to create chimes by hanging nails and other metal objects from a hanger with yarn.

Games

Musical Instrument Concentration
Invite the children to play Musical Instrument Concentration (see the appendix, page 423).

Discovery

Drumstick Differences
Invite the children to use a variety of objects as drumsticks (chopsticks, pencils, straws, etc.). How does the sound change with each stick?

Music

Maracas
Invite the children to pour beans into small plastic water bottles. Tape closed. Encourage the children to play their maracas to music, trying to keep the beat.

String Instruments

Materials

string instruments, two chairs and a strong piece of elastic

Morning Circle

1. Strum an instrument as the children enter the room.
2. Demonstrate the differences in tightness and thickness of strings. Stretch a piece of elastic between two chairs. Invite someone to pluck the elastic as the rest of you move the chairs farther apart.

Story Circle

Zin! Zin! Zin! A Violin by Lloyd Moss

Music and Movement

Invite the children to perform a scarf dance to violin or classical guitar music.

Learning Centers

Art

String Printing
Invite the children to dip lengths of string in paint and then arrange them in a design on a sheet of paper. Press another sheet of paper on top, then lift to see the print.

Language

String Instrument Puzzles
Make string instrument puzzles for the children to put together (enlarge instrument illustrations in the appendix, page 423).

Construction

Milk Carton Guitar
Invite the children to build guitars from milk cartons, rubber bands and paper towel tubes.

Listening

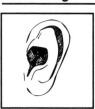

String Music
Provide recordings of different string instruments for the children to listen to.

Discovery

Can Telephones
Provide tin cans with holes poked in the bottoms and string for the children to make telephones. How does the sound change when they stretch the string tight?

Music

Washtub Bass
Poke a hole in the center of the bottom of the washtub, put a piece of string through the hole and tie a knot in the inside end. Attach the other end of the string to a stick. Turn the tub over and position the stick on the bottom of the upside-down tub, using it to adjust string tension.

Wind Instruments

Materials
wind instruments

Morning Circle
1. Encourage the children to try whistling their way to the circle.
2. Show the wind instruments.
3. Invite the children to make different wind sounds by changing the shape of their mouths.

Story Circle
Whistle for Willie by Ezra Jack Keats

Music and Movement
Invite the children to play harmonicas, panpipes and kazoos.

Learning Centers

Art

Straw Painting
Invite the children to blow paint through straws to create straw paintings.

Dramatic Play

Music Store
Invite the children to set up a music store in the center.

Construction

Kazoos
Provide wax paper and combs or toilet paper tubes for the children to make kazoos.

Games

Musical Instrument Concentration
Invite the children to play Musical Instrument Concentration (see the appendix, page 423).

Construction

Panpipes
Cut several sets of four to five cardboard tubes. Each one should be about an inch (3 cm) longer than the last. Encourage the children to arrange a set in order from shortest to longest and tape them together. Plug one end with playdough or clay. Blow across the other ends.

Listening

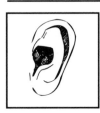

Horns and Flutes
Provide recordings of horns and flutes for the children to listen to.

Sing a Song

Materials
sheet music, tape and tape recorder

Morning Circle
1. Show the children the sheet music. Explain that the black shapes are called notes. Notes are like letters. Letters tell us what sounds to make, and notes tell us what sounds to sing or play and how to play them. Show the children where the lyrics (words) are written.
2. Sing a couple of the children's favorite songs and record them. If you play an instrument, provide accompaniment.
3. Help the children make up new words (lyrics) for a familiar tune.

Story Circle
The Wheels on the Bus by Maryann Kovalsky

Music and Movement
Invite the children to play Musical Mother, May I? or Simon Says by singing the commands (see the appendix, page 404).

Learning Centers

Art

Draw a Tune
Invite the children to illustrate their favorite song.

Listening
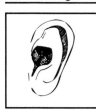

Name That Tune
Provide a tape of the first few bars of several familiar melodies. Ask the children to identify the song.

Dramatic Play

I'm a Singer
Provide props (microphone, tape recorder, musical instruments, headphones, etc.) for pretend professional singers.

Listening

Our Favorite Songs
Invite the children to listen to the tape they recorded during morning circle.

Library

Singing Stories
Fill the center with books based on songs (Itsy Bitsy Spider, The Wheels on the Bus, The Farmer in the Dell, etc.).

Writing

Tracing Notes
Provide tracing paper, pencils and musical notes drawn on index cards. Invite the children to trace the notes.

Additional Books for Sound and Movement

Animal Song by Marcia Sewall

Barn Dance! by Bill Martin

Ben's Trumpet by Rachel Isadora

The Breman Town Musicians by Jacob Grimm

Cat Goes Fiddle-I-Fee by Paul Galdone

Charlie Parker Played Be Bop by Chris Raschka

Crash! Bang! Boom! by Peter Spier

Dancers in the Garden by Joanne Ryder

Dreamsong by Alice McLerran

Flash, Crash, Rumble and Roll by Franklyn M. Branley

Georgia Music by Helen Griffith

Grandpa's Song by Tony Johnston

Hand Rhymes by Marc Brown

The Happy Hedgehog Band by Martin Waddell

I Like Music by Leah Komaiko

I See a Song by Eric Carle

Jingle Bells by Mary Ann Kovalski

Loudmouth George and the Cornet by Nancy Carlson

Making Sounds by Julian Rowe and Molly Perham

Music, Music for Everyone by V. Williams

Parade by Donald Crews

Peter's Song by Carol Saul

Seya's Song by Ron Hirschi

A Touch of Class

This unit presents a study of art in just the right proportions for a child to digest. The works of Picasso, O'Keeffe, Klee and others are used as a focus for daily activities and as a creative launching pad for the children's own works of art.

Unit at a Glance

Day	Focus	Centers	Story Circle	Music/Movement
1	Painting	At the Easel Oil Paints in Water Painted Cookies Oil and Water Finger Art Paintbrush Patterns	The Shepherd Boy (El Niño Pastor)	At the Easel
2	Watercolors	Watercolor Art Making Watercolors What Makes Black? Color Wash Dye Colors Tracing with a Brush	Emmett's Snowball	This Is a Song About Colors
3	Sculpting	Clay Modeling Trash Sculptures Ice Sculpting Papier-Mâché Soap Sculpting Playdough Creations	Josefina	Body Sculptures
4	Drawing	Pencil Sketches Doodle Art Colored Pencil Drawings What Kind of Illustrations Pencils Tall and Small Simple Lines	Alexander & the , Terrible, Horrible, No Good, Very Bad Day	Pencil March
5	Hand-Crafted Art	Mat Weaving Sewing Berry Basket Weaving Streamer Weaving Weave Classification Magnified Weaves	Nattie Parson's Good-Luck Lamb	Hokey Pokey

Day	Focus	Centers	Story Circle	Music/Movement
6	Georges Seurat	Pointillism Make It Round Hole Punch Big Dots Counting Dots Magnified Art	Nate's Treasure	Collective Shadows
7	Pablo Picasso	Blue Period Color Mixing Artist's Studio Art Concentration Cubism Through a Glass	The Art Lesson	Shadow Dancing
8	Paul Klee	Burlap Painting Nature in Watercolor Artist's Studio Both Hands Art Concentration Color Mixing	The Little Painter of Sabana Grande	Hokey Pokey
9	Piet Mondrian	Geo Paintings Building Art Geometric Collages Gelatin Shapes Flannel Geometrics What I See	Shapes	Body Shapes
10	Georgia O'Keeffe	Desert Themes Color Mixing Artist's Studio Artistic Patterns Collect to Paint Flowers and Bones	Coyote Dreams	Drop the Poppy

Painting Day 1

Materials
painting tools (brushes, palette, papers, paints, etc.), photographs of paintings, chart paper and paints

Morning Circle
1. Show the tools and the photos.
2. Demonstrate painting.

Story Circle
The Shepherd Boy (El Niño Pastor) by Kristine L. Franklin (the illustrations are paintings)

Music and Movement
"At the Easel" from *I Am Special* by Thomas Moore

Learning Centers

Art

At the Easel
Provide paint, brushes and paper for the children to paint at the easel.

Discovery

Oil and Water
Encourage the children to experiment with mixing oil and colored water. Provide a container of each, eyedroppers and small glass jars or bowls for mixing. What happens?

Construction

Oil Paints in Water
Invite the children to drop oil paints in a tub of water, swirl the water and then lay sheets of paper on top to make a print. Encourage them to experiment with several designs (swirling the paints, etc.).

Fine Motor

Finger Art
Invite the children to fingerpaint on a table top.

Cooking and Snack

Painted Cookies
Invite the children to make painted cookies (see the recipe in the appendix, page 390).

Math

Paintbrush Patterns
Provide paintbrushes of various widths, paints and paper. Invite the children to create painted patterns by alternating the brushes.

Watercolors

Day 2

Materials

chart paper, watercolor paints, paintbrushes, photographs of watercolor paintings

Morning Circle

1. Be busy painting when the children arrive.
2. Explain that many artists like to use watercolors in their paintings. Show the photos.

Story Circle

Emmett's Snowball by Ned Miller (illustrations are in watercolors)

Music and Movement

"This Is a Song About Colors" from *Basic Vocabulary, Volume I* by Hap Palmer

Learning Centers

Art

Watercolor Art
Provide watercolors, brushes and paper for the children to paint with.

Fine Motor

Color Wash
Encourage the children to make a crayon drawing and then paint over it with watercolors.

Construction

Making Watercolors
Invite the children to pour very thick tempera paint (pancake batter consistency) into egg carton sections. Let dry. You will have watercolors in about a week.

Science

Dye Colors
Invite the children to make and use paints from vegetable and fruit juices.

Discovery

What Makes Black?
Let the children experiment with mixing paints on paper or cleaning brushes in a jar of water.

Writing

Tracing with a Brush
Provide watercolors, brushes and tracing paper. Encourage the children to trace color words (written on index cards) with watercolors.

Sculpting

Materials
clay, photographs of sculptures

Morning Circle
1. Be sculpting with clay when the children arrive.
2. Show the photos.
3. Explain that sculpting is another form of art. It is three-dimensional, which means it has sides and depth.

Story Circle
Josefina by Jeanette Winter

Music and Movement
Invite the children to choose partners. One child poses and the other child sculpts his or her body pose.

Learning Centers

Art

Clay Modeling
Provide clay and a variety of objects for the children to copy as they practice sculpting. Pressing the clay through a garlic press makes stringy clay for hair.

Discovery

Papier-M chØ
Provide wheat paste and torn strips of newsprint for the children to make papier-mâché sculptures. What needs to be done to create three-dimensional sculptures?

Construction

Trash Sculptures
Provide an assortment of recyclables (Styrofoam trays, empty film canisters, fabric and wood scraps, food boxes, cans, etc.) for the children to use in a sculpture.

Fine Motor

Soap Sculpting
Encourage the children to create soap sculptures using Soapsuds Clay (see the recipe in the appendix, page 389).

Cooking and Snack

Ice Sculpting
Invite the children to sculpt and mold shaved ice. Place the sculpture on a cookie sheet or in a shallow pan. Pour cherry juice over it. Serve for snack.

Language

Playdough Creations
Invite the children to create with playdough. Help them make labels for, or write descriptions of, their work.

Drawing

Materials

chart paper and pencil, an artist's drawings

Morning Circle

1. Make some simple drawings on the chart paper.
2. Ask, "What am I doing?"
3. Explain that many artists sketch a picture of their work before they begin painting or sculpting.

Story Circle

Alexander and the Terrible, Horrible, No Good, Very Bad Day by Judith Viorst (illustrations are drawings)

Music and Movement

Invite the children to march like pencils.

Learning Centers

Art

Pencil Sketches

Provide pencils and paper for drawing. Teach the children how to shade a drawing by rubbing a tissue over it.

Library

What Kind of Illustrations

Provide an assortment of books. Encourage the children to find books that have illustrations that are drawings.

Games

Doodle Art

Encourage the children to make doodles on sheets of paper. Let them trade papers and draw something using the doodle as part of the "bigger" picture.

Math

Pencils Tall and Small

Provide an assortment of pencils of varying lengths. Encourage the children to place the pencils in order from smallest to longest.

Language

Colored Pencil Drawings

Invite the children to draw with colored pencils.

Writing

Simple Lines

Invite the children to trace simple line drawings.

Hand-Crafted Art Day 5

Materials
blankets, baskets, other woven materials; several 6"–8" (15–20 cm) pieces of ponytail yarn in two colors

Morning Circle
1. Show the children the blankets, baskets and other woven materials.
2. Have the children demonstrate the concepts of over and under and top to bottom.
3. Demonstrate weaving the two colors of yarn.

Story Circle
Nattie Parson's Good-Luck Lamb by Lisa Campbell Ernst

Music and Movement
"Hokey Pokey" from *Kidding Around with Greg and Steve*

Learning Centers

Art

Mat Weaving
Cut construction paper into 1" (3 cm) strips. Encourage the children to weave the strips into mats.

Fine Motor

Streamer Weaving
Give the children crepe paper streamers to weave into plastic milk crates or laundry baskets.

Dramatic Play

Sewing
Provide plastic needles, yarn and squares of burlap. Encourage the children to sew the yarn into the burlap.

Math

Weave Classification
Provide materials such as blankets, baskets, bowls and clothing for the children to classify as woven and nonwoven.

Fine Motor

Berry Basket Weaving
Provide ribbon, pipe cleaners and lace for the children to weave into berry baskets.

Science

Magnified Weaves
Let the children examine sweaters, blankets and baskets using a magnifying glass.

Georges Seurat (France, 1859 1891) Day 6

Materials
flashlight, black construction paper, hole punch or awl, pictures of Seurat's work

Morning Circle
1. Show the children pictures of Seurat's work.
2. Poke holes in black construction paper to create various designs and pictures.
3. Stand or hold the flashlight behind the hole-punched paper. Ask the children to talk about what they see.

Story Circle
Nate's Treasure by David Spohn

Music and Movement
Provide a light source. Have the children stand in a group in front of light and cast a collective shadow on the wall. Ask the children with blue on to sit down. How does the shadow change? Invite other groups to sit. Each time the shadow will change, just as Seurat's work was changed by the light coming through the dots on canvas.

Learning Centers

Art

Pointillism
Provide crayons and pencils for the children to experiment with pointillism.

Gross Motor

Big Dots
Cut 6″ (15 cm) circles from construction paper or plastic sheeting. Let the children arrange the dots on a large window or on the carpet.

Blocks

Make It Round
Encourage the children to construct a building using only round blocks.

Math

Counting Dots
Provide tiddly winks or cutout dots and paper plates with the numerals 1 through 5 written on them. Encourage the children to count and place the appropriate number of dots on each plate.

Fine Motor

Hole Punch
Provide a hole punch and construction paper. Invite the children to create designs of holes and then hold their paper up to the light.

Science

Magnified Art
Encourage the children to examine Seurat's work with a magnifying glass.

Pablo Picasso (Spain, 1881 1973) — Day 7

Materials
photographs of Picasso and his work

Morning Circle
1. Show the prints.
2. Discuss the distortions in Picasso's work. Explain that some people believe Picasso had a vision problem.
3. Talk about how Picasso's painting style changed during his life. When he was sad, he used a lot of blue (blue period). When he was happy, he used a lot of pink (rose period). Later, he developed cubism (a form that simplifies objects into shapes).

Story Circle
The Art Lesson by Tomie dePaola

Music and Movement
Invite the children to do a Shadow Dance. Encourage the children to vary their distance from the light source.

Learning Centers

Art

Blue Period
Encourage the children to paint a picture using different shades of blue only.

Games

Art Concentration
Invite the children to play Art Concentration (see the appendix, page 416).

Discovery

Color Mixing
Invite the children to experiment with color mixing. Put water and food coloring in the end cups of a Styrofoam egg carton. Pour water in the middle sections. Provide eyedroppers.

Math

Cubism
Provide pencils, paper and stencils. Encourage the children to trace around the stencils, section them as desired and paint each section a different color.

Dramatic Play

Artist's Studio
Provide props (easel, palette, paints, brushes, rags, smock, etc.) for the children to set up an artist's studio.

Science

Through a Glass
Provide magnifying glasses for the children to look through as they paint at the easel.

Paul Klee (Switzerland, 1879 1940) Day 8

Materials
photographs of Klee and his work

Morning Circle
1. Show the photos.
2. Ask, "What do you notice?"
3. Explain that Klee liked to make simple, childlike drawings. He loved to paint nature. He liked using watercolors and chalks. Sometimes he painted on things besides canvas, like burlap. Paul Klee could paint with both hands.

Story Circle
The Little Painter of Sabana Grande by Patricia Maloney Markun

Music and Movement
Sing and move to the "Hokey Pokey" (see the appendix, page 394).

Learning Centers

Art

Burlap Painting
Provide several jars of colored glue (mix with tempera) and a piece of burlap. Encourage the children to paint on burlap to create a wall hanging.

Art

Nature in Watercolor
Provide brushes, watercolors and an assortment of natural items for the children to paint.

Dramatic Play

Artist's Studio
Encourage the children to add to their artist's studio.

Fine Motor

Both Hands
Invite the children to explore painting with their nondominant hand. How is this different from painting with your dominant hand?

Games

Art Concentration
Invite the children to play Art Concentration (see the appendix, page 416).

Science

Color Mixing
Invite the children to experiment with color mixing using colored chalks on paper.

Piet Mondrian (Netherlands, 1872 1944) Day 9

Materials
photographs of Mondrian and his work

Morning Circle
1. Show the photos.
2. Ask "What do you notice?" They will probably say that most of the paintings use the same colors (red, yellow, black, blue, white).
3. Explain that Mondrian painted people and landscapes when he started painting. Later, he painted geometric shapes.

Story Circle
Shapes by John Reiss

Music and Movement
Invite the children to figure out ways to form shapes with their bodies.

Learning Centers

Art

Geo Paintings
Provide yellow, black, blue and red paints for the children to paint geometric designs at the easel.

Cooking and Snack

Gelatin Shapes
Invite the children to make red and yellow gelatin shapes (see the recipe in the appendix, page 391).

Blocks

Building Art
Cover blocks with red, yellow, blue, white and black contact paper. Invite the children to "build" a painting.

Language

Flannel Geometrics
Provide geometric shapes cut from red, blue, black, yellow and white felt. Encourage the children to arrange the shapes in different designs on the flannel board.

Construction

Geometric Collages
Provide a variety of geometric cutouts in red, black, blue, yellow and white. Invite the children to arrange the shapes on paper and glue them down.

Language

What I See
Ask the children to describe the paintings they created. Record what they say about their paintings.

Georgia O'Keeffe (United States, 1887 1986) Day 10

Materials
photographs of O'Keeffe and her work

Morning Circle
1. Show the photos.
2. Talk about the unique characteristics of O'Keeffe's work (desert themes, larger-than-life paintings, bold and colorful paintings, etc.). Explain that O'Keeffe never painted people. She often bleached bones she was going to paint to give them a worn look. One of her most famous paintings is of a poppy.

Story Circle
Coyote Dreams by Susan Nunes

Music and Movement
Play Drop the Poppy like Drop the Handkerchief (see the appendix, page 402).

Learning Centers

Art

Desert Themes
Place fossils, rocks and cactus plants in the center for the children to paint still lifes.

Math

Artistic Patterns
Provide flower-shaped sponges and two colors of paint. Encourage the children to create flower print patterns.

Discovery

Color Mixing
Invite the children to rub colored chalk over salt on paper plates. Provide a small spoon and extra plates for the children to mix the colored salts. How well do they mix? What happens when water is added?

Outside

Collect to Paint
Go on a walk outside to collect items such as flowers, leaves, twigs and pine cones to inspire the children's painting.

Dramatic Play

Artist's Studio
Encourage the children to add "O'Keeffe" props to their artist's studio.

Science

Flowers and Bones
Provide a variety of flowers and bleached bones for the children to examine through magnifying glasses. Explain that the sun bleaches the bones.

Additional Book for A Touch of Class

All I See by Cynthia Rylant
The Big Orange Splot by Daniel Pinkwater
Draw Me a Star by Eric Carle
Emma by Wendy Kesselman
Frederick by Leo Lionni
Grandma Moses: Painter of Rural America by Zibby O'Neal
The Legend of the Indian Paintbrush by Tomie dePaola
Linnea in Monet's Garden by Christina Bjork
Mary Cassatt by Mike Venezia
Mouse Paint by Ellen Stoll Walsh
No Good in Art by Miriam Cohen
Van Gogh by Mike Venezia
What Makes a Monet a Monet? by Richard Muhlberger

A Pot, a Pan & a Wooden Spoon

This is a "yummy" unit about food its source and its preparation. Children learn about textures and colors of foods. Everyone will enjoy the fruits of their labors.

Into 2 cup bowl, put 1 cup lukewarm water, 2 teaspoons sugar and 2 yeast cakes. Into larger bowl, put 3 cups lukewarm water, 3 teaspoons salt, and 4 tablespoons sugar, then add first mixture. Add 6 cups flour; mix partly, ball; let rise, then put into pans. Let rise, and bake at 350° for 1 hour. This recipe makes 4 loaves of bread.

* Coffee cake may be made out of this dough by adding 1 to 2 cups of sugar.

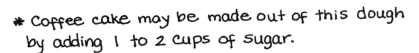

Unit at a Glance

Day	Focus	Centers	Story Circle	Music/Movement
1	Cooking Utensils	Gadget Painting Carrot Salad My Kitchen Bean Sweep Pancake Flippers Pans and Spoons	Pots and Pans	Kitchen Gadget Rhythm Band
2	Following Directions	Picture Recipes Beating Rolling and Cutting Kneading and Rolling Separate Measuring	Strega Nona	Birthday Cake
3	Cookies	No-Bake Cookies My Bakery Cookie Hunt Drop the Cookie Flannel Board Cookies Cookie Patterns	The Doorbell Rang	Who Stole the Cookie?
4	Candy	Candy Land Peanut Butter Balls Candy Store Candy Pick-Up Yummy, Yummy Books Candy Sort	The Chocolate-Covered- Cookie Tantrum	Candy Land Walk
5	Corn	Corn Cob Prints Popcorn Changes Shucking Corn Corn Sort Popping Sounds Corny Counting	Popcorn at the Palace	Popping Corn

Day	Focus	Centers	Story Circle	Music/Movement
6	Vegetables	Gardens Vegetable Dyes Vegetable Stand Shelling Peas Veggie Sort Veggies Up Close	The Carrot Seed	Hot Potato
7	Fruits	Applesauce Fruit Dyes Turnover Berry Pick-Up Toss the Pit Fruit Kabobs Up-Close Look	The Blueberry Pie Elf	Fruit Basket
8	Breads, Cereals & Pastas	Farmland Donut Making Tasty Letters Great Grains Bakery Cereal Sort	The Little Red Hen	Twister
9	Meats, Fish & Poultry	Butcher Paper Mural Tuna Boats Pizza Meat Collage Egg Roll Move Like Animals	Meat	Cow, Cow, Chicken
10	Dairy Products	Buttermilk Art Milk Crates Baggie Ice Cream Ice Cream Shop Cheesy Shapes What's the Answer?	Milk	Did You Feed My Cow?

Cooking Utensils

Day 1

Materials
pots, pans, assortment of utensils

Morning Circle
1. Show the pots, pans and utensils. Talk about what each is made of and used for.
2. Discuss sizes and shapes of bread pans, muffin tins, cake pans and so on. Talk about how the shape of the pan creates the shape of the product.
3. Encourage the children to think of different ways to use cookware and utensils.

Story Circle
Pots and Pans by Anne Rockwell

Music and Movement
Invite the children to perform in a Kitchen Gadget Rhythm Band.

Learning Centers

Art

Gadget Painting
Provide an assortment of kitchen gadgets, paints and paper for the children to create gadget prints.

Fine Motor

Bean Sweep
Provide a bowl, a scoop, a pastry brush and a pile of beans. Invite the children to sweep the beans into the scoop and pour them into the bowl.

Cooking and Snack

Carrot Salad
Provide carrots, a grater and raisins. Encourage the children to grate the carrots and then add raisins to make carrot salad.

Games

Pancake Flippers
Provide a spatula, frying pan and pancake shapes cut from sponges or vinyl wallpaper. Invite the children to flip the pancakes with the spatula and catch them in the frying pan.

Dramatic Play

My Kitchen
Provide pots, pans and other cooking utensils for the children to set up a kitchen.

Math

Pans and Spoons
Provide pans and spoons in various sizes for the children to arrange in order from largest to smallest.

Following Directions

Materials
recipe (preferably a rebus recipe—see the appendix, page 428, for an example)

Morning Circle
1. Show the recipe.
2. Explain that a recipe is a set of directions. A recipe tells us how to make something and it helps us make it the same way every time.
3. Give the children some simple directions to practice following.

Story Circle
Strega Nona by Tomie dePaola

Music and Movement
Invite the children to role-play mixing, baking and decorating a birthday cake.

Learning Centers

Cooking and Snack

Picture Recipes
Encourage the children to make cinnamon toast by following the rebus directions in the appendix, page 428.

Fine Motor

Kneading and Rolling
Provide playdough for the children to knead and roll.

Discovery

Beating
Provide a beater and a bucket of bubble soap. Invite the children to create bubbles.

Math

Separate
Provide dried beans, rice and salt mixed in one bowl. Invite the children to use strainers and colanders to separate the ingredients.

Dramatic Play

Rolling and Cutting
Provide a rolling pin, playdough and cookie cutters for the children to roll and cut playdough cookies.

Sand and Water Table

Measuring
Provide funnels, basters, measuring spoons and measuring cups at the water table for the children to practice measuring.

Cookies

Materials
tray of cookies

Morning Circle
1. Have the tray of cookies available when the children enter the room. Invite everyone to have a cookie.
2. Ask the children to tell about a time when they helped make cookies.

Story Circle
The Doorbell Rang by Pat Hutchins

Music and Movement
Invite the children to play Who Stole the Cookie from the Cookie Jar? (see the appendix, page 401).

Learning Centers

Cooking and Snack

No-Bake Cookies
Invite the children to make No-Bake Cookies by following the recipe in the appendix, page 389.

Dramatic Play

My Bakery
Provide playdough, rolling pins, mixing bowls, cookie cutters, cookie sheets and other supplies for the children to play bakery.

Games

Cookie Hunt
Hide paper cut-out cookies in the center. Invite the children to find them.

Games

Drop the Cookie
Encourage the children to drop playdough cookies into a mixing bowl. Try first from waist height, then from shoulder height.

Language

"My picture is about...."

Flannel Board Cookies
Provide felt pieces (round shapes, bar shapes, decorative elements, etc.) for the children to make cookies at the flannel board.

Math

Cookie Patterns
Provide cookie cutouts in various shapes and colors. Invite the children to arrange the cookies in patterns on a cookie sheet.

Candy

Materials
recording of "The Candy Man" by Sammy Davis, Jr.; candy thermometer

Morning Circle
1. Have "The Candy Man" playing as the children come into the classroom.
2. Find out what the children know about candy making. Show them the candy thermometer.

Story Circle
The Chocolate-Covered-Cookie Tantrum by Deborah Blumenthal

Music and Movement
Invite the children on a pretend walk through Candy Land. Try walking through caramel, sliding through chocolate syrup and hopping over peppermint patties. You could do this like "Going on a Bear Hunt."

Learning Centers

Art

Candy Land
Provide paper and colorful paints; invite the children to paint a Candy Land.

Fine Motor

Candy Pick-Up
Invite the children to use tongs to pick up hard candies and place them in a bowl.

Cooking and Snack

Peanut Butter Balls
Encourage the children to make Peanut Butter Balls by following the recipe in the appendix, page 390.

Library

Yummy, Yummy Books
Provide an assortment of books about candy.

Dramatic Play

Candy Store
Provide props for the children to set up a candy store.

Math

Candy Sort
Provide several types of hard, wrapped candies for the children to sort and classify.

Corn Day 5

Materials
ear of corn still in shuck, chart paper and marker

Morning Circle
1. Show the children how to shuck corn. Are they surprised at what's inside?
2. Help the children create a list of all the ways they can eat corn.

Story Circle
Popcorn at the Palace by Emily McCully

Music and Movement
Invite the children to pretend to be popping corn.

Learning Centers

Art

Corncob Prints
Provide tempera paints in shallow trays, paper and corncobs for the children to make prints.

Fine Motor

Corn Sort
Encourage the children to pick up kernels of corn with tweezers and drop them in a jar.

Cooking and Snack

Popcorn Changes
Provide popcorn and various seasonings for the children to try (e.g., cinnamon and sugar, parmesan cheese, brown sugar).

Listening

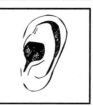

Popping Sounds
Record the children making popping sounds. Encourage the children to listen to all the popping sounds and try to identify who made each sound.

Discovery

Shucking Corn
Provide ears of corn for the children to shuck. If you use sweet corn, cook it for snack. If you use feed corn, feed it to squirrels.

Math

Corny Counting
Cut holes in the lids of five margarine tubs. Place one to five stick-on dots on each lid. Invite the children to use tweezers to put the appropriate number of corn kernels in each tub.

Vegetables

Materials
vegetables, chart paper and marker, cutting board and sharp knife (for teacher)

Morning Circle
1. Show the vegetables.
2. Help the children create a list of vegetables.
3. Invite the children to taste the vegetables you've provided.
4. Encourage the children to compare the vegetables and choose the ones they like best. Create a graph showing their favorites.

Story Circle
The Carrot Seed by Ruth Krauss

Music and Movement
Invite the children to play Hot Potato (see directions in the appendix, page 403).

Learning Centers

Art

Gardens
Provide paper, paints and paintbrushes for the children to create pictures of gardens where their favorite vegetables grow.

Fine Motor

Shelling Peas
Provide peas and bowls. Show the children how to shell the peas.

Discovery

Vegetable Dyes
Invite the children to make dyes from vegetable juices (beets, broccoli, etc.) using an eyedropper to drop the dyes onto coffee filters. Is it easy to predict the color dye the vegetable will produce?

Math

Veggie Sort
Provide an assortment of vegetables or pictures of vegetables for the children to sort.

Dramatic Play

Vegetable Stand
Provide props for the children to set up a vegetable stand (plastic vegetables, bags, baskets, scales, etc.).

Science

Veggies Up Close
Provide a variety of seeds and vegetables for the children to examine with magnifying glasses.

Fruits Day 7

Materials
fruits, chart paper and marker, cutting board and sharp knife (for teacher)

Morning Circle
1. Show the fruits. Ask, "How are fruits different from vegetables?"
2. Make a list of all the fruits the children can name.
3. Invite the children to taste the fruits you've provided.
4. Encourage the children to compare the fruits and choose the ones they like best. Make a graph showing their choices.

Story Circle
The Blueberry Pie Elf by Jane Thayer

Music and Movement
Invite the children to play Fruit Basket Turnover (see directions in the appendix, page 402).

Learning Centers

Cooking and Snack

Applesauce
Invite the children to make applesauce by following the directions in the appendix, page 389.

Discovery

Fruit Dyes
Provide several fruit juices that make dyes (blueberry, strawberry, etc.). Invite the children to drop the juices through an eyedropper onto coffee filters. Is it easy to predict what color the dyes will produce?

Fine Motor

Berry Pick-Up
Encourage the children to use tweezers to move blueberries from one bowl to another.

Gross Motor

Toss the Pit
Invite the children to toss peach pits into a berry basket.

Math

Fruit Kabobs
Provide two or three diced fruits. Encourage the children to arrange fruit pieces in patterns on skewers.

Science

Up-Close Look
Provide fruit seeds and skins for the children to examine with a magnifying glass.

Breads, Cereals & Pastas   Day 8

Materials
photographs and samples of grain products

Morning Circle
1. Ask the children to tell what they ate for breakfast. Note each mention of bread and cereal.
2. Explain the importance of grains to our health and nutrition.

Story Circle
The Little Red Hen by Paul Galdone

Music and Movement
Invite the children to play Twister. Do they end up looking like spaghetti?

Learning Centers

Blocks

Farmland
Encourage the children to build a farm where grains grow. Provide tractors and other props.

Discovery

Great Grains
Provide a mortar and pestle and several different grains (oats, rice, wheat, barley, etc.) for the children to grind. How are they similar? How are they different?

Cooking and Snack

Donut Making
Invite the children to cut holes in refrigerator biscuits, cook them in a deep fryer and then coat them with powdered sugar. Supervise closely. [Use caution.]

Dramatic Play

Bakery
Provide props (rolling pins, playdough, bread pans, muffin tins, etc.) for the children to set up a bakery.

Cooking and Snack

Tasty Letters
Provide letter-shaped cereal or pretzels for snack. Encourage the children to find a letter that is in their names or to make a word from the letters.

Math

Cereal Sort
Provide an assortment of empty boxes of cereal. Encourage the children to sort them according to what grain they contained. Help the children realize that cereals can also contain more than one type of grain.

Meats, Fish and Poultry — Day 9

Materials
photographs of different meats and the animals they come from, chart paper and marker

Morning Circle
1. Show the photos.
2. Talk about where beef, pork, chicken and fish come from.
3. Ask, "What other animals do we get meat from?"
4. Ask the children to name their favorite meat. Create a graph showing their responses.

Story Circle
Meat by Elizabeth Clark

Music and Movement
Invite the children to play Cow, Cow, Chicken like Duck, Duck, Goose (see the appendix, page 402).

Learning Centers

Art

Butcher Paper Mural
Provide fingerpaints and let the children paint on the shiny side of butcher paper. Does the shiny side feel different than the nonshiny side?

Fine Motor

Meat Collage
Invite the children to cut pictures of meat dishes and meat-giving animals from magazines and create a collage.

Cooking and Snack

Tuna Boats
Encourage the children to make tuna sandwiches and cut them diagonally. Stick a toothpick into an apple slice and add to each half sandwich.

Games

Egg Roll
Provide paper towel tubes, plastic eggs and juice cans with both ends cut out. Invite the children to putt the eggs through the cans. Are eggs difficult to roll? Try substituting Ping-Pong balls.

Dramatic Play

Pizza
Provide felt cutouts (pizza slices, pepperoni, mushrooms, peppers, etc.) and a pizza pan. Encourage the children to "build" a pizza.

Gross Motor

Move Like Animals
Encourage each child to pick an animal. For the whole day, whenever the children need to move around the classroom, encourage them to move like the animals they selected.

Dairy Products

Materials
photographs and samples of dairy products, chart paper and marker

Morning Circle
1. Make up riddles that will help the children begin a list of dairy products. For example, "I'm thinking of a drink that comes from cows. I'm thinking of something cold that you eat out of a cone."
2. Write responses on chart paper. Continue the list until the children catch on to the nature of the list.
3. Go through the list and circle the things that are better cold.

Story Circle
Milk by Donald Carrick

Music and Movement
"Did You Feed My Cow" from *You'll Sing a Song and I'll Sing a Song* by Ella Jenkins

Learning Centers

Art

Buttermilk Art
Add a little buttermilk to tempera paints and encourage the children to paint with it.

Blocks

Milk Crates
Invite the children to build with milk crates.

Cooking and Snack

Baggie Ice Cream
Encourage the children to make Baggie Ice Cream by following the recipe in the appendix, page 389.

Dramatic Play

Ice Cream Shop
Provide props (empty ice cream cartons, dippers, ice cream dishes, spoons, malt glasses, straws, etc.) for the children to set up an ice cream shop.

Fine Motor

Cheesy Shapes
Provide plastic knives and cookie cutters for the children to cut shapes from cheese slices. Serve with crackers for snack.

Listening

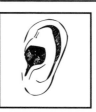

What's the Answer?
Record the children's own riddles for dairy products. Encourage the children to listen and guess the answer to the riddles.

Additional Books for A Pot, a Pan & a Wooden Spoon

Blueberries for Sal by Robert McCloskey
Bread and Jam for Frances by Russell Hoban
Bread Is for Eating by David and Phillis Gershator
Bread, Bread, Bread by Ann Morris
Bunny Cakes by Rosemary Wells
Chicken Soup With Rice by Maurice Sendak
Cloudy With a Chance of Meatballs by Judi Barrett
Corn Is Maize: The Gift of the Indians by Aliki
Daddy Makes the Best Spaghetti by Anna Grossnickle Hines
Eating the Alphabet: Fruits and Vegetables From A to Z by Lois Ehlert
Everybody Bakes Bread by Norah Dooley
Everybody Cooks Rice by Norah Dooley
Feast for Ten by Cathryn Falwell
The Giant Jam Sandwich by John Vernon Lord and Janet Burroway
Gregory, the Terrible Eater by Mitchell Sharmat
How Pizza Came to Queens by Dayal Kaur Khalsa
I Need a Lunch Box by Jeannette Caines
If You Give a Moose a Muffin by Laura Joffe Numeroff
If You Give a Mouse a Cookie by Laura Joffe Numeroff
Jamberry by Bruce Degan
Just Me and My Dad by Mercer Mayer
Lunch by Denise Fleming
The Magic Pretzel by James Magorian
Milk by Dorothy Turner
The Milk Makers by Gail Gibbons
Pancakes, Pancakes by Eric Carle
Peanut Butter and Jelly: A Play Rhyme by Nadine Bernard Westcott
Sam's Sandwich by David Pelham
Sitti's Secrets by Naomi S. Nye
Sofie's Role by Amy Heath
Stone Soup by Diane Paterson
Today Is Monday by Eric Carle
Tony's Bread by Tomie DePaola
Two Cool Cows by Toby Speed
Walter the Baker by Eric Carle

Good Morning, Sunshine

What child doesn't love warm sunshine and blue skies? The activities in this unit focus on the many interesting properties of the sun. Children will learn as they make sundials, play with shadows, study clouds, create suncatchers and more.

Unit at a Glance

Day	Focus	Centers	Story Circle	Music/Movement
1	Mr. Sun	You Are My Sunshine Sunbathing Fan Folding Sun Concentration Sun Puzzles Sun Ray Patterns	What the Sun Sees, What the Moon Sees	Good Morning
2	Sunshine Activities	Daytime Fun Sun Catchers Sunshine Sandwiches Prisms Picnic Time Day/Night Sort	Mimi and the Picnic	Jum Ropes and Hula Hoops
3	Clouds Above	Cloudy Sky Cloud Sculptures Cloud Cutouts Cloud Pick-Up Cloud Stories Fluffy Clouds	Little Cloud	Floating Clouds
4	It's Daytime	Daytime Art Individual Sundials Cinnamon Toast Alarm! It's Breakfast Make Sundials	The Napping House Wakes Up	Beach Ball Fun
5	Daytime Activities	PB & J Sandwiches Office Time Ball Roll Daytime Favorites Order of the Day Songs Throughout the Day	Bread and Jam for Frances	Morning Exercises

Day	Focus	Centers	Story Circle	Music/Movement
6	**Days of the Week**	Sweep the House Wash the Clothes Baking Bread Hungry Caterpillar Saturday Night Bath My Favorite Day	The Very Hungry Caterpillar	Days of the Week
7	**Animal Day Life**	Dam Building Home Building Looking for Worms Grazing Daytime Is For… Food Gathering	Busy Beavers	Ants
8	**Shadows All Around**	Shadow Painting Shadow Changes Shadow Puppets Shadow Designs Shadow Drama Hand Print Shadows	Me and My Shadow	Shadow Dance
9	**More Shadows**	My Shadow Shadow Puppets Reverse Shadows Shadow Concentration Shadow Order Sidewalk Shadows	Shadow Magic	Shadow Tag
10	**Sun's Heat and Light**	Melted Crayon Art Sun Art Make a Sun Visor Sunglasses Dress for Heat Heat and Ice	Sun Song	Mr. Sun Says

Mr. Sun

Day 1

Materials
sunglasses, sun hat, chart paper and marker

Morning Circle
1. Sit in the circle, wearing sunglasses and hat.
2. Tell the children that this unit is about daytime and sunshine is an important part of daytime. Therefore, you're starting the unit by talking about sunshine.
3. Encourage the children to create a list of things they know about the sun and sunshine.
4. Write down their responses.

Story Circle
What the Sun Sees, What the Moon Sees by Nancy Tafuri

Music and Movement
"Good Morning" from *We All Live Together, Volume II* by Steve and Greg

Learning Centers

Art

You Are My Sunshine
Provide yellow paint and paper for the children to paint pictures of the sun.

Games

Sun Concentration
Draw matching pairs of smiling faces on yellow circles. Invite the children to turn all the circles face down, then turn up two at a time to find matching pairs.

Dramatic Play

Sunbathing
Provide props for pretend sun-bathing (towels, lotion bottles, hats, glasses, cooler, umbrella, etc.).

Language

Sun Puzzles
Cut two large suns from poster board. Cut each into three or four puzzle pieces for the children to put together.

Fine Motor

Fan Folding
Provide wrapping paper and wallpaper for the children to fold into fans.

Math

Sun Ray Patterns
Place a big, yellow paper sun in the center of a table or on the floor. Provide 1" x 8" (3 cm x 20 cm) paper rays in two or three colors. Invite the children to arrange them around the sun in a pattern.

Sunshine Activities   Day 2

Materials
"Good Morning to You" (see the appendix, page 393), chart paper and marker

Morning Circle
1. Sing "Good Morning to You."
2. Invite the children to talk about things people do in the sunshine.
3. Make a list of their ideas.

Story Circle
Mimi and the Picnic by Martin Waddell

Music and Movement
Provide jump ropes and hula hoops for the children to play with.

Learning Centers

Art

Daytime Fun
Invite the children to draw pictures of their favorite daytime activities.

Discovery

Prisms
Put several prisms in the center for the children to explore and make rainbows.

Construction

Sun Catchers
Encourage the children to sprinkle crayon shavings on waxed paper. Fold the paper over and iron. Supervise closely. Hang the sun catcher in a sunny window. [Use caution.]

Dramatic Play

Picnic Time
Provide props for the children to have a pretend picnic (basket, plastic foods, glasses, dishes, napkins, blanket, etc.).

Cooking and Snack

Sunshine Sandwiches
Invite the children to make Sunshine Sandwiches (see the recipe in the appendix, page 391).

Science

Day/Night Sort
Provide pictures of day and night activities from magazines. Invite the children to sort the pictures.

Clouds Above

Day 3

Materials
poster board or construction-paper cloud shapes for the children to sit on

Morning Circle
1. Have cloud shapes around the circle area for the children to sit on.
2. Ask the children to tell you what they know about clouds. Ask, "What shapes have you seen in clouds?"
3. Look out the window or go outside and look for clouds.

Story Circle
Little Cloud by Eric Carle

Music and Movement
Play peaceful music and invite the children to move like floating clouds.

Learning Centers

Art

Cloudy Sky
Provide white paint and blue paper for the children to paint skies with clouds.

Fine Motor

Cloud Pick-Up
Invite the children to move clouds (cotton balls) from one sky (blue construction paper) to another.

Construction

Cloud Sculptures
Mix three parts Ivory Snow Flakes with one part water to make a molding paste. Invite the children to sculpt clouds. Do they look like familiar objects?

Language

"My picture is about...."

Cloud Stories
Provide white, cloud-shaped felt cutouts for the children to use on the flannel board. Encourage them to tell cloud stories.

Fine Motor

Cloud Cutouts
Provide white paper and scissors for the children to cut out cloud shapes.

Sand and Water Table

Fluffy Clouds
Put blue bulletin board paper in the empty sand and water table. Squirt shaving cream on the paper. Encourage the children to fingerpaint shaving cream clouds on the blue poster board "sky."

It's Daytime

Day 4

Materials
chart paper and marker

Morning Circle
1. Ask, "How do you know when it's daytime?" (The children will probably mention sun and activities.)
2. Make a list of daytime characteristics (sunlight, noise, activity, being awake, gardening, working, etc.).
3. Talk about routines (waking up, getting out of bed, getting dressed, etc.).

Story Circle
The Napping House Wakes Up by Audrey Wood

Music and Movement
Provide a couple of beach balls and challenge the children to keep them airborne.

Learning Centers

Art

Daytime Art
Encourage the children to paint a daytime picture with watercolors.

Discovery

Alarm!
Provide an assortment of wind-up alarm clocks. Encourage the children to discover how they work.

Construction

Individual Sundials
Invite the children to make individual sundials with paper plates and straws (cut an X in the center of each plate to push the straw through). Use stick-on dots for hour markers. Try the sundials in the sun.

Dramatic Play

It's Breakfast
Invite the children to set up the center with breakfast props for pretend play.

Cooking and Snack

Cinnamon Toast
Provide bread, margarine, sugar and cinnamon for the children to make cinnamon toast (see the rebus recipe in the appendix, page 428).

Outdoors

Make Sundials
Help the children stick a 6' (2 m) pole in the ground. Place twelve rocks in a circle around the pole. Check the pole regularly and adjust the placement of stones to show the hours.

GOOD MORNING, SUNSHINE • • • 293

Daytime Activities

Materials
song "Mr. Sun" (see the appendix, page 396), chart paper and marker

Morning Circle
1. Sing "Mr Sun."
2. Help the children make a list of things they are going to do today.

Story Circle
Bread and Jam for Frances by Russel Hoban

Music and Movement
Lead the children in morning exercises.

Learning Centers

Cooking and Snack

PB & J Sandwiches
Provide peanut butter, jelly and bread for the children to make sandwiches.

Language

Daytime Favorites
Invite the children to draw a picture of their favorite daytime activity and dictate a sentence about it.

Dramatic Play

Office Time
Provide props for the children to play office (papers, folders, typewriter, pencils, etc.).

Math

Order of the Day
Provide the children with pictures of things they do during the day (real photos or clippings from supply catalogs and magazines). Encourage them to put the pictures in the order in which they usually occur.

Gross Motor

Ball Roll
Encourage the children to roll a soft ball such as a Nerf ball back and forth.

Music

Songs Throughout the Day
Encourage the children to sing their favorite songs throughout the day. Make a list of their favorite songs and when they like to sing them.

Days of the Week

Materials
"Rock Around the Mulberry Bush" from *We All Live Together Volume III* by Steve and Greg; vinyl tiles and permanent markers or construction paper and markers

Morning Circle
1. Sing "Mulberry Bush" or listen to Steve and Greg's recording. Encourage the children to rewrite the lyrics to reflect things they do.
2. Ask the children if they do any special things on certain days of the week (e.g., church on Sunday, pizza on Friday nights, school Monday through Friday, Grandma's house on Sunday afternoon, etc.). Talk about traditional activities (e.g., Saturday night bath, Sunday napping and resting, etc.).
3. Write the names of days of the week on vinyl tiles and place them in order on the floor. Let the children take turns stepping on the days as you call them out.

Story Circle
The Very Hungry Caterpillar by Eric Carle

Music and Movement
"Days of the Week" from *We All Live Together Volume IV* by Steve and Greg

Learning Centers

Art

Sweep the House
Provide pastry brushes for the children to use as paintbrushes.

Language

Hungry Caterpillar Sequence
Provide felt cutouts of the foods from *The Very Hungry Caterpillar* for the children to sequence. Encourage them to retell the story.

Dramatic Play

Wash the Clothes
Provide props for the children to do pretend laundry (clothes, clothesline, clothespins, iron and ironing board, etc.).

Sand and Water Table

Saturday Night Bath
Invite the children to give the babies a bath (wash dolls).

Fine Motor

Baking Bread
Provide playdough, mixing bowls and bread pans for bread making.

Writing

My Favorite Day
Challenge the children to dictate a story about their favorite day of the week.

Animal Day Life

Materials
none

Morning Circle
1. Talk about the fact that some animals are active during the day and some are active at night.
2. Let the children brainstorm a list of animals that are active during the day (birds, dogs, cows, horses, ants, humans, deer, etc.).
3. When appropriate, talk about how the habits and livelihood of many animals depend on the daylight (e.g., hawks finding food, deer finding food, bees finding flowers to pollinate, etc.).

Story Circle
Busy Beavers by Lydia Dabcovich

Music and Movement
"Ants" from *Let's Pretend* by Hap Palmer

Learning Centers

Blocks

Dam Building
Provide twigs for the "beavers" to build a dam. Invite them to build on water (blue bulletin board paper).

Discovery

Grazing
Provide dry grass for the children to cut with scissors, one blade at a time. How long would it take to cut enough for a cow?

Construction

Home Building
Provide clay and pictures of a dirt dauber's nest. Invite the children to build a nest.

Listening

Daytime Is Fo r
Record the children's stories about what animals do in the daytime. Encourage the children to listen to the stories.

Cooking and Snack

Looking for Worms
Invite the children to crumble chocolate cookies (dirt) over gummy worms for snack.

Sand and Water Table

Food Gathering
Hide nuts and acorns in the sand table for the children to find.

Shadows All Around

Day 8

Materials
tracing of your shadow, overhead projector

Morning Circle
1. Show the children your shadow. Tell them how you made it. Ask, "Would you know it was my shadow if I hadn't told you?" If they answer yes, ask them to tell how.
2. Turn on the overhead projector. Let the children take turns standing in front of the light and making shadows.

Story Circle
Me and My Shadow by Arthur Dorros

Music and Movement
Invite the children to Shadow Dance between a sheet and a light source. Add streamers to make it even more fun.

Learning Centers

Art

Shadow Painting
Provide black paint for the children to paint shadows.

Fine Motor

Shadow Designs
Have the children cut a design from construction paper. Tape the design to the window and watch for shadows to come. Can the children find their design on the floor?

Discovery

Shadow Changes
Place an object in a window so that it casts a shadow from the sun. Encourage the children to watch the shadow change. Does it get shorter? Taller? Longer?

Language

Shadow Drama
Provide a light source behind a hanging sheet and invite the children to stage a shadow drama.

Dramatic Play

Shadow Puppets
Provide a light source and teach the children to make hand-shadow figures on the wall.

Science

Hand Print Shadows
Provide a light source. Invite the children to trace the shadow of their hand with white chalk on dark paper.

More Shadows

Materials
large sheet of paper, old sheet or window shade with a design cut out of it

Morning Circle
1. Place your design over the window. Discuss shadows again. Call attention to the sunlight that comes through the holes in your window covering.
2. Ask, "What makes the shadow?"
3. Talk about shadows. Ask, "Is shade created by shadows? Is it cooler in the shade? Why?"
4. Go on a shadow hunt. Can you find shadows that make patterns?

Story Circle
Shadow Magic by Seymour Simon

Music and Movement
Play Shadow Tag outside. IT tries to tag someone's shadow. Play while clouds are overhead, if possible.

Learning Centers

Construction

My Shadow
Encourage the children to trace their bodies on bulletin board paper and then color them black with crayons or paints to make shadows.

Games

Shadow Concentration
Make simple drawings of four familiar objects on index cards. Draw the objects' shadows on four more index cards. Invite the children to play concentration, matching each object to its shadow.

Dramatic Play

Shadow Puppets
Make shadow puppets (black paper cutouts glued onto tongue depressors) for a familiar song like "Itsy Bitsy Spider." Invite the children to put on a show.

Math

Shadow Order
Cut several sizes of gingerbread people from black construction paper. Invite the children to place them in order from smallest to largest.

Fine Motor

Reverse Shadows
Invite the children to cut a design from black paper and then glue the black paper to white paper.

Outdoors

Sidewalk Shadows
Invite the children to trace each other's shadows on the sidewalk with chalk.

Sun's Heat and Light

Materials
sunglasses, sun hat

Morning Circle
1. Sit around the circle in sunglasses and hat.
2. Discuss what the children know about the sun as a source of light and heat. Ask, "What happens when you leave your crayons in the sun? What happens when we get hot?"
3. Explain that people often dress to protect themselves from the direct heat and light of the sun (e.g., they wear sunglasses, hats, sunscreen, etc.).

Story Circle
Sun Song by Jean Marzollo

Music and Movement
Play Mr. Sun Says like Simon Says.

Learning Centers

Art

Melted Crayon Art
Invite the children to draw with crayons on paper that's on a warming tray. Is this what happens if you leave your crayons in the sun?

Art

Sun Art
Put out an assortment of scraps of paper. Encourage the children to place the scraps on dark pieces of construction paper. Put them in the sun. What happens when you remove the scraps later in the day?

Construction

Make a Sun Visor
Invite the children to cut the center out of a paper plate and then cut the center in half. Glue one half to the rim to make a sun visor.

Discovery

Sunglasses
Provide a template for a pair of glasses that the children can trace. Cut out the glasses and cover with colored cellophane. Encourage the children to try different colors. Which is best at keeping out the light?

Dramatic Play

Dress for Heat
Provide summer clothes for paper dolls and for people. Invite the children to dress for summer heat.

Science

Heat and Ice
Invite the children to place one ice cube in the sun and one in the shade. Which melts faster?

Additional Books for Good Morning, Sunshine

Alexander and the Terrible, Horrible, No Good, Very Bad Day by Judith Viorst

Bear Shadow by Frank Asch

Clare and Her Shadow by William Michaels

Dawn by Uri Shulevitz

The Day the Sun Danced by Edith T. Hurd

Early Morning in the Barn by Nancy Tafuri

Footprints and Shadows by Anne Wescott Dodd

I Can Hear the Sun: A Modern Myth by Patricia Polacco

Night Becomes Day by Richard McGuire

Pancakes for Breakfast by Tomie DePaola

Rise and Shine, Mariko-Chan by Chiyoko Tomioka

Shadowville by Michael Bartalos

Shine, Sun! by Carol Greene

The Sun's Day by Mordicai Gerstein

Sun Up, Sun Down by Gail Gibbons

Sunshine by Jan Ormerod

Under the Sun by Ellen Kandoian

What Is the Sun? by Reeve Lindburgh

What Makes a Shadow by Robert Clyde Bulla

What Makes Day and Night by Franklyn Branley

Who Gets the Sun Out of Bed? by Nancy Carlstrom

Why the Sun and Moon Live in the Sky by Elphinstone Dayrell

Good Night, Sleep Tight

Nighttime is a special time in a child's day. With its emphasis on the moon, the stars, dreams and stories, this unit focuses on the fun side of going to sleep.

Unit at a Glance

Day	Focus	Centers	Story Circle	Music/Movement
1	Ms Moon	Night Pictures Goodnight, Baby Moon Stencils Moon Puzzles Night Skies Bedtime Stories	Goodnight Owl	Nocturne
2	Moon Activities	Moon Pictures Constellation Tube Rockets to the Moon Moon Race Moon Skies Moon Views	Hildilid's Night	Grandma's Sleeping in My Bed Tonight
3	Stars Above	Starry Night Paintings Star Mobile Rolling Stars Playdough Stars Star Transfer Star Patterns	Stars in the Sky	Starlight
4	It's Nighttime	Toothbrush Art Build a Bed Dress the Baby for Bed Sleep Out Tooth Fairy Pillow Sticker Stars	Goodnight Moon	Last Night
5	Nighttime Activities	Hot Chocolate Dinner Time Television Favorite Nighttime Activity Lullabies Star Gazing	Moonlight	All Through the Night

Day	Focus	Centers	Story Circle	Music/Movement
6	Dreams	Dream Pictures Dream Catchers My Best Dream Dream Books Daydreams Dream Music	Where the Wild Things Are	Wild Things Dance
7	Animal Life at Night	Bat Drawings Owl Vision Night Shift Night Animal Concentration Lily Pad Jump Pictures of Night Animals	Creatures of the Night	Musical Lily Pads
8	Bedtime Stories	Goodnight, Baby Bedside Stories My Own Story Bedtime Stories A Listening Story Sleepy Eyes	Tell Me a Story, Mama	Roll Over
9	Totally Black	Black Art Everything in Black Light and Dark Black Clothes Black Playdough Dark, Darker, Darkest	Night in the Country	Streamer Dance
10	Special Nights	Stormy Night Halloween Mask Slumber Party Wrapping Presents Ring That Treat Celebration Music	Storm in the Night	Skater's Waltz

Ms Moon

Day 1

Materials
chart paper with Nighttime written at the top, marker, night clothes

Morning Circle
1. Sit in the circle in your night clothes and robe or with a pillow and blanket.
2. Ask the children to guess what unit they are beginning.
3. When the children say "nighttime," ask them to create a word web of all the things the word makes them think of.

Story Circle
Goodnight Owl by Pat Hutchins

Music and Movement
"Nocturne" from *We All Live Together Volume III* by Steve and Greg

Learning Centers

Art

Night Pictures
Invite the children to paint a night-time picture.

Language

Moon Puzzles
Cut several moons (full, half, quarter, etc.) from poster board. Cut each one into three or four pieces for the children to put together.

Dramatic Play

Goodnight, Baby
Provide props for the children to bathe babies and tuck them in.

Language

Night Skies
Provide moon and star felt cutouts for the children to arrange on the flannel board.

Fine Motor

Moon Stencils
Provide stencils of the moon at various stages (full, half, quarter, etc.) for the children to make moon pictures.

Library

Bedtime Stories
Fill the center with bedtime stories.

Moon Activities

Day 2

Materials
Moon Bear by Frank Asch

Morning Circle
1. Read the book to the children.
2. Discuss the shape of the moon and how it seems to change. Ask, "Has anyone seen a harvest moon? Who thinks they see a face in the moon?"

Story Circle
Hildilid's Night by Cheli Duran Ryan

Music and Movement
"Grandma's Sleeping in My Bed Tonight" from *Late Last Night* by Joe Scruggs

Learning Centers

Art

Moon Pictures
Provide circles cut from easel paper and white, gray, pale blue and yellow paints. Encourage the children to paint moons.

Gross Motor

Moon Race
Provide various size moons (balls). Invite the children to roll the moons around the room and follow them as they roll.

Construction

Constellation Tube
Give the children empty toilet paper tubes and black drawing paper. Encourage the children to wrap the paper over one end of the tube and secure it with a rubber band. Poke pin holes in the paper, then look through the other end.

Math

Moon Skies
Provide full-moon, half-moon and two quarter-moon (one facing each way) cutouts. Invite the children to arrange the cutouts in sequence.

Dramatic Play

Rockets to the Moon
Provide props for space play (paper sack helmets, boxes for building rockets, hoses, oatmeal boxes for air tanks and backpacks).

Science

Moon Views
Provide pictures of the moon in different stages for the children to look at.

Stars Above

Materials

"Twinkle, Twinkle, Little Star" (see the appendix, page 400), print of van Gogh's painting *Starry Night* or another nice picture of nighttime stars

Morning Circle

1. Sing "Twinkle, Twinkle, Little Star."
2. Show the print or the pictures.
3. Talk about stars. Why do we see more some nights? Are stars really star-shaped? Are stars near or far away?

Story Circle

Stars in the Sky by Allan Fowler

Music and Movement

"Starlight" from *One Elephant, Deux Elephants* by Sharon, Lois and Bram

Learning Centers

Art

Starry Night Paintings
Provide blue or black paper and white paint for the children to create a starry night.

Fine Motor

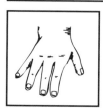

Playdough Stars
Invite the children to cut stars from playdough using star-shaped cookie cutters.

Construction

Star Mobile
Provide a hanger, monofilament and cutout stars of various sizes. Help the children create a mobile.

Fine Motor

Star Transfer
Encourage the children to use tweezers to move stars (rhinestones) from one sky (sheet of blue paper) to another. Supervise closely. [Use caution.]

Discovery

Rolling Stars
Provide cardboard cutouts of circles and stars. Encourage the children to try rolling both. Which rolls?

Math

Star Patterns
Cut out star-shaped sponges and provide two or three colors of tempera paint for the children to create star print patterns.

It's Nighttime

Day 4

Materials
none

Morning Circle
1. Talk about nighttime routines.
2. Tell the children what you do before you go to bed, then ask them to tell what they do.
3. Sing "Are You Sleeping?" (see the appendix, page 392).

Story Circle
Goodnight Moon by Margaret Wise Brown

Music and Movement
"Last Night" from *Late Last Night* by Joe Scruggs

Learning Centers

Art

Toothbrush Art
Provide toothbrushes, strainers and tempera paint for splatter paintings.

Blocks

Build a Bed
Provide small blankets and pillows and invite the children to build beds to fit them.

Dramatic Play

Dress the Baby for Bed
Provide night clothes for dressing paper dolls for bed.

Dramatic Play

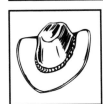

Sleep Out
Provide sleeping bags, pillows and flashlight for a pretend sleep out.

Fine Motor

Tooth Fairy Pillow
Provide 6" (15 cm) squares of fabric, needles, thread and cotton balls for stuffing. Invite the children to make pillows to put lost teeth under.

Math

Sticker Stars
Provide stick-on stars for the children to create star patterns.

Nighttime Activities

Day 5

Materials
chart paper and marker

Morning Circle
1. Lead the children in a discussion about nighttime activities.
2. Create a list of all nighttime activities the children mention.
3. Ask them what routine they would use if they were in charge of putting their parents to bed.

Story Circle
Moonlight by Jan Ormerod

Music and Movement
"All Through the Night" from *Peter, Paul, and Mommy* by Peter, Paul, and Mary

Learning Centers

Cooking and Snack

Hot Chocolate
Invite the children to make a bed-time cup of hot chocolate.

Language

Favorite Nighttime Activity
Encourage the children to draw a picture of their favorite nighttime activity and dictate a sentence that tells about it.

Dramatic Play

Dinner Time
Provide props for the children to make, serve and eat dinner.

Listening

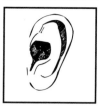

Lullabies
Place recordings of lullabies in the center for the children to listen to.

Dramatic Play

Television
Cut a television-screen shape from a big box. Let the children put on a puppet television show.

Science

Star Gazing
Place fluorescent stars inside the top of a large box. Put a black light inside and invite the children to star gaze.

Dreams

Materials
none

Morning Circle
1. Tell the children about a pleasant dream you had.
2. Invite the children to tell about their dreams.
3. Talk about the real and unreal aspects of dreams.
4. Ask, "Do you know what daydreams are?"

Story Circle
Where the Wild Things Are by Maurice Sendak

Music and Movement
Invite the children to create a dance from *Where the Wild Things Are.*

Learning Centers

Art

Dream Pictures
Invite the children to paint pictures of their dreams.

Library

Dream Books
Fill the center with books about dreams (*Where the Wild Things Are, Dream Catcher, Dreams, In the Night Kitchen, Harold and the Purple Crayon,* etc.).

Construction

Dream Catchers
Cut the inner circle from paper plates. Encourage the children to punch holes around the inside edge of the plate and thread yarn through and across the hole to create dream catchers.

Listening

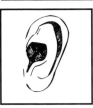

Daydreams
Provide music for daydreaming.

Language

My Best Dream
Encourage the children to dictate the end of this sentence: The best dream I ever had was. . . . Ask them to illustrate their dreams.

Music

Dream Music
Encourage the children to create dream music with rhythm instruments.

Animal Life at Night

Materials
"Hear the Lively Song" (see the appendix, page 394), photographs of night creatures and night workers, chart paper and marker

Morning Circle
1. Teach the children "Hear the Lively Song."
2. Show the photographs.
3. Let the children share stories about raccoons, opossums, bats, cats and other animals they might have seen at night. What about insects? Locusts sing at night, and so do others. Frogs croak at night.
4. Ask, "Does anyone have a relative who works at night?"
5. Make a list of night jobs.

Story Circle
Creatures of the Night by Judith E. Rinard

Music and Movement
Invite the children to play Musical Lily Pads like Musical Chairs. Cut lily pads from green construction paper.

Learning Centers

Art

Bat Drawings
Invite the children to draw a picture upside down. Does it look like they thought it would when they turn it right-side up?

Games

Night Animal Concentration
Invite the children to play Nocturnal Animal Concentration (use copies of appendix page 415 to make a set of cards).

Discovery

Owl Vision
Provide binoculars for the children to look through. Explain that this is the kind of vision owls have. It's how they spot food in the distance.

Gross Motor

Lily Pad Jump
Place paper lily pads 2' (60 cm) apart. Secure with tape. Challenge the children to jump from one to another. Gradually increase the distance.

Dramatic Play

Night Shift
Provide props for the children to play hospital (they stay open all night).

Science

Pictures of Night Animals
Provide pictures of nocturnal animals for the children to look at.

Bedtime Stories

Materials
chart paper and marker

Morning Circle
1. Ask the children to lie down. Tell them a bedtime story.
2. Ask the children to name their favorite bedtime story. Create a graph to show their choices.

Story Circle
Tell Me a Story, Mama by Angela Johnson

Music and Movement
"Roll Over" from *Where Is Thumbkin?* by The Learning Station. Encourage the children to act out the song, using bulletin board paper or a mat as the bed.

Learning Centers

Cooking and Snack

Goodnight, Baby
Invite the children to use a cookie cutter to cut a gingerbread baby from a slice of cheese. Lay the cheese on a slice of bread, cover with a half-slice (covers). Toast and eat for snack. Supervise closely. [Use caution.]

Dramatic Play

Bedside Stories
Invite the children to put babies to bed with a bedtime story.

Language

My Own Story
Challenge the children to make up a bedtime story. Write it down for them.

Library

Bedtime Stories
Fill the center with bedtime stories again.

Listening

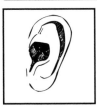

A Listening Story
Record a bedtime story for the children to listen to.

Math

Sleepy Eyes
Invite the children to toss a handful of wiggly eyes into a shallow box, then match open eyes (those right side up) to sleepy eyes (those upside down) using one-to-one correspondence.

Some children may want to count the eyes using tally marks to record their findings.

Totally Black

Materials
none

Morning Circle

1. Explain that on some nights, when there are clouds in the sky, you can't see the moon and stars.
2. Ask, "What is the darkest place or time you remember?" Encourage them to share their experiences. Ask, "Who has been on a carnival ride that was dark? Who has been in the country where there are no city lights? Who has been camping where it was very dark?"

Story Circle

Night in the Country by Cynthia Rylant

Music and Movement

Invite the children to dance with black streamers in a darkened room while listening to lullabies.

Learning Centers

Art

Black Art
Invite the children to paint with black paint while wearing dark sunglasses.

Dramatic Play

Black Clothes
Provide dark or black clothes and accessories for dress-up play.

Construction

Everything in Black
Provide black materials (film canisters, pipe cleaners, wall paper and fabric scraps, crayons, tissue paper, etc.) for the children to create a black collage.

Fine Motor

Black Playdough
Invite the children to work with black playdough. What will they make?

Discovery

Light and Dark
Put a flashlight inside a box. Cover it with screen and black paper. Encourage the children to use toothpicks to poke holes to make pictures and designs. How is this different from drawing dots on paper?

Math

Darker, Darker, Darkest
Put out crayons, paper or pieces of material in various shades of brown, tan, black, gray, etc. Encourage the children to order them from dark to darkest.

Special Nights

Materials
chart paper and marker

Morning Circle
1. Have familiar holiday songs playing as the children come to the circle.
2. Discuss special nights. Help the children make a list of special nights (e.g., Halloween, Christmas Eve, Hanukkah, nights before special days, slumber parties, etc.).
3. Talk about nighttime events like skating, going to the movies, dancing and so on.

Story Circle
Storm in the Night by Mary Stolz

Music and Movement
Invite the children to remove their shoes and pretend to skate as they listen to "Skater's Waltz."

Learning Centers

Art

Stormy Night
Invite the children to use black and gray finger paints to create a stormy picture.

Fine Motor

Wrapping Presents
Provide wrapping paper, scissors, tape, bows and ribbons. Invite the children to wrap presents.

Construction

Halloween Mask
Provide paper plates, paper sacks, yarn, markers, scissors and other art materials for the children to create Halloween masks.

Games

Ring That Treat
Scatter wrapped candies on the floor. Invite the children to toss plastic rings around the candies. They can eat the ones they ring.

Dramatic Play

Slumber Party
Fill the center with props for a slumber party.

Listening

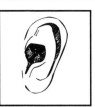

Celebration Music
Provide holiday music for the children to listen to.

Additional Books for Good Night, Sleep Tight

City Night by Eve Rice
The Dark at the Top of the Stairs by Sam McBratney
Dark Day, Light Night by Jan Carr
Fireflies for Nathan by Shulamith L. Oppenheim
Frog Is Frightened by Max Velthuijs
The Ghost-Eye Tree by Bill Martin, Jr.
Grandfather Twilight by Barbara Berger
If You Were My Bunny by Kate McMullen
In the Night Kitchen by Maurice Sendak
Ira Sleeps Over by Bernard Waber
K Is for a Kiss Goodnight by Jill Sardegna
Kate's Giants by Valiska Gregory
Moondance by Frank Asch
The Napping House by Audrey Wood
Night Noises by Mem Fox
Owl Moon by Jane Yolen
The Polar Express by Chris Van Allsburg
Raccoons and Ripe Corn by Jim Arnosky
Roll Over by Mordicai Gerstein
There's a Nightmare in My Closet by Mercer Mayer
There's an Alligator Under My Bed by Mercer Mayer
Wait Till the Moon Is Full by Margaret Wise Brown
What Is the Sun? by Reeve Lindbergh
What the Sun Sees, What the Moon Sees by Nancy Tafuri
You Be Good and I'll Be Night: Jump-on-the-Bed Poems by Eve Merriam

Tell Me a Story

We never get tired of hearing a story. This unit focuses daily activities around some of our favorite stories the ones we want to hear again and again.

Unit at a Glance

Day	Focus	Centers	Story Circle	Music/Movement
1	A Dozen Ways to Tell a Story	Story Pictures Puppets Flannel Board Story Story Songs Hula Shadow Stories	Favorite Story	Hula
2	Brown Bear, Brown Bear	Purple Cat Tracing Templates Flannel Books Brown Bear Tape Color Patterns Color Words	Color Dance	Cellophane Shadows
3	The Emperor's New Clothes	Crown Making Emperor's Court Emperor's Horses Tailor Emperor's Treasury Fanfare Music	The Emperor's New Clothes	Emperor's Processional
4	Paul Bunyan	Babe the Blue Ox Sawing Logs Lumberjack Breakfast Hot Cakes Tree Trunks Floating Logs	Paul Bunyon	Log Roll
5	Johnny Appleseed	Applesauce Johnny's Path Appleseed Pick-Up Apple Toss Johnny Appleseed Revisited Apple/Worm Match	Johnny Appleseed	Apple Toss

Day	Focus	Centers	Story Circle	Music/Movement
6	**The Princess and the Pea**	Green All Around A Crown for the Princess Green Peas Pea Under the Pillow Pea Pick-Up Pea Hunt	The Paper Bag Princess	Mashed Peas Dance
7	**Rumpelstiltskin**	Gold Collage Castle Tower Royal Wedding Golden Mats Coin Hunt I Can Write My Name	Rumpelstiltskin	The Name Game
8	**Chicka Chicka Boom Boom**	Palm Leaf Art Letter Pretzels Bright Colors Collage Letter Match Coconuts Up Close Tracing Letters	Alphabatics	Alphabet Boogie
9	**The Little Engine That Could**	Smoky Designs Train Building Train Station Up the Hill and Down the Hill I Think I Can Train Tracks	The Itsy Bitsy Spider	I've Been Working on the Railroad
10	**The Sneetches**	Starry, Starry Night Star Belly Machine Star Cutters Alike and Different Beaches Star Stencils	The Butter Battle Book	Drop the Star

A Dozen Ways to Tell a Story   Day 1

Materials
chart paper and marker

Morning Circle
Invite the children to brainstorm a list of ways to tell a story (e.g., books, puppets, role-play, songs, dances, videos, pictures, flannel boards, etc.).

Story Circle
Read or tell one of the children's favorite stories.

Music and Movement
Play Hawaiian music and invite the children to make up a hula dance to tell a story.

Learning Centers

Art

Story Pictures
Provide a chalkboard and colored chalk for the children to draw story pictures.

Listening
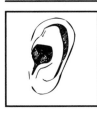
Story Songs
Provide a recording of a storytelling song like "Froggie Went a-Courtin'" or "The Itsy Bitsy Spider" for the children to listen to.

Dramatic Play

Puppets
Provide puppets and a stage for the children to put on a puppet show.

Music

Hula
Provide Hawaiian music, grass skirts (see the appendix, page 430), and leis. Encourage the children to practice their hula dance.

Language

Flannel Board Story
Provide felt characters for the children to use as they tell a favorite story.

Science

Shadow Stories
Provide a light source and props (e.g., feathers, hats, etc.) for the children to perform a shadow story.

Brown Bear, Brown Bear   Day 2

Materials
Brown Bear, Brown Bear by Bill Martin Jr., pictures or cutouts of animals in the story

Morning Circle
1. Use cutouts or pictures to help you tell the story.
2. Repeat the story, inviting the children to recite as much as they can with you.

Story Circle
Color Dance by Ann Jonas

Music and Movement
Invite the children to create colored shadows with cellophane strips outdoors.

Learning Centers

Art

Purple Cat
Invite the children to paint a picture of a purple cat or other favorite animal in the story.

Listening
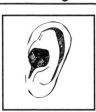
Brown Bear Tape
Provide a recording of *Brown Bear, Brown Bear* for the children to listen to as they look at the book.

Fine Motor

Tracing Templates
Provide animal-shaped templates for the children to trace around.

Math

Color Patterns
Provide crayons for the children to use in creating color patterns.

Language

Flannel Books
Stitch together several 8" X 10" (20 cm x 25 cm) pieces of felt to make a book. Sew a pocket on the top piece for the felt cutouts of the animals in *Brown Bear, Brown Bear*. Encourage the children to use the book and cutouts to retell the story.

Writing

Color Words
Write color words on index cards. Challenge the children to trace each word on acetate with colored markers.

The Emperor's New Clothes

Materials
a version of *The Emperor's New Clothes*

Morning Circle
1. Read the story.
2. Talk about the story. Why did everyone pretend to see the cloth?
3. Invite the children to act out the story.

Story Circle
The Principal's New Clothes by Stephanie Calmenson

Music and Movement
Lead the children in the Emperor's Processional. Encourage the children to march all around the town (classroom).

Learning Centers

Construction

Crown Making
Provide crowns cut from poster board. Encourage the children to decorate them with glitter and glue.

Fine Motor

Tailor
Provide burlap, yarn and large plastic needles, or 2" (5 cm) pipe cleaners wrapped around end of yarn, for the children to sew the emperor a new outfit.

Dramatic Play

Emperor's Court
Provide props for the royal palace (crown, throne, robes, jester clothes, gold scepter, etc.).

Math

Emperor's Treasury
Encourage the children to count the correct number of coins into treasure boxes numbered one through five.

Fine Motor

Emperor's Horses
Cut the torso and head of a horse from construction paper (see the pattern in the appendix, page 435). Provide clothespins for legs. Invite the children to stand their horses in a line.

Music

Fanfare Music
Provide "Pomp and Circumstance" style music for the children to listen to.

Paul Bunyan

Materials

Paul Bunyan by Steven Kellogg

Morning Circle

1. Read the book.
2. Talk about the exaggerations in the book. Are the things in this book real or make-believe?

Story Circle

Read another version of Paul Bunyan with different illustrations.

Music and Movement

Invite the children to lie on the floor and roll like logs. Encourage them to roll to a specified place.

Learning Centers

Art

Babe the Blue Ox

Provide blue chalk and buttermilk for the children to paint Paul's friend.

Construction

Sawing Logs

Provide a few logs for the children to saw. Supervise closely. [Use caution.]

Dramatic Play

Lumberjack Breakfast

Provide props for the children to prepare breakfast for Paul Bunyan (felt pancakes, egg cartons, large milk jug, etc.).

Games

Hot Cakes

Provide a skillet, spatula and several pancakes (cut from vinyl or carpet scraps). Encourage the children to divide into pairs. One of each pair flips the hot cakes with the spatula, the other tries to catch them in the skillet.

Gross Motor

Tree Trunk

Make the balance beam look like a log. Invite the children to practice walking it.

Sand and Water Table

Floating Logs

Invite the children to float play logs such as Lincoln logs on the water. Is there an easy way to move the logs?

Johnny Appleseed
Day 5

Materials
pot with a handle, sack, apple seeds, apples, shovel

Morning Circle
1. Use the props to tell the story.
2. Encourage the children to decide which parts of the story could be true.
3. Sing "Johnny Appleseed" (see the appendix, page 395).

Story Circle
Read a story about Johnny Appleseed.

Music and Movement
Provide wads of red construction paper (apples) and a towel for each pair of children. One child throws the apples and the other catches them in the towel.

Learning Centers

Cooking and Snack

Applesauce
Invite the children to make apple-sauce (follow the recipe in the appendix, page 389).

Gross Motor

Apple Toss
Provide wads of red construction paper (apples) for the children to toss into a basket.

Discovery

Johnny's Path
Encourage the children to put bare feet in red tempera paint, then walk across butcher paper on the floor. Have a pan of soapy water and tow-els at the end for cleaning feet. After the footprints are dry, challenge the children to identify theirs.

Language

"My picture is about..."

Johnny Appleseed Revisited
Provide props for the children to act out the story.

Fine Motor

Apple Seed Pick-Up
Encourage the children to use tweez-ers to move apple seeds from one field (brown construction paper) to another.

Math

Apple/Worm Match
Make a set of five paper apples. Punch one to five holes in each. Invite the children to stick a worm (Styrofoam peanut) in each hole.

The Princess and the Pea   Day 6

Materials
a copy of the story "The Princess and the Pea"

Morning Circle
1. Read the story.
2. Put a dried pea under a pillow. Invite the children to try it out. Can anyone feel the pea? Try a block. Can anyone feel that?

Story Circle
Read *The Paper Bag Princess* by Robert Munsch and compare this story to the other.

Music and Movement
Invite the children to do the Mashed Peas Dance like the Mashed Potato. Play "Mashed Potato" from *All Time Favorite Dances* from Melody House.

Learning Centers

Art

Green All Around
Provide green materials (paper, paint, markers, crayons, etc.) for the children to make green pea pictures.

Dramatic Play

Pea Under the Pillow
Provide pillows and peas for the children to experiment with. Who can feel the pea? Provide other objects for the children to try.

Construction

A Crown for the Princess
Invite the children to decorate poster board crowns with sequins, ribbon, rickrack and glitter.

Fine Motor

Pea Pick-Up
Encourage the children to pick up dried peas with tweezers. When done, rinse thoroughly, then make pea soup with the dried peas.

Cooking and Snack

Green Peas
Cook frozen peas. Supervise closely. Serve for snack with butter and salt. [Use caution.]

Games

Pea Hunt
Invite the children to take turns hiding peas and hunting for them.

Rumpelstiltskin

Day 7

Materials
Rumpelstiltskin by Paul O. Zelinsky

Morning Circle
1. If possible, invite a spinner to demonstrate how a spinning wheel works.
2. Read the story. (Let your guest read it, if possible.)
3. Talk about what could be real and what could be make-believe. Could someone spin straw into gold?

Story Circle
Rumpelstiltskin by Paul Galdone

Music and Movement
Teach the children to sing "The Name Game."

Learning Centers

Art

Gold Collage
Provide gold fabric, rickrack, yarn, glitter, sequins and so on. Invite the children to create a collage.

Fine Motor

Golden Mats
Provide a weaving board and gold rickrack, ribbon and yarn for the children to weave.

Blocks

Castle Tower
Encourage the children to build a castle with blocks, canisters and boxes.

Sand and Water Table

Coin Hunt
Spray paint straw gold and place it in the table. Hide shiny pennies in the straw for the children to find. Supervise closely. [Use caution.]

Dramatic Play

Royal Wedding
Provide props for a royal wedding (crowns, robes, scepters, etc.).

Writing

I Can Write My Name
Write the children's names on index cards for tracing. Include Rumpelstiltskin's name.

Chicka Chicka Boom Boom   Day 8

Materials
Chicka Chicka Boom Boom by Bill Martin Jr., letters drawn on index cards (punch a hole in each one and put it on a yarn necklace)

Morning Circle
1. Invite the children to wear the letter cards and act out the story.
2. Ask, "How are the mama and papa letters different from the other letters?"

Story Circle
Alphabatics by Suse MacDonald

Music and Movement
"Alphabet Boogie" from *I Am Special* by Thomas Moore

Learning Centers

Art

Palm Leaf Art
Provide butcher paper and paints. Invite the children to paint with actual palm fronds or paper cut in the shape of palm fronds.

Games

Letter Match
Write upper and lowercase letters on pieces of paper. Write each pair of upper and lower case letters in the same color. Invite the children to match the pairs.

Cooking and Snack

Letter Pretzels
Invite the children to make letter pretzels (see the recipe in the appendix, page 390).

Science

Coconuts Up Close
Provide a coconut for the children to examine. Encourage them to weigh it on the balance scale.

Fine Motor

Bright Colors Collage
Provide construction paper in bright colors, scissors, hole punch and glue. Encourage the children to make collages.

Writing

Tracing Letters
Provide letters for the children to trace or sandpaper letters for the children to make crayon rubbings.

The Little Engine That Could   Day 9

Materials
The Little Engine That Could by Watty Piper

Morning Circle
1. Read the story. Invite the children to join in on the repetitive lines.
2. Encourage the children to think of another character with the same kind of persistence. What about the Itsty Bitsy Spider?

Story Circle
Read a favorite version of "The Itsy Bitsy Spider."

Music and Movement
"I've Been Working on the Railroad" from *More Singable Songs* by Raffi

Learning Centers

Art

Smoky Designs
Provide black and gray paints for the children to create smokestack designs.

Blocks

Train Building
Fill the center with shoe boxes for train building. Add plastic animals for car loading.

Dramatic Play

Train Station
Provide props for the children to set up a train station (tickets, luggage, hats, etc.).

Fine Motor

Up the Hill and Down the Hill
Draw a couple of hills on a piece of poster board. Cut out a small train engine and glue a magnet to the back. Encourage the children to hold a second magnet on the back side of the poster board to move the train over the hills.

Language

"My picture is about..."

I Think I Can
Challenge the children to dictate a sentence about something difficult they accomplished. Put the papers together in a resealable plastic bag book. (Staple the non-zip closure side.)

Math

Train Tracks
Provide popsicle sticks (spray-painted black) for the children to make train tracks. Can they see a pattern?

The Sneetches

Day 10

Materials
The Sneetches and Other Stories by Dr. Seuss, star stickers

Morning Circle
1. As the children enter the room, place a star sticker on each child's hand.
2. Read the story.

Story Circle
The Butter Battle Book by Dr. Seuss

Music and Movement
Invite the children to play Drop the Star (cut from poster board) like Drop the Handkerchief (see the directions in the appendix, page 402).

Learning Centers

Art

Starry, Starry Night
Invite the children to paint stars with fluorescent paint. Provide a black light and watch the stars shine.

Language

"My picture is about..."
Alike and Different
Draw lines on index cards to divide them in half. Draw shapes, letters and simple designs on each half (draw the same thing on some cards, different things on others). Invite the children to sort the cards.

Construction

Star Belly Machine
Provide wire, sticks, paper, glue, clay and other materials for the children to build a star belly machine.

Sand and Water Table

Beaches
Encourage the children to create a beach.

Fine Motor
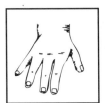
Star Cutters
Invite the children to cut star shapes from playdough.

Writing

Star Stencils
Provide star-shaped stencils for the children to trace.

Additional Books for Tell Me a Story

Abiyoyo by Pete Seeger

Alexander and the Terrible, Horrible, No Good, Very Bad Day by Judith Viorst

Annie and the Wild Animals by Jan Brett

Are You My Mother? by P.D. Eastman

The Bear's Toothache by David McPhail

Best Friends by Miriam Cohen

The Carrot Seed by Ruth Krauss

A Chair for My Mother by Vera B. Williams

Chicken Soup with Rice by Maurice Sendak

The Doorbell Rang by Pat Hutchins

Frederick by Leo Lionni

Friends by Helme Heine

The Happy Day by Ruth Krauss

Little Blue and Little Yellow by Leo Lionni

Mike Mulligan and His Steam Shovel by Virginia Lee Burton

The Mitten by Alvin Tresselt

Sam Who Never Forgets by Eve Rice

Swimmy by Leo Lionni

Tell Me a Story, Mama by Angela Johnson

The Three Bears by Paul Galdone

The Three Billy Goats Gruff by Ellen Appleby

The Three Little Pigs by Paul Galdone

Thunderstorm by Mary Szilagyi

A Tree Is Nice by Janice Udry

The Turnip by Janina Domanska

Fun and Fantasy

The world of make-believe is a wonderful place for children. This unit is filled with fantasy and also offers lots of opportunities to distinguish between what is real and what is unreal.

Unit at a Glance

Day	Focus	Centers	Story Circle	Music/Movement
1	Let's Pretend	Pretend Pretend Architects Pretend Grocery Pretend Grown-Ups Puppet Show Pretend Pets	Pretend You're a Cat	Let's Pretend
2	Fairy Tales	Jack's Beanstalk Three Pig's Houses Porridge Riding Hood's Basket Fairy Tales Fairy Tales	The Three Little Pigs	Three Bear's Rap
3	Toy Time	My Favorite Toy Moving Toys Toy Room Toy Collage Tiddly Winks Puzzles	Corduroy	Wind-Up Toys
4	What If?	Only Red Only Paper Only Broccoli Only Toes Blank Puzzles Finger Print	Imogene's Antlers	Go Backward
5	Magicians	Magic Paint Magic Wand Held by a Thread Magicians at Work Water Trick Making It Appear	Abiyoyo	Abiyoyo

Day	Focus	Centers	Story Circle	Music/Movement
6	Real and Make-Believe	Fantasy Art Make-Believe Real and Make-Believe Sort Tall Tales Fiction and Nonfiction Mud Pies	A Fish Out of Water	True, Not True
7	Dragons	Fire-Spitting Dragon Box Dragon Create a Dragon Dragon Fire Salad Pin the Tail on the Dragon Dragon Stories	The Judge: An Untrue Tale	Puff the Magic Dragon
8	Monsters	Monster Art Shadow Monsters Monster Stencils Eye Toss Giant Monster Puzzle My Favorite Monster	There's a Monster Under My Bed	Monster Mash
9	Giants	Painting by Giants Small Town A Giant's View Guess Who's Coming to Dinner? Giant Concentration Giant Footprints	David's Father	Mother, May I?
10	What Can This Be?	Doodle Art My Creation Mystery Box Pipe Cleaners Guess What I Am Mystery Puzzles	Look, Look Again!	I Spy

Let's Pretend

Day 1

Materials
dress-up clothes or costume

Morning Circle
1. Be in costume or in exaggerated clothes when the children arrive.
2. Let the children guess what you are pretending to be.
3. Invite the children to discuss things they have pretended were real.
4. Ask, "What does it meant to pretend?"

Story Circle
Pretend You're a Cat by Jean Marzollo

Music and Movement
Let's Pretend by Hap Palmer

Learning Centers

Art

Pretend
Invite the children to pretend to be artists painting pictures.

Blocks

Pretend Architects
Invite the children to pretend to be architects designing and building a city.

Dramatic Play

Pretend Grocery
Set up props (cash register, play money, empty food containers, etc.) for the children to role-play running a grocery store.

Dramatic Play

Pretend Grown-Ups
Provide dress-up clothes for the children to pretend to be grown-ups.

Dramatic Play

Puppet Show
Encourage the children to put on a puppet show.

Fine Motor

Pretend Pets
Invite the children to sculpt pretend pets in clay or playdough.

Fairy Tales

Materials
none

Morning Circle
1. Talk about fairy tales like "Little Red Riding Hood," "The Three Little Pigs" and "Jack and the Beanstalk."
2. Discuss the make-believe elements of the stories.

Story Circle
"The Three Little Pigs" (any version)

Music and Movement
Three Bears Rap (see the appendix, page 400)

Learning Centers

Art

Jack's Beanstalk
Invite the children to paint a beanstalk for Jack.

Dramatic Play

Red Riding Hood's Basket
Provide props for the children to pack Red Riding Hood's basket.

Blocks

Three Pig's Houses
Invite the children to build houses for the three pigs.

Library

Fairy Tales
Fill the center with books of fairy tales.

Cooking and Snack

Porridge
Encourage the children to follow the directions for making cream of wheat found on the box and to eat it for snack.

Listening
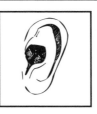
Fairy Tales
Provide recordings of favorite fairy tales for the children to listen to.

Toy Time

Day 3

Materials
an assortment of toys

Morning Circle
1. Show the toys.
2. Tell the children about your favorite toy when you were young. Do you still have a favorite toy?
3. Invite the children to tell about their favorite toys.

Story Circle
Corduroy by Don Freeman

Music and Movement
Invite the children to pretend to be wind-up toys.

Learning Centers

Art

My Favorite Toy
Encourage the children to draw pictures of their favorite toys.

Fine Motor

Toy Collage
Invite the children to cut pictures of toys from magazines, catalogs and coloring books. Encourage them to assemble a toy collage.

Discovery

Moving Toys
Provide several toys with moving parts for the children to examine. How do the toys work?

Games

Tiddly Winks
Provide a set of tiddly winks for the children to play with.

Dramatic Play

Toy Room
Provide a toy box and toys for the children to create a toy room.

Language

Puzzles
Provide several puzzles for the children to work.

What If?

Materials
none

Morning Circle
1. Pose "What if" questions. For example, "What if there were only one color? What if animals were smarter than people? What if the only food we had was broccoli?"

Story Circle
Imogene's Antlers by David Small

Music and Movement
Challenge the children to do things backward like walk, crawl, roll over, skip and jump.

Learning Centers

Art

Only Red
What if red were the only color? Provide red crayons, paints, pencils and chalks for the children to draw with.

Blocks

Only Paper
What if blocks were made of paper? Stuff grocery sacks 3/4 full with crumpled newspapers. Fold the tops down and staple or tape to make blocks. Invite the children to build with the paper bag blocks.

Cooking and Snack

Only Broccoli
What if the only food we had was broccoli? Invite the children to dip broccoli florets in Ranch dip and eat for snack.

Fine Motor

Only Toes
What if we had no hands? Invite the children to pick up beads and drop them in a basket using their toes.

Language

Blank Puzzles
What if puzzles had no pictures? Cut blank poster board into puzzle pieces for the children to put together. (Cut a few large pieces for beginners and smaller pieces for more advanced children.)

Writing

Finger Print
What if we wrote with our fingers? Provide fingerpaint and paper and encourage the children to make letters.

Magicians

Day 5

Materials
materials to perform a simple magic trick

Morning Circle
1. Perform a simple magic trick.
2. Find out what the children know about magic.

Story Circle
Abiyoyo by Pete Seeger

Music and Movement
"Abiyoyo" from *Miss Jackie and Her Friends* by Miss Jackie

Learning Centers

Art

Magic Paint
Invite the children to create paintings using chalk and buttermilk. What happens?

Dramatic Play

Magicians at Work
Provide props for the children to have a pretend magic show (wand, stuffed rabbit, hat, cape, etc.).

Construction

Magic Wand
Invite the children to decorate the cardboard tubes from pants hangers with sequins, glitter and paint to make magic wands. Supervise closely. [Use caution.]

Science

Water Trick
Teach the children this trick. Fill a deep bowl with water. Turn a drinking glass upside down and put it in the water. Slowly pull the glass out until just the rim is under water. What happens?

Discovery

Held by a Thread
Have the children choose partners. One child lies down. The other child holds a 2' (60 cm) length of string over her with the end just under her nose. Ask the child on the floor to get up. What happens?

Writing

Make It Appear
Encourage the children to write with lemon juice on white paper. The teacher then holds the paper up to a heat source. The writing will magically appear. Supervise closely. [Use caution.]

Real and Make-Believe   Day 6

Materials
Abuela by Arthur Dorros

Morning Circle
1. Read the story.
2. Discuss real and make-believe situations in the book. Then talk about real and make-believe situations in everyday life.

Story Circle
A Fish Out of Water by Helen Palmer

Music and Movement
Invite the children to play True, Not True. IT stands and makes a statement. The other children decide if it's true or not true. IT sits down after an untrue statement is correctly named.

Learning Centers

Art

Fantasy Art
Provide paint and collage materials for the children to create a fantasy picture.

Language

Tall Tales
Give the children a one-sentence story starter. Challenge them to dictate or record the rest of the story. For example, "I met a giant on a motorcycle on my way to school this morning."

Dramatic Play

Make-Believe
Provide props for pretend play. Maybe a costume box!

Library

Fiction and Nonfiction
Fill the center with fiction and nonfiction books. Challenge the children to sort the books by looking at the illustrations.

Language

Real and Make-Believe Sort
Provide pictures of real and make-believe objects for the children to sort.

Sand and Water Table

Mud Pies
Provide small pans, spoons, forks and decorations like acorns leaves and pebbles. Encourage the children to make and decorate mud pies.

Dragons

Materials
recording of "Puff the Magic Dragon," pictures of dragons

Morning Circle
1. Ask, "Has anyone here seen a dragon?"
2. Discuss dragons in movies (*Pete's Dragon, Dragonheart,* etc.).
3. Explain that in China the dragon is a symbol of good luck and is used in many festivals and celebrations.

Story Circle
The Judge: An Untrue Tale by Margot and Harve Zemach

Music and Movement
"Puff the Magic Dragon" from *Peter, Paul and Mommy* by Peter, Paul and Mary

Learning Centers

Art

Fire-Spitting Dragon
Provide brown, yellow, orange and red paints for the children to paint fire-spitting dragons.

Cooking and Snack

Dragon Fire Salad
Encourage the children to grate carrots and mix them with a few raisins to make a snack.

Blocks

Box Dragon
Encourage the children to build a dragon with cardboard boxes.

Games

Pin the Tail on the Dragon
Draw a dragon on a sheet of poster board. Cut a tail from another sheet. Invite the children to take turns blindfolding each other and pinning on the tail.

Construction

Create a Dragon
Provide egg cartons, paper, pipe cleaners and other art materials for the children to create dragons.

Library

Dragon Stories
Fill the center with books about dragons.

Monsters

Materials

There's a Monster in My Closet by James Howe

Morning Circle

1. Read the book.
2. Ask, "How many of you think you have seen a monster?" Encourage the children to share their stories.

Story Circle

There's a Monster Under My Bed by James Howe

Music and Movement

Invite the children to create a dance to "Monster Mash" on *All Time Favorite Dances*

Learning Centers

Art

Monster Art
Invite the children to create a monster by splatter painting. Encourage them to add red eyes, scary hands and other features.

Dramatic Play

Shadow Monsters
Provide a light source. Challenge the children to create hand shadow monsters.

Fine Motor

Monster Stencils
Provide monster-shaped stencils for the children to trace around.

Gross Motor

Eye Toss
Draw a monster face on poster board. Glue strips of Velcro where the eyes should be. Glue strips of Velcro around Ping Pong balls. Invite the children to Toss the Eyes on the Monster.

Language

Giant Monster Puzzle
Draw a monster on poster board. Cut the picture into four or five pieces for the children to put together.

Language

My Favorite Monster
Invite the children to dictate a make-believe story about a pet monster.

Giants

Materials

Morning Circle

Talk about how it might feel to be a giant living among normal-sized humans. Would things look different? How many cheeseburgers would it take to fill you up? Where would you buy your clothes? What kinds of toys would you play with? What kind of car could you drive? How good would you be at basketball?

Story Circle

David's Father by Robert Munsch

Music and Movement

Invite the children to play Mother, May I (see the appendix, page 404). Help them focus on taking small and giant steps.

Learning Centers

Art

Painting by Giants

Encourage the children to pretend to be giants as they paint a house or other familiar thing.

Dramatic Play

Guess Who's Coming to Dinner?

Provide large plates and utensils for the children to set a place at the table for a giant.

Blocks

Small Town

Invite the children to build a small town and walk through it pretending to be giants.

Games

Giant Concentration

Make a set of large color cards (8" x 10" or 20 cm x 25 cm) for the children to play concentration.

Discovery

A Giant's View

Help the children climb a 4' (1 m) ladder and look down at a penny. What does it look like? Is it hard to see? Supervise closely. [Use caution.]

Math

Giant Footprints

Cut a huge footprint about 8' or 2 m long from butcher paper or vinyl. Challenge the children to walk the length of the print and count the number of footsteps it takes to get across.

What Can this Be?

Day 10

Materials
empty paper towel tubes, coffee cans, paper sacks, food boxes, etc.; *Bored, Nothing to Do* by Peter Spier

Morning Circle
1. Read *Bored, Nothing to Do* by Peter Spier.
2. Hold up the throw-away items you gathered one at a time. Invite the children to think of uses for each item.
3. Discuss looking at things in new and different ways.

Story Circle
Look, Look Again! by Tana Hoban

Music and Movement
Invite the children to play I Spy.

Learning Centers

Art

Doodle Art
Invite the children to draw doodles on sheets of paper. Challenge them to trade papers and create drawings from the doodles.

Fine Motor

Pipe Cleaners
Provide an assortment of colored pipe cleaners for the children to twist into anything they choose.

Construction

My Creation
Provide throw-away items for the children to use to create a mystery object.

Games

Guess What I Am
Glue a picture inside a file folder. Cut several small windows (flaps) in the cover of the folder. How many windows do the children have to open before they can identify the object in the picture?

Discovery

Mystery Box
Place several familiar objects in a box. Invite the children to stick their hand in the box without looking, pick up an object and identify it by touch only. How difficult is this task?

Language

Mystery Puzzles
Draw something on poster board and cut it out. Then cut it into puzzle pieces. Challenge the children to guess what it is before they put the pieces together.

Additional Books for Fun and Fantasy

Alexander and the Wind-up Mouse by Leo Lionni
The Bear's Toothache by David McPhail
Cloudy With a Chance of Meatballs by Judi Barrett
The Day Jimmy's Boa Ate the Wash by Trinka Hakes Noble
Doctor De Soto by William Steig
The Fortune Tellers by Lloyd Alexander
The Giant Jam Sandwich by John Vernon Lord and Janet Burroway
Go Away, Big Green Monster! by Ed Emberley
If You Give a Mouse a Cookie by Laura Joffe Numeroff and Felicia Bond
Little Bear's Trousers by Jane Hissey
Louie by Ezra Jack Keats
The Popcorn Dragon by Jane Thayer
Pueblo Storyteller by Diane Hoyt-Goldsmith
Sheep in a Jeep by Nancy Shaw
Teeny Tiny by Jill Bennett
A Treeful of Pigs by Arnold Lobel
Why a Disguise? by Laura Joffe Numerof

Wheels and Wings

Travel intrigues children. Boats, airplanes, space ships and even the old family car seem mysterious to them. This unit explores the many ways people move from one place to another.

Unit at a Glance

Day	Focus	Centers	Story Circle	Music/Movement
1	Planning a Trip	Vehicle Match Suitcase Packing Travel Bingo Story Dictation Transportation Graph Suitcase Weighing	Ira Sleeps Over	It's a Small World
2	Motor Vehicles	Car Tracks Travel Tracking Car Building Shape Comparisons Key Classification Word Tracing	Sheep in a Jeep	Red Light, Green Light
3	Land Travel: Carrying Many People	Bus Building Bus Role-Play Making Buses Circle Rolling Bus Story Dictation Coin Classification	The Wheels on the Bus	The Wheels on the Bus
4	Land Travel on Tracks	Shoe Box Train Pretend Play Train Role-Play Hole-Punch Tickets Shape Train Crossing Signs	Trains	Locomotion
5	Water Travel	Sail Making Boat Building Celery Boats Boat Carving Sail Patterns Sink or Float	Who Sank the Boat?	Row, Row, Row Your Boat

Day	Focus	Centers	Story Circle	Music/Movement
6	**Air Travel**	Decorating Machines Flying Machines Float and Drop Airline Role-Play Air Travel Concentration Parachutes	Bored, Nothing to Do	Flying
7	**Traveling with the Wind**	Straw Blowing Air Movers Feather Lift Story Starter Wind Blow Sort Seed Blowing	When the Wind Blew	The Wind
8	**Traveling on Foot**	Stepping Around Shoe Sort Left/Right Foot Tracks Map Making Magnified Feet Measuring Steps	The Story of Johnny Appleseed	The Ants Go Marching
9	**Animal Travel**	Crayon Rubbings Dog Sled Role-Play Wagon Role-Play Peanut/Dog Bone Sort Animal Sort Saddle Patterns	Seventeen Kings and Forty-Two Elephants	She'll Be Comin' 'Round the Mountain
10	**Kid-Sized Travel**	Path Signs Wheel Machines Pizza Cutters Bike Horn Honk Moving! Wheels	D. W. Rides Again!	The Bicycle Song

Planning a Trip

Materials
travel brochures, suitcase packed with travel items, chart paper and marker

Morning Circle
1. Bring a small, packed suitcase and some travel brochures to the circle.
2. Talk with the children about trips they have taken. How many of them helped pack their own suitcase? What did they pack?
3. Go through the items in the suitcase. Explain that what you pack is related to where you are going (e.g., swimsuit to the beach, snow boots to the mountains).
4. Choose a destination from the travel brochures and brainstorm a list of items you would pack for the trip.

Story Circle
Ira Sleeps Over by Bernard Waber

Music and Movement
"It's a Small World" from *Miss Jackie and Her Friends* by Miss Jackie

Learning Centers

Blocks

Vehicle Match
Decorate the block center with travel posters. Provide a variety of toy vehicles and encourage the children to decide which vehicle they might use to get to each place pictured.

Language

Story Dictation
Let the children dictate stories about places they have traveled to or places they'd like to travel to.

Dramatic Play

Suitcase Packing
Provide small suitcases and dress-up clothes for the children to pack.

Math

Transportation Graph
Make a graph showing several means of transportation (car, bus, boat, plane, etc.). Encourage the children to place a mark beside those they have experienced.

Fine Motor

Travel Bingo
Play Transportation Bingo. Make game boards using pictures of different vehicles.

Science

Suitcase Weighing
Have the children weigh a small, packed suitcase on a bathroom scale. Ask them what item(s) in the suitcase they might take out to make the suitcase lighter.

Motor Vehicles

Materials
pictures and/or models of different motor vehicles, chart paper and marker

Morning Circle
1. Discuss car travel. Show pictures of different types of motor vehicles. Ask each child to describe the family car.
2. Make a chart illustrating how many children have trucks, vans and cars for family travel.

Story Circle
Sheep in a Jeep by Nancy Shaw

Music and Movement
Play Red Light, Green Light (see the appendix, page 404).

Learning Centers

Art

Car Tracks
Let the children paint car tracks on drawing paper. Provide small toy cars and tempera paint in shallow containers. Roll the cars through the paint and across the paper.

Blocks

Travel Tracking
Place butcher paper on the floor. Using a rubber band, attach a felt-tip marker to a toy car so that the marker rests on the paper. Encourage the children to roll the car across the paper to make a track.

Construction

Car Building
Provide large cardboard boxes and other materials for the children to create a car.

Discovery

Shape Comparisons
Provide round and square cardboard shapes for the children to roll across the floor. Which rolls easier? Why? How do the round shapes compare to car wheels?

Math

Key Classification
Provide a collection of car keys for the children to explore, sort and classify.

Writing

Word Tracing
Write the words STOP and YIELD on 5″ x 8″ (13 cm x 20 cm) cards. Provide tracing paper and encourage the children to trace the words.

Land Travel: Carrying Many People

Day 3

Materials
pictures of buses

Morning Circle
1. Sing "The Wheels on the Bus."
2. Talk about buses and uses of buses (e.g., taking people to and from school, work and far-away places). Show any pictures you can find.
3. Ask, "How is a school bus different from a city bus?"

Story Circle
The Wheels on the Bus by Raffi

Music and Movement
"The Wheels on the Bus" from *Rise and Shine* by Raffi

Learning Centers

Blocks

Bus Building
Fill the center with large cardboard boxes. Let the children make buses.

Games

Circle Rolling
Encourage the children to have a button-rolling contest. Have two children stand at one end of a table and attempt to roll a button off the other side.

Dramatic Play

Bus Role-Play
Arrange several chairs in short bus-like rows. Let the children role-play riding on a bus.

Language

Bus Story Dictation
Provide bus shapes for book pages and covers. Allow the children to write (or dictate) stories and draw pictures about riding on a bus.

Fine Motor

Making Buses
Provide a yellow construction-paper bus shape with cut-out windows. Encourage the children to cut pictures of people from magazines and glue them inside the windows.

Math

Coin Classification
Provide a box with real coins inside. Let the children sort and classify the coins.

Land Travel on Tracks

Day 4

Materials

simple picture cards showing people and various cargoes carried by train, red and black construction paper

Morning Circle

1. Identify the various cars of a train (engine, caboose, passenger, cargo, tanker, livestock, etc.).
2. Discuss differences between cargo and passenger trains.
3. Divide the children into two groups. Let one group be a passenger train and the other a cargo train.
4. Give each child a simple picture card to show a kind of car. Passenger cars can show pictures of stick figures and cargo cars can show pictures of cars, lumber, grain, etc. Use black construction paper to identify the engines and red to identify the cabooses.

Story Circle

Trains by Gail Gibbons

Music and Movement

Have the children line up. Call the first child the Engine. Let the children follow the Engine around the room, moving their arms to indicate train wheel movement.

Learning Centers

Art

Shoe Box Train
Provide shoe boxes and art materials for the children to build a train.

Fine Motor

Hole-Punch Tickets
Suggest that the children use hole-punchers to punch holes in construction paper train tickets.

Blocks

Pretend Play
Provide blocks, toy trains and tracks for pretend play.

Fine Motor

Shape Train
Provide small construction-paper shapes and encourage the children to combine them to make a train collage.

Dramatic Play

Train Role-Play
Let the children arrange chairs like train seats and use toilet-paper-tube megaphones to call "All Aboard!"

Language

Crossing Signs
Provide construction-paper shapes for the children to make railroad crossing signs. Attach to popsicle sticks.

Water Travel

Materials
toy boats and/or pictures of boats

Morning Circle
1. Sing "Row, Row, Row Your Boat."
2. Discuss different kinds of boats and how they're powered. Show pictures or models to the children.
3. Sing "Row, Row, Row Your Boat" again. Have the children sit facing a partner, holding hands and feet together. Encourage them to "row" together as they sing.

Story Circle
Who Sank the Boat? by Pamela Allen

Music and Movement
"Row, Row, Row Your Boat" from *Bert and Ernie's Sing Along*

Learning Centers

Art

Sail Making
Provide the children with large triangles from which they can create fancy sails by painting, coloring or creating a collage.

Fine Motor

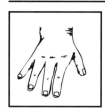

Boat Carving
Encourage the children to make soap boats, using a spoon to carve a small area out of the center of a bar of soap.

Blocks

Boat Building
Provide blue bulletin board paper cut into a "water shape." Encourage the children to use blocks to build boats on the water.

Math

Sail Patterns
Provide a variety of paper or cardboard boat sails of different colors and shapes. Let the children create patterns.

Cooking and Snack

Celery Boats
Make celery boats. Let the children spread peanut butter in celery sticks. Add toothpicks with white paper sails.

Science

Sink or Float
Provide materials for the children to experiment with sinking and floating.

Air Travel

Day 6

Materials
pictures of different aircraft, wood scraps, popsicle sticks and bottle caps

Morning Circle
1. Show the children pictures of airplanes. Try to include some pictures of the first airplane or other early models. Also include pictures of hot-air balloons, rockets, helicopters and other aircraft.
2. Show the children wood scraps, popsicle sticks and bottle caps.
3. Discuss ways to put the materials together to make a flying machine.

Story Circle
Bored, Nothing to Do by Peter Spier

Music and Movement
The children move around the room to music, arms outstretched to fly.

Learning Centers

Art

Decorating Machines
Encourage the children to decorate their flying machines using markers, paints and stickers.

Dramatic Play

Airline Role-Play
Arrange chairs to resemble seats in an airplane cabin. Provide props such as trays, cups, soft drink cans and napkins for role-play.

Construction

Flying Machines
Provide blocks of wood, popsicle sticks, bottle caps, hammers and nails for the children to construct flying machines.

Games

Air Travel Concentration
Make cards for an Air Travel Concentration game (use patterns from the appendix, page 414).

Discovery

Float and Drop
Provide tissues, feathers, washers, sticks and so on. Let the children experiment with the materials and determine whether they fall at the same rate or not.

Science

Parachutes
Cut an old sheet into 12" (30 cm) squares. Tie a 12" piece of yarn to each corner. Run the loose ends through an empty spool and knot them together. Let the children throw their parachutes into the air and watch them land.

WHEELS & WINGS • • • 351

Traveling with the Wind
Day 7

Materials
seeds (use pine if available), small fan, tissues or other lightweight material, chart paper and marker

Morning Circle
1. Let the children watch things blowing in the wind. Make a list of all the things the wind might blow.
2. If there is no wind, demonstrate how wind moves things using the fan and tissues.
3. Show the children the seeds. Explain that the wind often carries seeds to new locations and that is often how flowers and trees come up in new places. (You may want to go outside later for a "seed-hunt" walk.)
4. Drop the seeds in front of the fan and watch them blow. Pine seeds are great. Any wind will move them.

Story Circle
When the Wind Blew by Margaret Wise Brown

Music and Movement
"The Wind" from *One Elephant, Deux Elephants* by Sharon, Lois and Bram

Learning Centers

Art

Straw Blowing
Provide the children with straws, tempera paint and paper. Let them blow small puddles of paint across their paper to make designs.

Language

Story Starter
Encourage the children to finish a story that starts, "The little leaf fell from the tree. Just as it was about to hit the ground, the wind picked it up. Its journey had begun."

Discovery

Air Movers
Provide basters, fans, straws, eye-droppers, empty detergent bottles, paper towel tubes, a tire pump and Ping-Pong balls. Let the children experiment moving the balls with air.

Math

Wind Blow Sort
Provide a leaf, seed, tissues, feather, block, scissors and eraser. Let the children classify them as things a normal wind could/could not blow.

Gross Motor

Feather Lift
Give the children a folded fan and a feather. Let them try to keep the feather afloat with the fan.

Science

Seed Blowing
Let the children use straws to blow seeds across the table.

Traveling on Foot

Day 8

Materials
none

Morning Circle
1. Select two children to walk from the circle to the door and back to the circle.
2. Ask the other children if their friends have traveled or just walked a distance.
3. Explain that the dictionary says travel is to go from one place to another.

Story Circle
The Story of Johnny Appleseed by Aliki

Music and Movement
"The Ants Go Marching" from *Singing and Swinging* by Sharon, Lois and Bram

Learning Centers

Construction

Stepping Around
Cut out a foot shape from an inner sole. Glue to a wood block. Dab on ink pad or tempera paint-soaked pad of paper towels. Encourage the children to add footstep printing to their drawings.

Dramatic Play

Shoe Sort
Fill the center with different kinds of shoes such as boots, heels, tennis shoes, galoshes and sandals.

Gross Motor

Left/Right Foot Tracks
Cut out left (red) and right (blue) footprints out of construction paper. Make a trail for the children to follow.

Language

Map Making
Provide crayons and paper and encourage the children to make a map of a route they could walk, such as the parking lot to the classroom or the art center to the playground.

Science

Magnified Feet
Encourage the children to look at their toes through a magnifying glass.

Science

Measuring Steps
Place two pieces of masking tape 6' (2 m) apart. Ask the children to see how many small steps and how many giant steps it takes to get from one to the other.

Animal Travel

Animal Travel   Day 9

Materials
chart paper and marker

Morning Circle
1. Write the words *Animal Travel* on a sheet of chart paper.
2. Ask the children to list as many animals as they can think of that people use for transporting themselves or their equipment and supplies.

Story Circle
Seventeen Kings and Forty-Two Elephants by Margaret Mahy

Music and Movement
"She'll Be Comin' 'Round the Mountain" from *Joe Scruggs in Concert* by Joe Scruggs

Learning Centers

Art

Crayon Rubbings
Give the children cardboard shapes of dogs and horses to make crayon rubbings.

Construction

Dog Sled Role-Play
Provide boxes and ropes for the children to make dog sleds.

Dramatic Play

Wagon Role-Play
Provide a sheet and some materials for a covered wagon. Encourage the children to make their wagon and pack it for travel.

Fine Motor

Peanut/Dog Bone Sort
Provide tongs and bowls. Let the children sort peanuts and dog biscuits.

Language

Animal Sort
Provide animal pictures and let the children sort them according to whether or not they are used for transportation.

Math

Saddle Patterns
Let the children make felt saddles and elephants and then pattern the elephants according to saddle color.

Kid-Sized Travel

Materials
chart paper and marker

Morning Circle
1. Ask the children to brainstorm a list of ways kids travel, such as roller blades, bikes, tricycles, pogo sticks and skateboards.
2. Ask questions such as, "How many items have wheels? What moves those things without wheels?"

Story Circle
D.W. Rides Again! by Marc Brown

Music and Movement
"The Bicycle Song" from *Traffic Jam* by Joe Scruggs

Learning Centers

Art

Path Signs
Make path signs to decorate a bike trail outdoors or bike flags for bikes at home.

Gross Motor

Bike Horn Honk
Place a bike horn on the floor. Let the children honk it by tossing bean-bags and hitting it.

Construction

Wheel Machines
Provide spools, dowels and other wood scraps for building wheel machines.

Gross Motor

Moving!
Encourage the children to move around the room as if they were on a pogo stick (hopping), then on roller blades (gliding), etc.

Fine Motor

Pizza Cutters
Give the children playdough and pizza wheels to cut through the dough.

Science

Wheels
In the center, puts lots of things with wheels like roller skates, egg beaters and small cars.

Additional Books for Wheels and Wings

Boats by Anne Rockwell

The Caboose Who Got Loose by Bill Peet

Cars by Anne Rockwell

Cars by Richard Scarry

First Flight by David McPhail

Flying by Donald Crews

Freight Train by Donald Crews

How Many Trucks Can a Tow Truck Tow? by Charlotte Pomerantz

I Love Boats by Flora McDonnell

I Want to Be a Pilot by Teddy Slater

The Little Red Lighthouse and the Great Gray Bridge by Hildegarde Swift

On the Go by Ann Morris

Sarah's Boat: A Young Girl Learns the Art of Sailing by Douglas Alvord

School Bus by Donald Crews

This Is the Way We Go to School by Edith Baer

Train Song by Diane Siebert

Truck by Donald Crews

The Wheels on the Bus by Maryann Kovalski

William the Vehicle King by Laura Newton

Celebrating Little Things

Learning new things is part of growing up. This unit celebrates the special accomplishments and events that are part of every child's life.

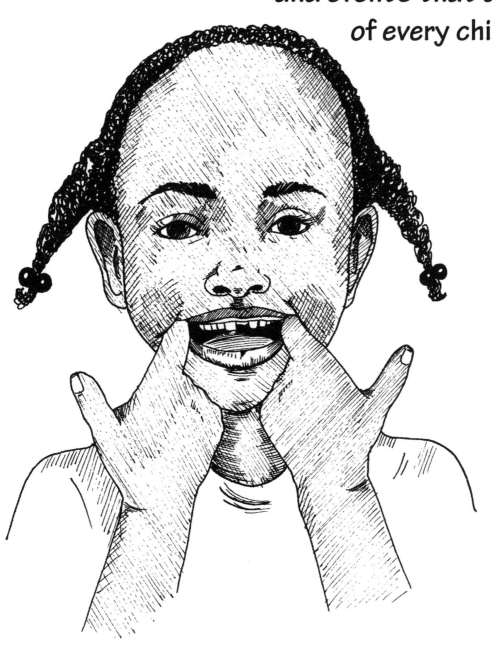

Unit at a Glance

Day	Focus	Centers	Story Circle	Music/Movement
1	Growing Up	Baby Days Food Sort Who's Who I Can Book Growing, Growing Measure Up	Now I'm Big	So Big
2	Losing a Tooth	Splatter Paint Tooth Fairy Pillow Giant Teeth Toothpaste Tooth Fairy Dust Tooth Hunt	Little Rabbit's Loose Tooth	Tooth Fairy Hide and Seek
3	It's My Birthday	Cupcakes Birthday Party Wrapping Presents Drop the Clothespin Mylar Balloon Book How Many Candles?	Moira's Birthday	Musical Chairs
4	Learning to Tie and Button	Shoelace Printing I Can Tie Button Up Tiddly Button Lacing Boards Shoelace Seriation	How Do I Put it On?	Tug of War
5	Learning to Whistle, Snap, Clap and Blow	Straw Painting I Can Snap Tracing Hands Feathers Up Hand/Foot Patterns Bubble Blowing	Whistle for Willie	Rhythm Band

Day	Focus	Centers	Story Circle	Music/Movement
6	**Balancing and Spinning**	Balance Beam Balancing and Spinning Top Spinning Twister Name the Pattern Balance Scale	D.W. Rides Again!	Flying Statues
7	**Spring Is Here**	Kite Time Raindrop Race Spring Tea Spring Colors Spring Rain Flower Seeds	The Boy Who Didn't Believe in Spring	Kites
8	**Summer Time**	My Favorite Summer Activity Zoo Visit Sunglasses Lemonade Summer Vacation Beach Play	Henry and Mudge in the Green Time	We're On Our Way
9	**Fall in for Fall**	Fall Leaves Fall Colors Apple Cider Colorful Gourds Counting Acorns Leaf Sort	Autumn Harvest	Pass the Pumpkin
10	**Winter's Coming**	Ice Painting North Pole Snowy Prints Ice Skating Season Sort Sensory Bottles	Henrietta's First Winter	Freeze Tag

Growing Up

Day 1

Materials

baby pictures of you and the children (send a note home asking parents to send them in)

Morning Circle

1. Show the children your baby picture.
2. Hold up baby pictures of the children. Can the children guess who is who?
3. On a yardstick, show the children how long they were at birth (probably 18"–24" or 45–60 cm).
4. Discuss things the children can do now that they could not do as babies. What a celebration!
5. Talk about healthy habits for growing.

Story Circle

Now I'm Big by Margaret Miller

Music and Movement

So Big by Hap Palmer

Learning Centers

Art

Baby Days

Invite the children to paint pictures of themselves as babies.

Language

I Can Book

Invite the children to draw pictures of things they can do. Help them compile their pictures into resealable plastic bag books.

Cooking and Snack

Food Sort

Provide pictures of healthful food and junk food for the children to sort.

Math

Growing, Growing, Growing

Provide playdough people in various sizes for the children to arrange in order from smallest to largest.

Games

Who's Who?

Make photocopies of the children's baby pictures and their recent pictures. Invite the children to match the pairs.

Science

Measure Up

Weigh and measure each child. Encourage the children to compare their measurements with those you took at the beginning of the year.

Losing a Tooth

Materials
dentist or oral hygienist (if possible)

Morning Circle
1. If possible, invite a dentist or oral hygienist to discuss taking care of teeth.
2. Invite the children who have lost a tooth to tell about the "happening."
3. Teach the children "I Had a Loose Tooth" (see the appendix, page 394).

Story Circle
Little Rabbit's Loose Tooth by Lucy Bates

Music and Movement
Invite the children to play Tooth Fairy Hide and Seek. The child who is IT becomes the Tooth Fairy, and the other children are the teeth.

Learning Centers

Art

Splatter Paint
Provide toothbrushes, tempera paints, paper and screen for splatter painting.

Discovery

Toothpaste
Encourage the children to make toothpaste. Add water to baking soda until you have a paste consistency. Add a couple of drops of peppermint extract.

Cooking and Snack

Giant Teeth
Invite the children to spread peanut butter over apple slices, then top with miniature marshmallows (teeth).

Fine Motor

Tooth Fairy Dust
Invite the children to mix two tablespoons (30 ml) of fine sand with blue chalk dust (rub two pieces of chalk together). They can put their fairy dust in a small plastic bag and take it home.

Construction

Tooth Fairy Pillow
Cut 6" (15 cm) felt squares and use fabric glue to attach two squares together on three sides. Invite the children to decorate them with glitter glue and stuff them with old hose. Glue the open side closed. Finish by gluing a small pocket in the center of one side (to hold that special tooth).

Games

Tooth Hunt
Hide tooth-shaped Styrofoam chips in a tub of seashells, marbles, feathers, teddy bear counters or other material. Invite the children to find the hidden teeth.

It's My Birthday

Materials
none

Morning Circle
1. Make a pretend birthday cake. Act out all the steps it takes to mix, bake and decorate the cake. Measure, stir, pour, place in oven, wait, remove from oven, ice, put on candles and so on. Can the children guess what you are doing?
2. Discuss birthday party activities.

Story Circle
Moira's Birthday by Robert Munsch

Music and Movement
Invite the children to play Musical Chairs or other traditional party games.

Learning Centers

Cooking and Snack

Cupcakes
Invite the children to ice cupcakes with powdered sugar icing.

Dramatic Play

Birthday Party
Provide props for a pretend birthday party (hats, wrapped boxes, party favors, plates and cups, etc.).

Fine Motor

Wrapping Presents
Provide boxes, wrapping paper, scissors, tape, bows and ribbons for the children to wrap presents.

Games

Drop the Clothespin
Provide a wide-mouthed jar and a tub of clothespins. Encourage the children to drop the clothespins into the jar from waist height and then from shoulder height.

Language

Mylar Balloon Book
Cut apart a Happy Birthday mylar balloon so that you have a front and back. Put several sheets of paper between and staple it all together. Invite the children to draw pictures of their favorite birthday activities inside.

Math

How Many Candles?
Provide felt cakes with the numerals 1 to 5 on them. Encourage the children to put the corresponding number of felt candles on each cake.

Learning to Tie and Button   Day 4

Materials
none

Morning Circle
1. Let the children talk about their latest successes in dressing themselves. Can they remember when things were more difficult?
2. Invite older children into the room to help the younger ones learn and practice tying their shoes.

Story Circle
How Do I Put it On? by Shigeo Watanabe

Music and Movement
Invite the children to play Tug of War with a giant's shoelace (rope).

Learning Centers

Art

Shoelace Printing
Encourage the children to dip shoelaces in paint and then arrange them on a sheet of paper to create a picture or design. Lay a second sheet over the design and press. Lift to find a print.

Dramatic Play

I Can Tie
Provide several pairs of shoes with laces for the children to practice tying.

Fine Motor

Button Up
Cut slots in the lids of several empty coffee cans. Provide a bowl of buttons for the children to push through the slots.

Games

Tiddly Button
Challenge the children to play Tiddly Winks with buttons.

Language

Lacing Boards
Invite the children to lace around poster board cutouts with shoelaces.

Math

Shoelace Seriation
Provide shoelaces of several lengths for the children to arrange in order from shortest to longest.

Learning to Whistle, Snap, Clap and Blow

Materials
create a rebus direction for a clap, stomp and snap pattern (Cut hands, feet and snapping fingers from construction paper and arrange them in a pattern; glue them to cardboard strips.)

Morning Circle
1. Teach the children some simple clapping and snapping patterns.
2. Use the pattern cards to lead the children through patterns of clapping, stomping and snapping.

Story Circle
Whistle for Willie by Ezra Jack Keats

Music and Movement
Invite the children to perform in a rhythm band, using only clapping, snapping, whistling and blowing sounds.

Learning Centers

Art

Straw Painting
Put dabs of tempera paints on paper and invite the children to blow on it through straws.

Games

Feathers Up
Challenge the children to keep a feather airborne by blowing on it.

Fine Motor

I Can Snap
Encourage the children to choose partners and practice snapping with them.

Math

Hand/Foot Patterns
Provide cutouts of hands and feet for the children to create patterns.

Fine Motor

Tracing Hands
Provide pencils and paper for hand tracing. Some children may want to cut out their prints with scissors.

Science

Bubble Blowing
Provide bubble soap (see the appendix, page 388) and a variety of wands for the children to blow bubbles.

Balancing and Spinning   Day 6

Materials
none

Morning Circle
1. Invite the children to balance on one foot and then on their tiptoes. Can anyone do a somersault?
2. Talk about how difficult it is to keep your balance when you first start walking.
3. Discuss activities that require balance (bike riding, walking, skating, dancing, gymnastics, etc.).
4. Ask, "Who can spin all the way around? Do you need balance for that?"

Story Circle
D.W. Rides Again! by Marc Brown

Music and Movement
Invite the children to play Flying Statues (see the appendix, page 404).

Learning Centers

Blocks

Balance Beam
Invite the children to walk the balance beam. Can anyone walk it backward?

Gross Motor

Twister
Provide a Twister game and invite the children to play.

Discovery

Balancing and Spinning
Provide objects for the children to balance and spin (coins, spools, tops, straws, etc.). Are some easier to balance and spin than others? Why?

Math

Name That Pattern
Challenge the children to create and copy patterns of disk magnets (sides repel and attract). Encourage the children to slide the magnets onto a dowel anchored in playdough.

Fine Motor

Top Spinning
Provide a variety of tops for the children to spin. Which top spins the longest? Fastest? Which one travels farthest?

Science

Balance Scale
Provide a balance scale and an assortment of objects for the children to experiment with.

Spring Is Here

Materials
chart paper and marker

Morning Circle
1. Make a word web for spring. Invite the children to brainstorm a list of activities, games, foods and holidays that represent spring.
2. Ask, "What are reasons to celebrate spring?"

Story Circle
The Boy Who Didn't Believe in Spring by Lucille Clifton

Music and Movement
Provide kite streamers and let the children run outside.

Learning Centers

Construction

Kite Time
Invite the children to make a kite by gluing crepe paper streamers around a paper sack opening. Then they can decorate the rest of the sack and "fly" it.

Fine Motor

Spring Colors
Provide pastel tissue paper for the children to create a spring collage.

Discovery

Raindrop Race
Provide two eyedroppers, a cookie sheet and a cup of water. Encourage the children to drop water on the tilted cookie sheet and see whose raindrop gets to the bottom first.

Language

Spring Rain
Cut raindrops from blue construction paper. Glue pictures of objects with rhyming names on the raindrops. Challenge the children to match the rhyming raindrops.

Dramatic Play

Spring Tea
Provide tea cups and fancy hats for the children to have a Spring Tea.

Science

Flower Seeds
Provide flower pots, potting soil, spoons and an assortment of flower seeds for the children to plant. Don't forget the watering can.

Summer Time

Materials
chart paper and marker

Morning Circle
1. Brainstorm a list of summer activities, foods, holidays and so on.
2. Record the children's responses.
3. Ask, "What are reasons to celebrate summer?"

Story Circle
Henry and Mudge in the Green Time by Cynthia Rylant

Music and Movement
We're on Our Way by Hap Palmer

Learning Centers

Art

My Favorite Summer Activity
Encourage the children to paint a picture of their favorite summer time activity.

Cooking and Snack

Lemonade
Provide lemons, sugar, water and a pitcher for the children to make fresh lemonade.

Blocks

Zoo Visit
Invite the children to build a zoo with blocks and plastic or stuffed animals.

Dramatic Play

Summer Vacation
Provide suitcases, clothes to pack, maps, travel books and other props for the children to take a pretend vacation.

Construction

Sunglasses
Provide an eyeglass template for the children to trace around. After they cut out the frames, encourage them to cover the "eyes" with colored cellophane and decorate the frames with glitter glue, feathers and so on.

Sand and Water Table

Beach Play
Provide shovels, buckets and other containers for beach play.

Fall in for Fall

Materials
chart paper and marker

Morning Circle
1. Help the children brainstorm a list of fall activities, holidays, foods and so on.
2. Record the children's responses.
3. Ask, "What are reasons to celebrate fall?"

Story Circle
Autumn Harvest by Alvin Tresselt

Music and Movement
Play Pass the Pumpkin. Pass a real or plastic pumpkin around the circle to the beat of a drum. Vary the tempo, slow, fast, slow, fast.

Learning Centers

Art

Fall Leaves
Provide paper, sponges and tempera paint in fall colors. Invite the children to sponge paint fall leaves.

Construction

Fall Colors
Provide tissue paper in fall colors for the children to create a fall collage.

Cooking and Snack

Apple Cider
Encourage the children to make apple cider by following the recipe in the appendix on page 389.

Discovery

Colorful Gourds
Provide a variety of gourds for the children to examine. Be sure to cut a couple of them open for an inside look. How are the inside and outside different?

Math

Counting Acorns
Place one to six (or one to eight) stick-on dots in each section of a muffin tin. Challenge the children to count the corresponding number of acorns into each section.

Math

Leaf Sort
Provide a pile of leaves of different shapes and colors. Challenge the children to sort the leaves into two categories. Can they sort each of those two into two more?

Winter's Coming
Day 10

Materials
chart paper and marker

Morning Circle
1. Help the children brainstorm a list of winter activities, holidays, foods and so on.
2. Record their responses.
3. Ask, "What are reasons to celebrate winter?"

Story Circle
Henrietta's First Winter by Rob Lewis

Music and Movement
Invite the children to play Freeze Tag.

Learning Centers

Art

Ice Painting
Invite the children to paint using ice cubes with popsicle sticks as a "paintbrush." Provide paper, tempera paint, ice cubes and tongs.

Blocks

North Pole
Fill the center with Styrofoam packing chips. (Make sure you have some kind of "fence" to keep them inside the center.) Challenge the children to build a village at the North Pole.

Fine Motor

Snowy Prints
Encourage the children to paint with snow (shaving cream) on the table top.

Gross Motor

Ice Skating
Glue a magnetic strip to the feet of a plastic person. Stand it on a mirror. Challenge the children to hold a second magnet on the underside of the mirror and use it to move the skater around the ice.

Language

"My picture is about..."

Season Sort
Provide pictures of people doing seasonal activities. Encourage the children to sort them according to season.

Science

Sensory Bottles
Mix ¼ cup (60 ml) white corn syrup, 2 tablespoons (30 ml) silver and white glitter, and water in a 12-ounce (350 g) plastic bottle. In a second bottle, mix ¼ cup (60 ml) detergent with water. Invite the children to shake the bottles and watch the snow fall. Which looks more like snow?

Additional Books for Celebrating Little Things

Anna's Red Sled by Patricia Quinlan

Apples and Pumpkins by Anne Rockwell

The Birthday Swap by Loretta Lopez

The Chipmunk Song by Joanne Ryder

Frederick by Leo Lionni

The Happy Day by Ruth Krauss

Keep Looking! by Millicent Selsam and Joyce Hunt

Marmalade's Yellow Leaf by Cindy Wheeler

My Favorite Time of Year by Susan Pearson

My Spring Robin by Anne Rockwell

Something Special by Nicola Moon

Spring Is Here by Taro Gomi

Squirrels by Brian Wildsmith

Surprise! by Sally Noll

Wild Wild Sunflower Child Anna by Nancy White Carlstrom

Wintertime by Ann Schweninger

The Year at Maple Hill Farm by Alice and Martin Provensen

Summertime Fun

Summer is filled with unstructured, creative activities. . . everything from bubbles to time alone. This unit focuses on the lazy, hazy days of the good ol' summertime.

Unit at a Glance

Day	Focus	Centers	Story Circle	Music/Movement
1	Kites and Frisbees			
		Kite Making Floaters and Droppers Frisbee Kite and Frisbee Puzzles Tail Count Kite Tracing	Curious George Flies a Kite	Kite Flying
2	Bubbles			
		Bubble Wrap Art Bubble Sculpture Bubble Machine Beater Bubbles Bubble Stories Bubble Mix	Bubble, Bubble	Bubble Dance
3	Games			
		My Own Game Pick-Up Sticks Tiddly Winks Tic-Tac-Toe Drop the Clothespin Game Pieces Pattern	Look What I Can Do	Freeze
4	Water Fun			
		Mud Pie Bake Sponge Puppets Water Spray Balloon Toss Sprinkler Fun Make a Rainbow	No More Water in the Tub	Shadow Tag
5	Being Alone			
		Alone Activities Quiet Place Solitaire My Diary Cozy Reading A Story Just for Me	The Very Lonely Firefly	Solo Dance

Kites and Frisbees   Day 1

Materials
kites (several different kinds, if possible) or pictures of kites

Morning Circle
1. Have the kite(s) in the circle for the children to examine as they come in.
2. Invite the children to tell you about their kite flying adventures. Ask, "Does anyone have a funny story to tell about getting a kite out of a tree?"
3. Explain how kites float on currents of air and how they only fly in breezes.

Story Circle
Curious George Flies a Kite by Margaret E.W. Rey

Music and Movement
Go outside. Fly kites and throw Frisbees.

Learning Centers

Construction

Kite Making
Provide paper sacks, crayons, tape, hole punch and yarn. Invite the children to decorate their sacks and then reinforce the open edge with tape. Punch holes to tie on the yarn.

Language

Kite and Frisbee Puzzles
Make kite- and Frisbee-shaped puzzles for the children to put together.

Discovery

Floaters and Droppers
Provide an assortment of objects that will float (tissue, feather, scarf) and drop (penny, button, bead). Encourage the children to drop each object from waist height. Does it float or drop?

Math

Tail Count
Cut five kites from poster board. Write a numeral 1 to 5 on each kite. Punch a hole in the bottom of each and attach a piece of yarn. Invite the children to clip the appropriate number of clothespins onto each kite tail.

Fine Motor

Frisbee
Provide plastic plates for the children to decorate as flying discs.

Writing

Kite Tracing
Provide kite-shaped stencils. Encourage the children to trace the kites and then turn them into pictures of kites flying in the breeze.

Bubbles

Materials
bubble soap (purchased or made from recipe in the appendix, page 388)

Morning Circle
1. Blow bubbles as the children enter the classroom.
2. Let the children discuss how bubble soap and bubbles are made.
3. Explain that bubbles float because they are lighter than air.

Story Circle
Bubble, Bubble by Mercer Mayer

Music and Movement
Play lullaby music and invite the children to float around the room like bubbles.

Learning Centers

Art

Bubble Wrap Art
Provide 6" (15 cm) squares of bubble wrap and shallow pans of tempera paints. Invite the children to make prints with the bubble wrap by painting the bubble wrap and then printing with it.

Fine Motor

Beater Bubbles
Provide an egg beater and bubble solution. Encourage the children to beat the bubbles.

Construction

Bubble Sculpture
Place bubble soap (recipe in the appendix, page 388) in a shallow pan. Give the children large straws. How high can they blow the bubble sculpture?

Language

Bubble Stories
Encourage the children to tell stories from the point of view of a bubble. For example, "From way up here in the trees, I can see…".

Discovery

Bubble Machine
Poke two straw-size holes in the lid of a margarine tub. Fill the tub halfway with bubble soap. Invite the children to push a straw into one hole and blow. Bubbles will pop out of the other hole.

Science

Bubble Mix
Invite the children to mix bubble soap and blow bubbles. Encourage them to examine the bubbles in the sunlight. Can they find rainbows?

Games

Day 3

Materials
none

Morning Circle
1. As the children come to the circle, invite them to join in a game of Telephone or I Spy.
2. Encourage the children to help you create a list of games. Point out the different types of games: action, table, competitive, noncompetitive and so on.
3. Discuss the role games play in our lives.

Story Circle
Look What I Can Do by José Aruego

Music and Movement
Invite the children to play Freeze Tag (see the appendix, page 402).

Learning Centers

Construction

My Own Game
Provide file folders, markers and stencils. Encourage the children to create their own board games.

Games

Tic-Tac-Toe
Provide a felt board (glue felt to cardboard, then section off with rickrack) and felt O's and X's for the children to play Tic-Tac-Toe.

Discovery

Pick-Up Sticks
Invite the children to play Pick-Up Sticks. Ask, "What do you need to know about balance and spatial relationships in order to pick up one stick without moving the others?"

Gross Motor

Drop the Clothespin
Provide clothespins and bowls or other containers for the children to play Drop the Clothespin.

Fine Motor

Tiddly Winks
Provide tiddly winks or buttons and a bowl. Challenge the children to play.

Math

Game Pieces Pattern
Provide game pieces from board games. Encourage the children to create patterns with the pieces.

Water Fun

Day 4

Materials
none

Morning Circle
1. Invite the children to the playground for circle time.
2. Introduce the water center activities.
3. Discuss safety.

Story Circle
No More Water in the Tub by Tedd Arnold

Music and Movement
Invite the children to play Shadow Tag.

Learning Centers

Dramatic Play

Mud Pie Bake
Provide damp sand or dirt, pie tins, plastic spoons and knives, craft sticks, acorns, leaves and other decorative ingredients. Invite the children to make mud pies.

Dramatic Play

Sponge Puppets
Provide sponges cut in the shapes of animals or people. Encourage the children to create stories about water and people, or water and animals.

Fine Motor

Water Spray
Provide empty spray bottles and butcher paper. Draw a circle on the paper. Invite the children to fill their bottles with water and then try to hit the circle with streams and sprays of water.

Gross Motor

Balloon Toss
Provide water balloons and a basket. Challenge the children to toss the balloons into the basket.

Gross Motor

Sprinkler Fun
Provide a sprinkler for the children to run through. Challenge them to see who can stay the driest (or the wettest).

Science

Make a Rainbow
Teach the children to spray water from a hose in such a way as to create a rainbow.

Being Alone

Materials
none

Morning Circle
1. Describe some activities you like to do when you're alone (reading, cooking, sewing, hiking, etc.).
2. Invite the children to discuss things they like to do alone.
3. Ask, "What would it feel like to always be alone?"

Story Circle
The Very Lonely Firefly by Eric Carle

Music and Movement
Play music and invite the children to dance without partners.

Learning Centers

Art

Alone Activities
Encourage the children to draw a picture of something they like to do alone.

Blocks

Quiet Place
Provide a washing machine box for the children to prepare a quiet place.

Games

Solitaire
Teach the children to play a game of matching cards (matching either the number or the color). Teach more experienced children an abbreviated game of solitaire.

Language

My Diary
Let the children dictate an entry for their own private diary.

Library

Cozy Reading
Fill a cozy corner with books and invite the children to retreat.

Listening

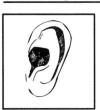

A Story Just for Me
Provide a tape and book for quiet listening.

Additional Books for Summertime Fun

Do Not Disturb by Nancy Tafuri
A Great Day for Up! by Dr. Suess
A Little House of Your Own by Beatrice de Regniers
Look! Look! Look! by Tana Hoban
On My Beach There Are Many Pebbles by Leo Lionni
Soap Bubble Magic by Seymour Simon
Summer by Ron Hirschi
Take Me Out to the Ballgame by Maryann Kovalski
Time of Wonder by Robert McCloskey
Yellow Ball by Molly Bang

Appendix

Flannel Board Stories and Patterns
Recipes
Songs, Chants and Fingerplays
Games
Drawings, Patterns and Instructions

Flannel Board Stories and Patterns

My First Day of School

It was the first day of school. Tamera woke up early. She was excited, but she was also a little bit afraid. Her mother said there was nothing to be afraid of. Her brother said there was nothing to be afraid.
But Tamera was still just a little bit afraid. She ate her breakfast, dressed up in her new school clothes and helped her mom pack her lunch. Finally, it was time to go.

Tamera's mother drove her to school. Tamera was surprised at how big the school looked. She held on to her mother's hand as they walked down the hall and to the door of Tamera's new classroom. Mrs. Marotta met Tamera at the door with a big, friendly smile.

Tamera bravely waved good-bye to her mother, although she didn't want to. She walked with Mrs. Marotta to where all the other children were seated in a big circle. She sat down.

Mrs. Marotta told the children about all the things they would be doing at school: painting at the easel with brightly colored paints in the art center, playing with playdough in the fine motor center, dressing up in clothes in the dramatic play center, building with blocks, working puzzles and dancing to happy music. They were even going to listen to a story or two.

Tamera began to think that school might be fun. She looked at the other boys and girls. They looked happy. When the teacher said everyone could choose a center, a nice girl named Julie asked Tamera to come play with her. Tamera and Julie did all the activities Mrs. Marotta described. They had a wonderful day. When Tamera's mother came for her, Tamera didn't want to go. She bravely waved good-bye to Julie and said, "I'll see you tomorrow."

Tamera's Mother

Tamera

brother

Julie

Mrs. Marotta

Enlarge patterns as needed.

And the Green Grass Grew All Around

In the park there was a hole,
Oh, the prettiest hole you ever did see.
Hole in the park,
Hole in the ground,
And the green grass grew all around,
All around,
The green grass grew all around.

And in that hole there was a sprout,
Oh, the prettiest sprout you ever did see.
Sprout in a hole,
Hole in the ground,
And the green grass grew all around,
All around,
The green grass grew all around.

And from that sprout there grew a tree,
Oh, the prettiest tree you ever did see.
Tree from a sprout,
Sprout in a hole,
Hole in the ground,
And the green grass grew all around,
All around,
The green grass grew all around.

And on that tree there was a branch,
Oh, the prettiest branch you ever did see.
Branch on a tree,
Tree from a sprout,
Sprout in a hole,
Hole in the ground,
And the green grass grew all around,
All around,
The green grass grew all around.

And on that branch there was a nest,
Oh, the prettiest nest you ever did see.
Nest on a branch,
Branch on a tree,
Tree from a sprout,
Sprout in a hole,
Hole in the ground,
And the green grass grew all around,
All around,
The green grass grew all around.

bird

And in that nest there was an egg,
Oh, the prettiest egg you ever did see.
Egg in a nest,
Nest on a branch,
Branch on a tree,
Tree from a sprout,
Sprout in a hole,
Hole in the ground,
And the green grass grew all around,
All around,
The green grass grew all around.

And in that egg there was a bird,
Oh, the prettiest bird you ever did see.
Bird in an egg,
Egg in a nest,
Nest on a branch,
Branch on a tree,
Tree from a sprout,
Sprout in a hole,
Hole in the ground,
And the green grass grew all around,
All around,
The green grass grew all around.

Enlarge patterns as needed.

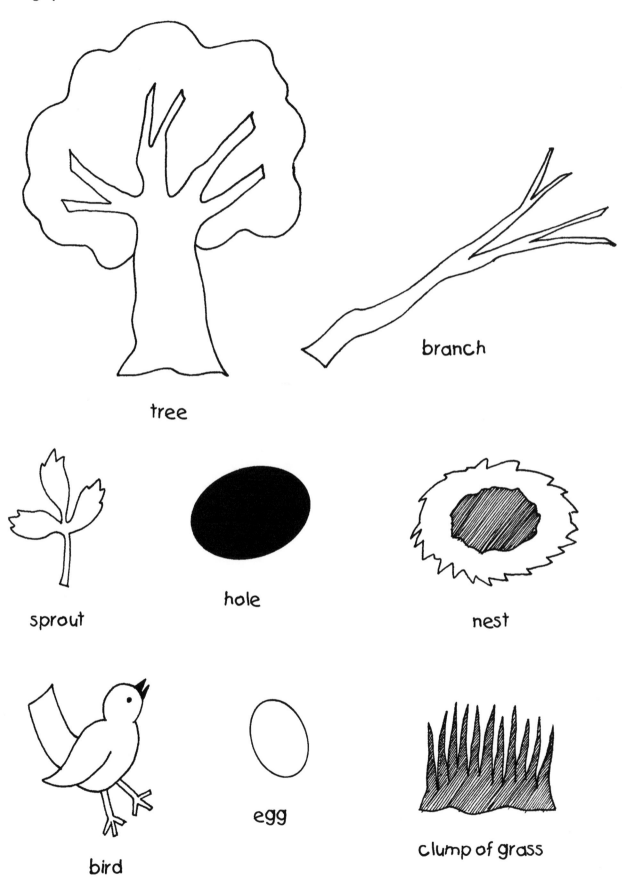

tree

branch

sprout

hole

nest

bird

egg

clump of grass

I Know an Old Woman

I know an old woman who swallowed a fly.
I don't know why she swallowed the fly.
Perhaps she'll die.

I know an old woman who swallowed a spider.
It wiggled and jiggled and tickled inside her.
She swallowed the spider to catch the fly.
I don't know why she swallowed the fly.
Perhaps she'll die.

I know an old woman who swallowed a bird.
My, how absurd to swallow a bird.
She swallowed the bird to catch the spider
That wiggled and jiggled and tickled inside her.
She swallowed the spider to catch the fly.
I don't know why she swallowed the fly.
Perhaps she'll die.

I know an old woman who swallowed a cat.
Imagine that—she swallowed a cat.
She swallowed the cat to catch the bird.
She swallowed the bird to catch the spider
That wiggled and jiggled and tickled inside her.
She swallowed the spider to catch the fly.
I don't know why she swallowed the fly.
Perhaps she'll die.

I know an old woman who swallowed a dog.
Oh, what a hog to swallow a dog.
She swallowed the dog to catch the cat.
She swallowed the cat to catch the bird.
She swallowed the bird to catch the spider
That wiggled and jiggled and tickled inside her.
She swallowed the spider to catch the fly.
I don't know why she swallowed the fly.
Perhaps she'll die.

I know an old woman who swallowed a cow.
I don't know how she swallowed a cow.
She swallowed the cow to catch the dog.
She swallowed the dog to catch the cat.
She swallowed the cat to catch the bird.
She swallowed the bird to catch the spider
That wiggled and jiggled and tickled inside her.
She swallowed the spider to catch the fly.
I don't know why she swallowed the fly.
Perhaps she'll die.

I know an old woman who swallowed a horse.
She died, of course.

Enlarge patterns as needed.

old woman

spider

cow

fly

horse

bird

dog

cat

Use the patterns that follow the story to make sequence cards or to make a flannel-board story.

This Is the House That Jack Built

This is the house that Jack built.

This is the malt
That lay in the house that Jack built.

This is the rat
That ate the malt
That lay in the house that Jack built.

This is the cat
That chased the rat
That ate the malt
That lay in the house that Jack built.

This is the dog
That worried the cat
That chased the rat
That ate the malt
That lay in the house that Jack built.

This is the cow with the crumpled horn
That tossed the dog
That worried the cat
That chased the rat
That ate the malt
That lay in the house that Jack built.

This is the maiden all forlorn
That milked the cow with the crumpled horn
That tossed the dog
That worried the cat
That chased the rat
That ate the malt
That lay in the house that Jack built.

This is the man all tattered and torn
That kissed the maiden all forlorn
That milked the cow with the crumpled horn
That tossed the dog
That worried the cat
That chased the rat
That ate the malt
That lay in the house that Jack built.

This is the priest all shaven and shorn
That married the man all tattered and torn
That kissed the maiden all forlorn
That milked the cow with the crumpled horn
That tossed the dog
That worried the cat
That chased the rat
That ate the malt
That lay in the house that Jack built.

This is the cock that crowed in the morn
That waked the priest all shaven and shorn
That married the man all tattered and torn
That kissed the maiden all forlorn
That milked the cow with the crumpled horn
That tossed the dog
That worried the cat
That chased the rat
That ate the malt
That lay in the house that Jack built.

This is the farmer sowing his corn
That kept the cock that crowed in the morn
That waked the priest all shaven and shorn
That married the man all tattered and torn
That kissed the maiden all forlorn
That milked the cow with the crumpled horn
That tossed the dog
That worried the cat
That chased the rat
That ate the malt
That lay in the house that Jack built.

Enlarge patterns as needed.

Recipes

*Use caution when children are helping with the recipes, especially when sharp utensils, electric appliances and hot pans are a necessary part of the recipe. In addition, check for allergies before serving food, especially nuts, dairy products and fruit.

Playdough, Clay and Other Non-edible Recipes

Bubble Soap

1 teaspoon (5 ml) glycerin
½ cup (125 ml) liquid detergent
½ cup (125 ml) water
measuring cups and spoons
mixing bowl and spoon

Mix glycerin with liquid detergent and water. Gather bubble wands to make bubbles galore!

Face Paint

2 tablespoons (30 grams) cold cream
½ teaspoon (2.5 ml) glycerin
1 teaspoon (5 grams) cornstarch
1 teaspoon (5 grams) dry tempera paint
measuring spoons
mixing bowl and spoon

Stir these ingredients until they are well mixed.

Gak

2 cups (500 ml) glue
1½ cups (375 ml) tap water
2 teaspoons (10 grams) borax
1 cup (250 ml) hot water
food coloring
measuring cups and spoons
small and large mixing bowls
mixing spoons
tray

Combine glue, tap water and food coloring in a bowl. In a larger bowl, dissolve the borax in the hot water. Slowly add the glue mixture. It will thicken quickly and be difficult to mix. Mix well and drain off excess water. Let stand for a few minutes, then pour into a tray. Let dry for ten minutes. Store in resealable plastic bags. It will keep for two to three weeks.

Modeling Goop

2 cups (600 grams) salt
1 cup (250 ml) water
1 cup (150 grams) cornstarch
measuring cups
saucepan
stove or hot plate

Cook salt and ½ cup (125 ml) of water 4–5 minutes. Remove from heat. Add cornstarch and ½ cup (125 ml) water. Return to heat. Stir until mixture thickens. Store in plastic bag or covered container.

Playdough

3 cups (420 grams) flour
1½ cups (450 grams) salt
3 tablespoons (45 ml) oil
2 tablespoons (30grams) cream of tartar
3 cups water (750 ml)
measuring cups and spoons
saucepan
mixing spoon
stove or hot plate

Combine all ingredients. Cook over very low heat until mixture is no longer sticky to the touch.

Variation

Add 1 teaspoon (5 ml) of flavored extract to make fragrant playdough.

Soapsuds Clay

3/4 cup soap powder (Ivory Snow works well)
1 tablespoon (15 ml) warm water
electric mixer
bowl

Mix soap powder and water in bowl. Beat with electric mixer until it has consistency of clay. Mold into shapes.

Edible Recipes

Apple Cider

32 oz. (4 cups or 1 L) apple juice
1 teaspoon (5 grams) cinnamon
1/4 cup (60 ml) lemon juice
2 tablespoons (30 ml) honey
measuring cups and spoons
large saucepan
mixing spoon
stove or hot plate

Mix, heat and serve.

Applesauce

6 apples
1/2 cup (125 ml) water
pinch of cinnamon
1 teaspoon (5 ml) lemon juice
sugar to taste
cutting board and knife
large saucepan
stove or hot plate

Peel, core and cut up apples. Put in large saucepan. Add water, sugar and lemon juice. Cook until tender. Add cinnamon. Press through a colander.

Baggie Ice Cream (one serving)

1/2 cup (125 ml) milk
1 tablespoon (12 grams) sugar
1/4 teaspoon (1 ml) vanilla
small resealable plastic bag
large resealable plastic bag
3 tablespoons rock salt
measuring cups and spoons

Place the milk, sugar and vanilla in a small plastic bag and seal. Fill a large plastic bag with rock salt and ice. Shake. Make one recipe for each child.

Buckaroo Cookies (No-Bake Cookies)

1/2 cup raisins
1/2 cup chopped dates
2 tablespoons (30 ml) honey
graham crackers
mixing bowl and spoon
resealable plastic bag
rolling pin

Pour raisins, dates and honey into mixing bowl. Put several graham crackers in a plastic bag. Crush them with a rolling pin. Add to honey-fruit mixture until the mixture is dry enough to roll into balls.

Donuts

1 can biscuits
4 cups (1 L) oil in deep fryer
shaker of cinnamon and sugar or powdered sugar
knife
tongs

Make a hole in the center of each biscuit. Drop in deep fryer set at 375°F (190°C). Cook two minutes. Remove with tongs and sprinkle with sugar.

Haystacks

small package of butterscotch chips
small package of chocolate chips
package of Chinese noodles
large saucepan
mixing spoon
stove or hot plate

Combine one small package of butterscotch chips and one small package of chocolate chips. Melt over low heat. Add one package of Chinese noodles. When cool enough to touch shape into haystacks. Let set.

Letter Pretzel Cookies

1½ sticks margarine (175 grams), at room temperature
½ cup (175 grams) sugar
1 teaspoon (5 ml) vanilla
1¾ cups (250 grams) enriched all-purpose flour
2 tablespoons (30 ml) milk
measuring cups and spoons
mixing bowl and spoon
oven

Beat margarine and sugar until blended. Add the flour and milk. Chill. Divide dough into four parts. Divide each part into 8 pieces. Roll each piece into an 8" (20 cm) strand. Twist into letter shapes. Bake at 375°F (190°C) for 8-10 minutes.

Lumberjack Pancakes

1¼ cups (175 grams) sifted flour
1½ teaspoons (8 grams) baking powder
2 tablespoons (24 grams) sugar
¾ teaspoon (5 grams) salt
1 egg
1¼ cups (310 ml) milk
3 tablespoons (45 ml) oil
maple syrup
sifter
large and small mixing bowls
mixing spoons
griddle or frying pan
stove or hot plate

Sift flour, baking powder, sugar and salt into the large mixing bowl. In a smaller bowl, beat the egg, then add the milk and oil. Stir liquid into flour mixture until dry ingredients are wet. Cook on griddle or frying pan.

Painted Cookies

2½ cups (350 grams) all purpose flour
1 teaspoon (5 grams) baking soda
1 teaspoon (5 grams) cream of tartar
1 cup (220 grams) margarine
1½ cups (180 grams) sifted powdered sugar
1 egg
¼ teaspoon (1 ml) orange extract
sifter
large mixing bowl and spoon (or electric mixer)
cookie sheet

Sift dry ingredients together. Cream margarine and sugar in large mixing bowl. Stir in egg and extract. Blend in dry ingredients. Cover and chill 2–3 hours. Divide in half. On a lightly floured board, roll to ¼" (6 mm) thickness. Cut into shapes. Place on ungreased cookie sheet. Decorate with Cookie Paint. Bake at 375°F (190°C) for 8–10 minutes. Makes about three dozen.

Cookie Paint

Place small amounts of evaporated milk into separate custard cups. Tint with food coloring. Paint on cookies with small brush.

Peanut Butter

1½ tablespoons (23 ml) vegetable oil
1 cup roasted peanuts
½ teaspoon (3 grams) salt
blender

Mix in electric blender. Blend to desired smoothness.

Peanut Butter Balls or Playdough

½ cup (125 ml) peanut butter
½ cup (125 ml) honey
1 cup (75 grams) nonfat powdered milk
measuring cups
mixing bowl and spoon
refrigerator

Mix well. Squeeze and pull until shiny and soft. Roll into balls and chill to set. Yummy!

Pudding

1 package instant pudding
2 cups (500 ml) milk
1 large plastic jar with lid
measuring cups

Mix pudding and milk together in the large jar. Shake, shake, shake. Pour into dishes and serve.

Sunshine Sandwich

¼ cup (60 ml) undiluted frozen orange juice
½ cup (125 ml) peanut butter
8 slices bread
measuring cups
mixing bowl and spoon
toaster
knife

Mix orange juice and peanut butter. Spread on toasted bread. Cut into small pieces.

Trail Mix

½ cup (120 grams) margarine
1 envelope salad dressing mix
2 cups bite-size shredded wheat
2 cups Rice Chex
1 cup pretzel sticks
2 cups salted peanuts
measuring cups
saucepan
mixing spoon
large baking pan
oven

Melt margarine in a saucepan. Pour in dressing mix. Mix well. Measure the dry ingredients into a large baking pan. Pour margarine mixture over the dry ingredients in the baking pan. Stir with fork until all is coated. Bake at 300°F (150°C) for 30 minutes. Stir every 10 minutes.

Gelatin Wobblers

4 oz. (110 grams) package of gelatin
1½ (375 ml) cups boiling water
stove or hot plate
mixing bowl and spoon
molds
refrigerator

Dissolve gelatin in boiling water. Pour into lightly oiled molds and refrigerate for 3 hours.

Songs, Chants and Fingerplays

Are You Sleeping?

Are you sleeping, are you sleeping?
Brother John? Brother John?
Morning bells are ringing.
Morning bells are ringing.
Ding, ding, dong.
Ding, ding, dong.

The Calliope Song

(Divide children into four groups to make a human carousel. Group One says, "Oom-pah-pah," as they bend and then straighten their knees. Group Two says, "Oomp-tweedle-dee-dee," as they raise up on their tip-toes and back down. Group Three says, "Oom-Shh-Shh," as they rock back and forth. Group Four hums as they sway side to side.)

Doodle-li-do

(Perform these movements in rhythm with the music. Clap thighs twice. Clap hands twice. Cross hands in front of you four times (left hand on top twice, then right hand on top twice). Touch nose, then right shoulder with left hand. Touch nose, then left shoulder with right hand. Move hands in "talking" motion just above shoulders, then above head. Repeat throughout the song.)

Please sing to me that sweet melody
Called Doodle-li-do, Doodle-li-do.
I like the rest, but the one I like best
Goes Doodle-li-do, Doodle-li-do.
It's the simplest thing, there isn't much to it.
All you gotta do is Doodle-li-do it.
I like it so that wherever I go
It's the Doodle-li, Doodle-li-do.

Come on and Waddle-li-atcha, Waddle-li-atcha,
Waddle-li-o, Waddle-li-o.
Waddle-li-atcha, Waddle-li-atcha
Waddle-li-o, Waddle-li-o.

It's the simplest thing, there isn't much to it.
All you gotta do is Doodle-li-do it.
I like it so that wherever I go
It's the Doodle-li-Doodle-li-do.

Five in the Bed

There were five in the bed, *(hold up five fingers)*
And the little one said,
"Roll over! Roll over!"
So they all rolled over and one fell out.

There were four in the bed. . .
There were three in the bed. . .
There were two in the bed. . .
There was one in the bed,
And the little one said,
"GOOD NIGHT!"

Five Little Monkeys

Five little monkeys, jumping on the bed. *(hold up five fingers)*
One fell off and bumped her head. *(rub head)*
Mamma called the doctor and the doctor said, *(pretend to make telephone call)*
"No more monkeys jumping on the bed!" *(scolding motion)*

Four little monkeys. . .
Three little monkeys. . .
Two little monkeys. . .
One little monkey. . .

Five Little Monkeys (Teasing Mr. Crocodile)

Five little monkeys sitting in a tree, *(hold up five fingers)*
Teasing Mr. Crocodile.
"You can't catch me! You can't catch me!"
Along came Mr. Crocodile, quiet as can be.
Snap! *(put elbows together and clap hands together, making the motion of a crocodile's jaws snapping shut)*

Four little monkeys. . .
Three little monkeys. . .
Two little monkeys. . .
One little monkey. . .

Gobble, Gobble, Gobble

Gobble, gobble, gobble
Quack, quack, quack.
A turkey says gobble,
And a duck says quack.

Good Morning to You

Good morning to you.
Good morning to you.
We're all in our places
With bright, shiny faces.
Oh, this is the way
To start a great day.

Grandfather's Clock

My grandfather's clock was too large for the shelf,
So it stood ninety years on the floor.
It was taller by half than the old man himself,
Tho' it weighed not a penny weight more.
It was bought on the morn of the day that he was born
And was always his treasure and pride.
But it stopped short, never to go again
When the old man died.

Ninety years without slumbering,
Tick, tock, tick, tock.
His life seconds numbering,
Tick, tock, tick, tock.
But it stopped short, never to go again
When the old man died.

In watching its pendulum swing to and fro,
Many hours he had spent as a boy.
And in childhood and manhood
the clock seemed to know
And to share both his grief and his joy.
For it struck twenty-four as he entered at the door
With a blooming and beautiful bride.
But it stopped short, never to go again
When the old man died.

Ninety years without slumbering
Tick, tock, tick, tock...

Now my grandfather said that of those he could hire,
Not a servant so faithful he found.
It wasted no time and it had but one desire,
At the end of each week to be wound.
And it stayed in its place, not a frown upon its face
And its hands never hung by its side.
But it stopped short, never to go again
When the old man died.

Ninety years without slumbering,
Tick, tock, tick, tock...

It rang an alarm in the dead of the night,
An alarm that for years had been dumb.
And we knew that his spirit was pluming its flight,
That his hour of departure had come.
Still the clock kept the time, with a soft and muffled chime,
As we silently stood by his side.
But it stopped short, never to go again
When the old man died.

Going on a Bear Hunt

We're going on a bear hunt.
Want to come along?
Well, come on then.
Let's go! *(walk in place)*
Look! There's a river.
Can't go over it.
Can't go under it.
Can't go around it.
We'll have to go through it. *(pretend to walk into river, swim through the water and walk up other bank; then resume walking in place)*
Look! There's a tree.
Can't go under it.
Can't go through it.
We'll have to go over it. *(pretend to climb up and over tree; then resume walking in place)*
Look! There's a wheat field.
Can't go over it.
Can't go under it.
Can't go around it.
We'll have to go through it. *(pretend to walk through field, make swishing sounds with hands against thighs, and then resume walking in place)*

(Add verses with actions to make the story as long as you like.)
Look! There's a cave.
Want to go inside?
Ooh, it's dark in here. *(look around, squinting)*
I see two eyes.
Wonder what it is. *(reach hands to touch)*
It's soft and furry.
It's big.
It's a bear! Let's run! *(retrace steps, running in place, through wheat field, in place, over tree, in place, across river, in place, then stop)*
Home safe.
Whew!

Hear the Lively Song

Hear the lively song
Of the frog in yonder pond.
Crick-crick-crickety-crick-barrump!

Hello! My Name Is Joe!

Hello! My name is Joe!
I have a wife, one kid and I work in a button factory.
One day, my boss said, "Are you busy?"
I said, "No."
"Then turn a button with your right hand." *(make turning gesture with right hand)*

Hello! My name is Joe!
I have a wife, two kids and I work in a button factory.
One day, my boss said, "Are you busy?"
I said, "No."
"Then turn a button with your left hand." *(make turning gesture with left hand as you continue with the right hand)*

(Continue adding number of children and adding right and left feet and head.)

Hello! My name is Joe!
I have a wife, six kids and I work in a button factory.
One day, my boss said, "Are you busy?"
I said, "Yes!"

The Hokey Pokey

(form a circle and act out the words)
You put your right foot in,
You put your right foot out,
You put your right foot in,
And you shake it all about.
You do the Hokey Pokey *(hold hands in the air and shake them)*
And you turn yourself around.
That's what it's all about.
Hey!

(Repeat, using other body parts.)

I Had a Loose Tooth

I had a loose tooth
A wiggly, jiggly loose tooth.
I had a loose tooth
Hanging by a thread.

I pulled my loose tooth,
My wiggly, jiggly loose tooth.
Now I have a dollar
And a hole in my head.

I'm a Little Teapot

I'm a little teapot, short and stout.
Here is my handle, *(put one hand on hip with elbow out to the side to make handle)*
Here is my spout. *(put other arm up with elbow bent and hand facing out to the side to make spout)*
When I get all steamed up hear me shout.
Just tip me over and pour me out. *(tip over to spout side)*

If You're Happy and You Know It

(act out motions that words indicate)
If you're happy and you know it,
Clap your hands.
If you're happy and you know it,
Clap your hands.
If you're happy and you know it,
Then your face will surely show it.
If you're happy and you know it,

Clap your hands.
If you're happy and you know it,
Stomp your feet…
Pat your head…
Say hello…
(create as many verses as you like)

It's Raining, It's Pouring

It's raining, it's pouring,
The old man is snoring.
He went to bed with a pain in his head
And didn't get up until morning.

The Itsy, Bitsy Spider

The itsy, bitsy spider climbed up the water spout. *(put the tip of the forefinger of each hand to the tip of the thumb of the other hand, creating an oblong diamond; then release the forefinger and thumb that are on the bottom and swing them up to the top of the diamond. Do this repeatedly.)*
Down came the rain and washed the spider out. *(wiggle fingers while streaming down)*
Out came the sun and dried up all the rain. *(create the arch of the sun with hands)*
And the itsy, bitsy spider climbed up the spout again. *(repeat first movement with forefingers and thumbs)*

I've Been Working on the Railroad

I've been workin' on the railroad all the livelong day.
I've been workin' on the railroad just to pass the time away.
Can't you hear the whistle blowing? Rise up so early in the morn.
Can't you hear the captain shouting, "Dinah, blow your horn!"

Dinah, won't you blow?
Dinah, won't you blow?
Dinah, won't you blow your horn?
(Repeat)

Someone's in the kitchen with Dinah.
Someone's in the kitchen, I know.
Someone's in the kitchen with Dinah,
Strummin' on the old banjo.

And singing, fee fie fiddle-y I O
Fee fie fiddle-y I O O O O
Fee fie fiddle-y I O
Strummin' on the old banjo.

Johnny Appleseed Song

Oh, the Lord is good to me.
And so I thank the Lord
For giving me the things I need,
The sun, and the rain, and the appleseed.
The Lord is good to me.

Johnny Works With One Hammer

Johnny works with one hammer, *(make hammering motion with right hand)*
One hammer, one hammer.
Johnny works with one hammer,
Then he works with two.

Johnny works with two hammers . . . *(make hammering motion with left and right hands)*

Johnny works with three hammers . . . *(motion with both hands and right foot)*

Johnny works with four hammers . . . *(motion with both hands and both feet)*

Johnny works with five hammers . . . *(motion with both hands and feet and with head)*
Then he goes to bed.

(There is another variation of this song that uses the name "Peter" instead of "Johnny" and ends each verse with the words, "all day long."

Little Boy Blue

Little Boy Blue, come blow your horn.
The sheep are in the meadow, the cow's in the corn.
But where is the boy who looks after the sheep?
He's under a haystack, fast asleep.

Mary Had a Little Lamb

Mary had a little lamb,
Little lamb, little lamb,
Mary had a little lamb,
Its fleece was white as snow.

And everywhere that Mary went,
Mary went, Mary went,
Everywhere that Mary went,
The lamb was sure to go.

It followed her to school one day,
School one day, school one day,
It followed her to school one day,
Which was against the rules.

It made the children laugh and play,
Laugh and play, laugh and play,
It made the children laugh and play,
To see a lamb at school.

And so the teacher turned it out,
Turned it out, turned it out,
And so the teacher turned it out,
But still it lingered near.

It waited patiently about,
Ly about, ly about,
It waited patiently about,
Till Mary did appear.

"What makes the lamb love Mary so,
Mary so, Mary so,
What makes the lamb love Mary so?"
the eager children cried.

"Why, Mary loves the lamb, you know,"
Lamb you know, lamb you know,
Why, Mary loves the lamb, you know,"
The teacher did reply.

Miss Mary Mack

Miss Mary Mack, Mack, Mack
All dressed in black, black, black,
With silver buttons, buttons, buttons
All down her back, back, back.
She asked her mother, mother, mother
For fifteen cents, cents, cents
To see the elephants, elephants, elephants
Jump over the fence, fence, fence.
They jumped so high, high, high,
They touched the sky, sky, sky,
And they didn't come back, back, back
'Til the Fourth of July, ly, ly
And they never came down, down, down,
'Til the Fourth of July.

The More We Get Together

The more we get together, together, together,
The more we get together, the happier we'll be.
For your friends are my friends,
And my friends are your friends.
The more we get together, the happier we'll be.

Mr. Sun

Oh Mr. Sun, Sun, Mr. Golden Sun,
Please shine down on me.
Oh Mr. Sun, Sun, Mr. Golden Sun,
Hiding behind a tree,
These little children are asking you
To please come out so we can play with you.
Oh Mr. Sun, Sun, Mr. Golden Sun,
Please shine down on me!

The Muffin Man

Oh, do you know the muffin man,
The muffin man, the muffin man?
Oh, do you know the muffin man
Who lives on Drury Lane?

Oh, yes, we know the muffin man,
The muffin man, the muffin man.
Oh, yes, we know the muffin man
Who lives on Drury Lane.

The Mulberry Bush

Here we go round the mulberry bush, *(hold hands and walk in circle)*
The mulberry bush, the mulberry bush.
Here we go round the mulberry bush,
So early in the morning.

(act out motions)
This is the way we wash our clothes,
Wash our clothes, wash our clothes.
This is the way we wash our clothes,
So early Monday morning.

This is the way we iron our clothes. . .Tuesday morning.
This is the way we scrub the floors. . .Wednesday morning.
This is the way we mend our clothes. . .Thursday morning.
This is the way we sweep the house. . .Friday morning.
This is the way we bake our bread. . .Saturday morning.
This is the way we go to church. . . Sunday morning.

The North Wind Doth Blow

The north wind doth blow
And we shall have some snow.
And what will the robin do then, poor thing?
He will sit in the barn and keep himself warm,
With his little head tucked under his wing, poor thing!

Old MacDonald Had a Farm

Old MacDonald had a farm. E-I-E-I-O.
And on that farm, he had some chicks. E-I-E-I-O.
With a chick, chick here,
And a chick, chick there.
Here a chick,
There a chick,
Everywhere a chick, chick.
Old MacDonald had a farm. E-I-E-I-O.

Other verses:
Ducks—quack
Horses—neigh
Cows—moo
Pigs—oink
Donkeys—heehaw

One Elephant

(Children sit in a circle. One child places one arm out in front of herself to make a trunk, then walks around the circle while the group sings the song. When the group sings "called for another elephant to come," the first child chooses another child to join her and become an "elephant." The first "elephant" extends her other hand between her legs to make a tail. The second "elephant" extends one arm out in front to make a trunk and grabs hold of the first "elephant's" tail. The two walk trunk to tail as the song continues and more elephants join.)

One elephant went out to play.
Out on a spider's web one day.
He had such enormous fun,
He called for another elephant to come.

Open, Shut Them

(hands perform the motions described)
Open, shut them.
Open, shut them.
Give a little clap.

Open, shut them.
Open, shut them.
Put them in your lap.

Walk them, walk them, *(walk fingers up chest to chin)*
Walk them, walk them.
Way up to your chin.

Walk them, walk them, *(walk fingers around face, but not into mouth)*
Walk them, walk them,
But don't let them walk in.

Punchinello

Here Comes Punchinello, Punchinello. *(children walk in a circle)*
Here comes Punchinello, funny you.

What can you do Punchinello, Punchinello? *(child in the center of the circle initiates a movement)*
What can you do, Punchinello, funny you?

We can do it, too, Punchinello, Punchinello. (children in
    the circle copy the movement)
We can do it, too, Punchinello, funny you.

Who do you choose, Punchinello, Punchinello? (child in
    the center chooses another child to take his place)
Who do you choose, Punchinello, funny you?

The Raindrop Song

If all of the raindrops (wiggle fingers in the air)
were lemon drops and gum drops (tap one index finger
    against palm of other hand)
Oh, what a rain it would be. (wiggle fingers in the air)
I'd stand outside with my mouth open wide.
Ah-ah-ah-ah-ah-ah-ah-ah-ah! (stand, looking up with
    mouth open)

If all of the snowflakes (wiggle fingers in the air)
Were candy bars and milkshakes, (make biting and sip-
    ping motions)
Oh, what a snow it would be. (wiggle fingers in the air)
I'd stand outside with my mouth open wide.
Ah-ah-ah-ah-ah-ah-ah-ah. (stand, looking up with mouth
    open)

Rain on the Green Grass

Rain on the green grass
And rain on the tree.
Rain on the housetop
But not on me.

Rain, Rain, Go Away

Rain, rain, go away.
Come again another day.

Rain, rain, go away.
Little Johnny wants to play.

She'll Be Comin' Round the Mountain

She'll be comin' round the mountain when she comes,
Toot, toot! (make motion as if pulling a train's whistle)
She'll be comin' round the mountain when she comes,
Toot, toot! (make motion as if pulling a train's whistle)
She'll be comin' round the mountain,
She'll be comin' round the mountain,
She'll be comin' round the mountain, when she comes,
Toot, toot! (make motion as if pulling a train's whistle)

She'll be ridin' six white horses, when she comes,
Whoa back!… (make motion as if pulling back the
    horses' reins)

She'll be wearin' pink pajamas, when she comes,
Scratch, scratch!… (scratch)

O, we'll all go out to meet her, when she comes,
"Hi, babe!"… (wave "hello")

O, we'll kill the old, red rooster when she comes,
Hack, hack!… (make motion as if hacking with a knife)

O, we'll all have chicken and dumplings, when she
    comes,
Yum, yum!… (rub stomach in contentment)

O, she'll have to sleep with grandpa, when she comes,
Snore, snore!… (put palms of hands together and lay
    head on back of hands as if sleeping)

Shoo, Fly, Don't Bother Me

Shoo, fly, don't bother me.
Shoo, fly, don't bother me.
Shoo, fly, don't bother me,
For I belong to somebody.

I feel, I feel, I feel like a morning star.
I feel, I feel, I feel like a morning star.
I feel, I feel, I feel like a morning star.
I feel, I feel, I feel like a morning star.

Shoo, fly, don't bother me.
Shoo, fly, don't bother me.
Shoo, fly, don't bother me,
For I belong to somebody.

Skip to My Lou

Lost my partner, what'll I do?
Lost my partner, what'll I do?
Lost my partner, what'll I do?
Skip to my Lou, my darling.
Lou, Lou, skip to my Lou,
Lou, Lou, skip to my Lou,
Lou, Lou, skip to my Lou,
Skip to my Lou, my darling.

I'll get another one prettier than you…
Little red wagon painted blue…
Flies in the buttermilk, two by two…
Cow's in the barnyard, moo, moo, moo…
Flies in the sugar, shoo, fly, shoo!…
Going to Texas, two by two…
Cat's in the cream jar, what'll I do?…

The Smoky Bear Song

by Steve Nelson and Jack Rollins, reprinted with permission from United States Department of Agriculture, Forest Service.

With a ranger's hat and shovel and a pair of dungarees,
You will find him in the forest always sniffin' at the breeze.
People stop and pay attention when he tells them to beware,
'Cause everybody knows that he's the Fire Prevention Bear.

Chorus
Smokey the Bear, Smokey the Bear.
Prowlin' and a growlin' and a sniffin' the air.
He can find a fire before it starts to flame.
That's why they call him Smokey, that was how he got his name.

You can take a tip from Smokey that there's nothin' like a tree,
'Cause they're good for kids to climb in and they're beautiful to see.
You just have to look around you and you'll find it's not a joke,
To see what you'd be missing if they all went up in smoke.

You can camp upon his doorstep and he'll make you feel at home
You can run and hunt and ramble anywhere you care to roam.
He will let you take his honey and pretend he's not so smart,
But don't you harm his trees for he's a Ranger in his heart.

If you've ever seen the forest when a fire is running wild,
And you love the things within it like a mother loves her child,
Then you know why Smokey tells you when he sees you passing through,
"Remember, please, be careful. It's the least that you can do."

Teddy Bear, Teddy Bear Turn Around

Teddy Bear, Teddy Bear, turn around.
Teddy Bear, Teddy Bear, touch the ground.
Teddy Bear, Teddy Bear, read the news.
Teddy Bear, Teddy Bear, shine your shoes.
Teddy Bear, Teddy Bear, go upstairs.
Teddy Bear, Teddy Bear, say your prayers.
Teddy Bear, Teddy Bear, turn out the light.
Teddy Bear, Teddy Bear, say GOOD NIGHT!

This Is a Snowman

This is a snowman as round as a ball.
He has two large eyes, but he's not very tall.
If the sun shines down on him today,
My jolly snowman will melt away.

This Little Piggy

This little piggy went to market,
This little piggy stayed home,
This little piggy had roast beef,
This little piggy had none.
And this little piggy cried,
"Wee, wee, wee, wee," all the way home.

This Old Man

This old man, he played one,
He played knick-knack on my thumb.
With a knick-knack paddy-whack, give your dog a bone.
This old man came rolling home.

This old man, he played two,
He played knick-knack on my shoe…
Three–on my knee
Four–on my door
Five–on my hive
Six–on my sticks
Seven–up in heaven
Eight–on my gate
Nine–on my spine
Ten–once again

Three Bears Rap

Shh, shh, shh, shh, shh, shh, shh, shh, shh, shh.
Out in the forest in a wee little cottage lived the three
    bears.
Shh, shh, shh, shh, shh, shh, shh, shh, shh, shh.
One was the Mama Bear, one was the Papa Bear and
    one was the wee bear.
Shh, shh, shh, shh, shh, shh, shh, shh, shh, shh.

Out of the forest came a walking, stalking, pretty little
    Goldilocks
and upon the door she was a-knockin'.
Clack, clack, clack.
But no one was there, unh-unh, no one was there.
So she walked right in and had herself a bowl.
She didn't care, unh-unh, she didn't care.

Home, home, home came the three bears.

"Someone's been eating my porridge," said the Mama
    Bear.
"Someone's been eating my porridge," said the Papa
    Bear.
"Baa-baa Barebear," said the little Wee Bear.
"Someone's broken my chair."
Crash!

Just then Goldilocks woke up.
She broke up the party and she beat it out of there.

"Good-bye, good-bye, good-bye," said the Mama Bear.
"Good-bye, good-bye, good-bye," said the Papa Bear.
"Baa-baa Barebear," said the little Wee Bear.
That's the story of the three little bears! Yeah!

Twinkle, Twinkle, Little Star

Twinkle, twinkle, little star,
How I wonder what you are.
Up above the world so high,
Like a diamond in the sky.
Twinkle, twinkle, little star,
How I wonder what you are.

Two Little Ducks

Two little ducks that I once knew,
Fat ones, skinny ones, there were too,
But the one little duck with the feathers on his back,
He led the others with a quack, quack, quack.

Down to the river they would go,
Wibble, wobble, wibble, wobble, to and fro.
But the one little duck with the feathers on his back,
He led the others with a quack, quack, quack.
He led the others with a quack, quack, quack.

Wee Willie Winkie

Wee Willie Winkie runs through the town,
Upstairs and downstairs in his nightgown.
Rapping at the window, crying through the lock,
"Are the children in their beds?
For it's past eight o'clock!"

Where Is Thumbkin?

Where is thumbkin? *(hands behind back)*
Where is thumbkin?
Here I am. Here I am. *(bring out right thumb, then left)*
How are you today, sir? *(bend right thumb)*
Very well, I thank you. *(bend left thumb)*
Run away. *(put right thumb behind back)*
Run away. *(put left thumb behind back)*

Other verses:
(use similar motions, changing fingers as the words
   indicate)
Where is pointer?
Where is middle one?
Where is ring finger?
Where is pinky?
Where are all of them?

Where, Oh, Where Has My Little Dog Gone

Where, oh, where has my little dog gone?
Oh, where, oh where can he be?
With his tail cut short and his ears cut long,
Oh, where, oh, where can he be?

Who Stole the Cookie From the Cookie Jar?

Who stole the cookie from the cookie jar?
(Name) stole the cookie from the cookie jar.
Who, me?
Yes, you.
Couldn't be.
Then who?
(Different child, chosen by the first child accused) stole
   the cookie from the cookie jar.
Who, me?
Yes, you.
Couldn't be.
Then who?

(Say this chant as you pat your thighs and snap in a
   rhythmic motion. Continue until everyone has been
   "accused" at least once.)

Games

Drop the Handkerchief

Choose one child to be "it" while the other children sit in a circle facing the center. The child who is "it" skips or walks around the outside of the circle and casually drops the handkerchief behind one of the children sitting in the circle. This child picks up the handkerchief and chases the first child around the circle. The first child tries to run around the circle and sit in the second child's spot without being tagged. If he is not tagged, then he sits in his new spot in the circle and the child with the handkerchief is now "it." If the first child is tagged, then he is "it" for another round.

The Farmer in the Dell

The children all stand in a circle facing the center, except for one child who stands in the middle and is the "farmer." The children in the circle join hands and walk or skip in a circle around the farmer while singing the song below. The "farmer" chooses a "wife" from the children in the circle to join him in the middle; the "wife" chooses a "child," etc. The child chosen to be the "cheese" stands alone (the "farmer," his "wife," etc. all rejoin the circle) and becomes the "farmer" in the next round of "The Farmer in the Dell."

The farmer in the dell,
The farmer in the dell,
High-ho the derry-o,
The farmer in the dell.

The farmer takes a wife…
The wife takes a child…
The child takes a nurse…
The nurse takes a dog…
The dog takes a cat…
The cat takes a rat…
The rat takes the cheese…
The cheese stands alone…

Duck, Duck, Goose

For this game everyone but one child who is "it" sits in a circle facing the center. The child who is "it" walks around the outside of the circle, tapping each child's head as she passes; every time she taps a head she says "duck." (She can say "duck" as few or as many times as she wants.) When she taps a child's head and says "goose," the goose has to get up and chase her around the circle. The first child tries to run around the circle and sit in the goose's spot without being tagged. If she is tagged, then she has to sit in the "stew pot" in the center of the circle until another comes to replace her. If she is not tagged, she joins the circle in the goose's empty space. In both cases, the child who was chasing becomes the new one to walk around the circle tapping heads and saying, "duck, duck, goose!"

Flying Statues (see Statues)

Freeze Tag

One child is chosen to be "it." He chases the other children trying to tag them. When he tags a child, she must freeze. She may run again when another child touches her to unfreeze her. The object of the game is for the child who is "it" to freeze all of the other players. Then the player who was frozen first is "it" in the next game of "Freeze Tag."

Fruit Basket Turnover

One child is chosen to be "it." He stands in the middle of a circle of children who are each standing on a carpet square. "It" calls out "Fruit Basket Turnover." All the children run to another carpet square. The child who is not standing on a carpet square becomes "it."

Giant Steps (see Mother, May I?)

Go Fish

Two or more players can play this card game. The object is to get as many pairs of cards as possible. Deal seven cards to each player and spread out the rest of the cards in a stack in the middle of the table. The players all look at their cards and if they have any pairs (e.g., two 7's, two Jacks, two Aces, etc.), they lay them down on the table face up. The person to the dealer's right goes first. She asks any player she chooses if he has a card she needs to make a pair. (Note: She may only ask for a card if she is already holding one with the same number on it in her hand; for example, if Susan has a 3 in her hand she may ask, "Jose, do you have any 3's?") If the player asked has the card he must give it to the player who asked for it. If he does not have the card, then he says, "Go fish," and the player who asked must draw a card from the pile on the table. If the player gets the card she asked for, either from the other player or from the pile, then she lays the pair of cards face up on the table and her turn continues. If the card she picks up from the pile is not the card she asked for but makes a pair with another card in her hand, she may lay the pair face up on the table, but her turn is over. If she does not get the card she asked for, she adds the card to the ones in her hand and her turn is over. Then the person to her right gets to go. If a player runs out of cards before the pile is gone, he may pick up a card when it is his turn and ask a player if she has a card to pair with it. The game is over when all of the cards in the pile are gone. Then the players each count the numbers of pairs of cards they have placed face up on the table. The player with the most pairs wins.

Hot and Cold

Two or more children can play this game. All of the children who are not "it" must leave the room. The child who is "it" hides a small object somewhere in the room. This object, such as a button or an acorn, must be seen by everyone before they leave the room. When everyone returns to the room they begin to hunt for the object. The child who is "it" gives hints as to the object's hiding place by saying, "hot," "cold" and "warm." If no one is near the object he says, "cold"; if someone gets closer he says, "warmer"; and if someone is very close, he says "hot!" The child who finds the object is the one to hide it in the next game of "Hot and Cold."

Hot Potato

The children stand in a circle and, while music is played, they pass a "hot potato" (a ball or a beanbag) around the circle as quickly as they can without dropping it. When the music stops, the child holding the potato must sit down. The last child holding the potato wins.

I Spy

One child is chosen to be "it." This child chooses something in the room and says, "I spy with my little eye something that is...(give a characteristic of the object chosen, e.g., "something that is round or red or smooth or hot"). The other children raise their hands and when chosen guess at different objects. When the object is guessed correctly, the first child sits down and the child who guessed correctly becomes the next one to "spy with his little eye..." and choose the object.

In and Out the Windows

This game must have at least seven players. All but one of the children stand in a circle facing the center, holding hands and raising them high to create arched "windows." One child is chosen to be the "dancer," and she stands in the middle. As the song indicates, on the first verse, the "dancer" skips around the circle going in and out of the windows. On the second verse, she stands and faces a child in the circle. On the third verse, she follows her new partner in and out of the windows. And on the final verse they go to the center of the circle together and curtsey/bow to each other. The child who was chosen to be the partner then becomes the next one to go "In and Out the Windows."

In and out the windows,
In and out the windows,
In and out the windows,
As we have done before.

Stand and face your partner...
Now follow her/him to London...
Bow before you leave her/him...

Leap Frog

As few as two children can play this game. One child crouches down on the ground like a frog *(knees bent and hands on the ground between and a little in front of his feet)*. The next child crouches down as well and then leaps and puts her legs on either side of the first child and her hands on the first child's back. Then she leaps onto the ground in front of the first child. The first child is now behind the second child and he leaps over her in the same way. If you are playing with many children, they can line up so that one child can leap over several "frogs" in one turn, landing on the ground between each frog.

Mother, May I?

Choose one child to be "Mother." The other children line up side by side about 30 feet (9 meters) away from and facing Mother. Mother chooses an individual child and gives her an order *(e.g., "Susan, you may take three little hops forward.")*. Before following the order, the child must say, "Mother, may I..." and repeat the order she was given *(e.g., "Mother, may I take three little hops forward?")*. If she does not say, "Mother, May I..." and carries out the order anyway, then she may not move forward and must stay where she is. But if she does ask, "Mother, may I...," then Mother either says, "Yes" or "No." If Mother says "Yes," then the child may carry out the order; if Mother says "No," and nothing more, then the child must stay where she is. However, if the child playing Mother says "No, but you may..." and gives another order, then the child given the order must remember to say, "Mother, may I..." again before carrying out this new order. If she forgets, she will have to go back to the beginning. The first one to reach Mother wins and plays Mother in the next game of "Mother, May I?".

One Elephant

Children sit in a circle. One child places one arm out in front of herself to make a trunk, then walks around the circle while the group sings the song. When the group sings "called for another elephant to come," the first child chooses another to join her and become an "elephant." The first "elephant" extends her other hand between her legs to make a tail. The second "elephant" extends one arm out in front to make a trunk and grabs hold of the first "elephant's" tail. The two walk trunk to tail as the song continues and more elephants join.

One elephant went out to play.
Out on a spider's web one day.
He had such enormous fun,
He called for another elephant to come.

Red Light! Green Light!

Choose one child to be the "stoplight." The other children line up side by side about 30 feet (9 meters) away from and facing the stoplight. When the child playing the stoplight turns his back to the other children he says, "Green light!" and the children may run toward him. When he turns back around and says, "Red light!" all of the children must stop. If the child playing the traffic light sees any of the other children move after he has said "Red light!" then he says the child's name and she must go back to the beginning. The first child to reach the stoplight is the stoplight in the next game of "Red Light! Green Light!"

Simon Says

Choose one child to be "Simon." All the other children stand side by side in a line facing Simon. The child playing Simon gives the other children orders that they have to carry out, but only when the orders follow the phrase "Simon says..." *(e.g., "Simon says touch your nose")*. If a child follows an order that Simon did not say *(e.g., "Touch your nose")*, then he is out and must sit down. The last child standing becomes the new Simon for the next game of "Simon Says."

Statues

Everyone dances around the room to music. When the music stops, everyone must freeze and hold that position, usually becoming a very funny looking "statue." If a child moves, he must sit down. When the music starts again, those who are still standing start to dance again. The last one standing wins. *(In another variation of this game, a dancer must become a "statue" when she is tapped on the head by the leader, usually an adult; she may start to dance again when she is tapped on the head again. The music does not stop in this version.)*

Telephone

Have the children sit in a circle facing the center. One child is chosen to "start the telephone conversation." This child thinks of a word or short phrase and whispers it in the ear of the child next to him. The second child whispers what she heard in the ear of the child next to her. And so the word or phrase continues around the circle. If a child was not able to hear what was whispered in his hear, he may say "operator" and the word can be whispered in his ear again. *(Note: a child may only say "operator" if he has not been able to hear the whispered word, not if he did not understand the whispered word. Not understanding the words is half the fun of the game!)* When the word is finally whispered in the ear of the last child in the circle, she then announces the word out loud. Then the child who "started the telephone conversation" repeats the original phrase so all can compare and see how it changed. Choose a new child to "start the telephone conversation" and play again.

Concentration Games

The concentration game patterns on the following pages can be used in a variety of ways.

Concentration Games

Make two copies. Color, cut and laminate. Encourage the children to place all the cards face down, then turn them over two at a time to find matching pairs.

Matching Games

Make two copies. Color, cut and laminate. Invite the children to sort the cards into matching pairs.

Make two copies. Color, cut and laminate. Punch a hole in the top of each card, tie on a piece of yarn and hang from a clothes hanger. Provide clothespins for the children to clip on to matching cards.

Bowling Games

Make enlarged copies of desired cards. Color and cut out. Attach to potato chip cans such as Pringles and set up like bowling pins. Provide soft balls such as Nerf balls or rubber balls for bowling.

Puzzles

Make enlarged copies of desired cards. Color and mount on poster board. Cut into pieces for the children to put together.

Happy Face

Sad Face

Mad Face

Scared Face

Surprised Face

Bored Face

Firefighter

Doctor

Police Officer

Office Worker

Baker

Barber

cloudy

Sunny

Snow

Rain

Windy

Tornado

Cow

Pig

Chicken

Duck

Horse

Sheep

Farm House

Barn

Haystack

Tractor

Field

Farmer

Mushroom

Tree

Stream

Fungi

Moss

Flowers

Diplodocus

Stegosaurus

Parasaurolphus

Dimetrodon

Triceratops

Pteranodon

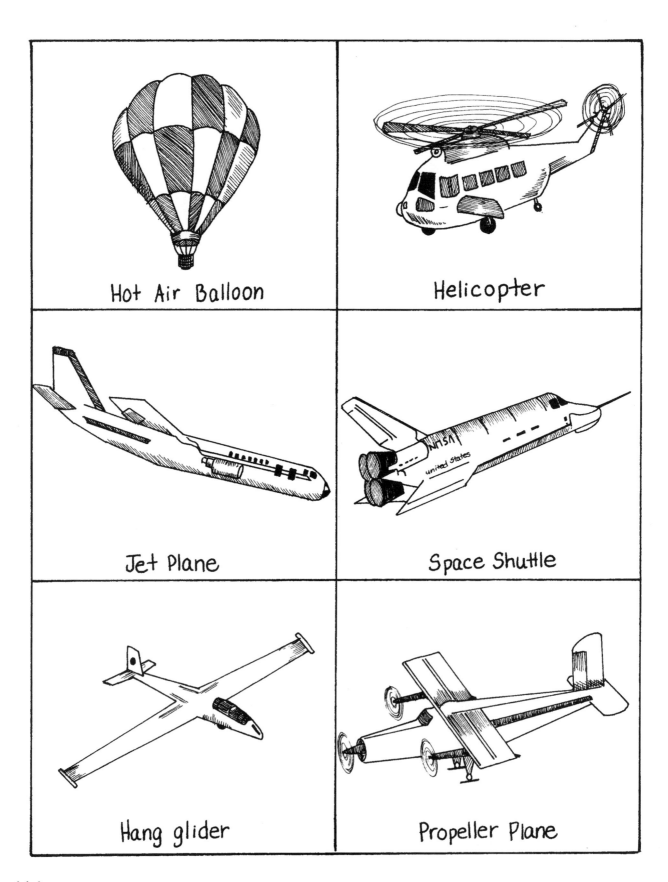

Hot Air Balloon

Helicopter

Jet Plane

Space Shuttle

Hang glider

Propeller Plane

Owl

Raccoon

Cat

Bat

Opossum

Mouse

Easel

Paintbrush

Palette

Sculpting Knife

Watercolors

Paint Jar

Fish

Crab

Octopus

Whale

Dolphin

Sea Horse

Body Parts Concentration

Write the name of each body part on an index card to make your drawing/calling cards. Provide buttons for children to cover the body parts you call out.

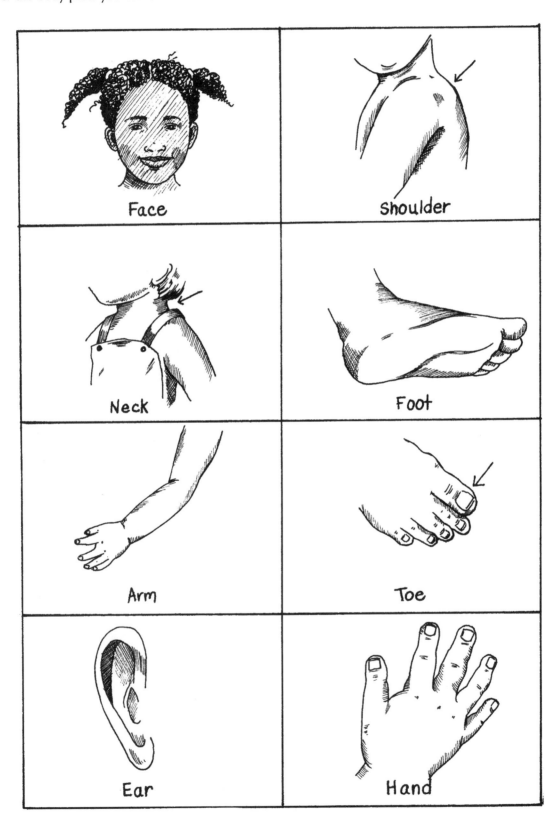

Face

Shoulder

Neck

Foot

Arm

Toe

Ear

Hand

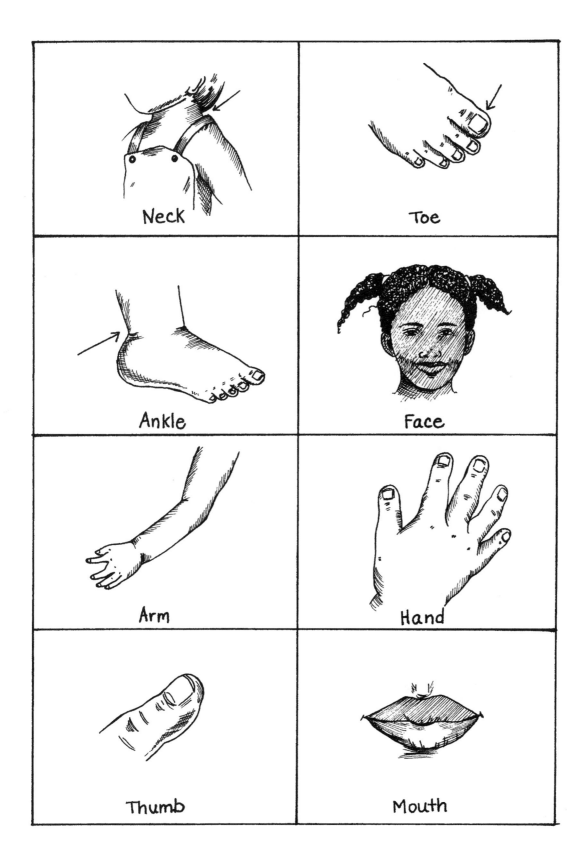

Neck

Toe

Ankle

Face

Arm

Hand

Thumb

Mouth

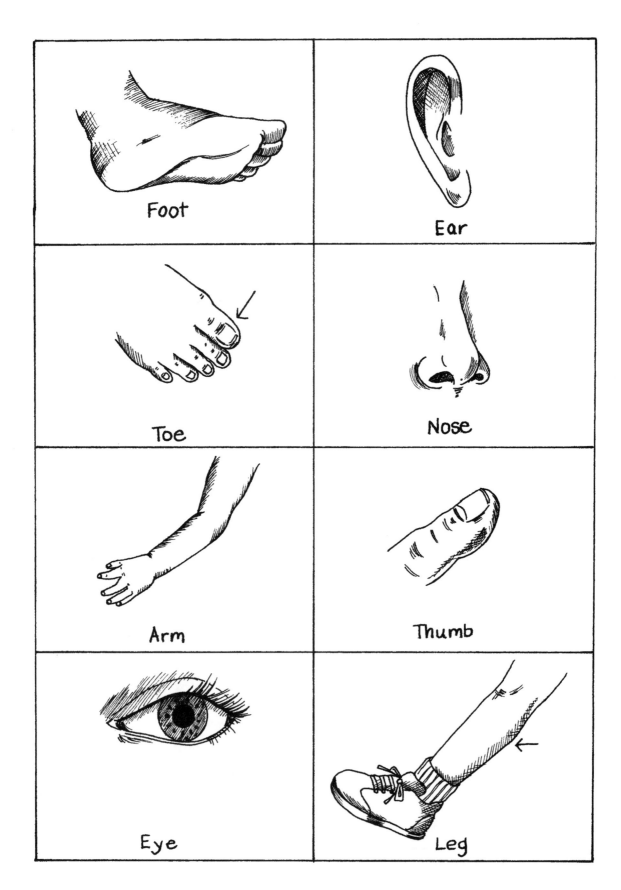

Foot

Ear

Toe

Nose

Arm

Thumb

Eye

Leg

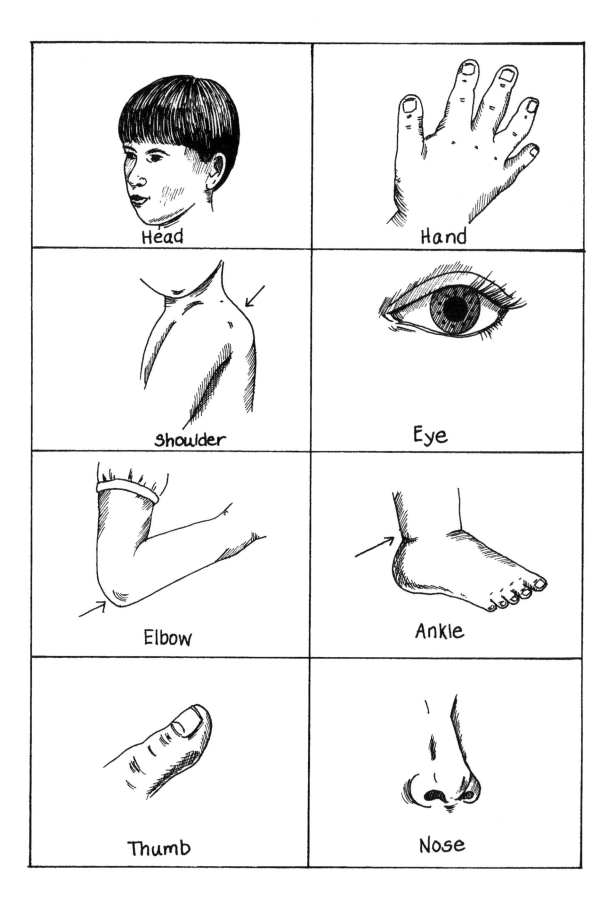

Head

Hand

Shoulder

Eye

Elbow

Ankle

Thumb

Nose

Ant

Fly

Bee

Ladybug

Butterfly

Cricket

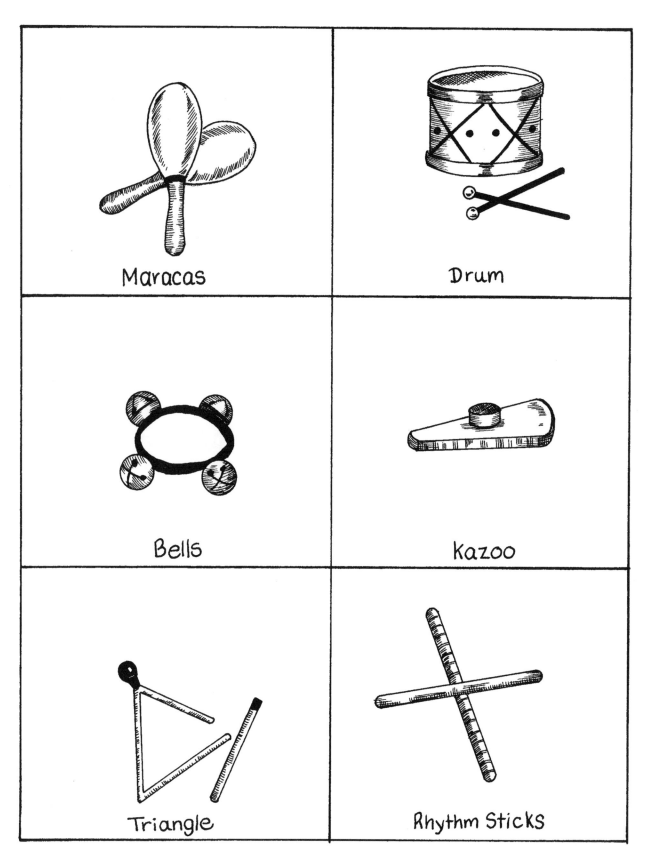

Maracas

Drum

Bells

Kazoo

Triangle

Rhythm Sticks

Use this blank concentration form to make up your own game.

Drawings, Patterns and Instructions

Family Tree

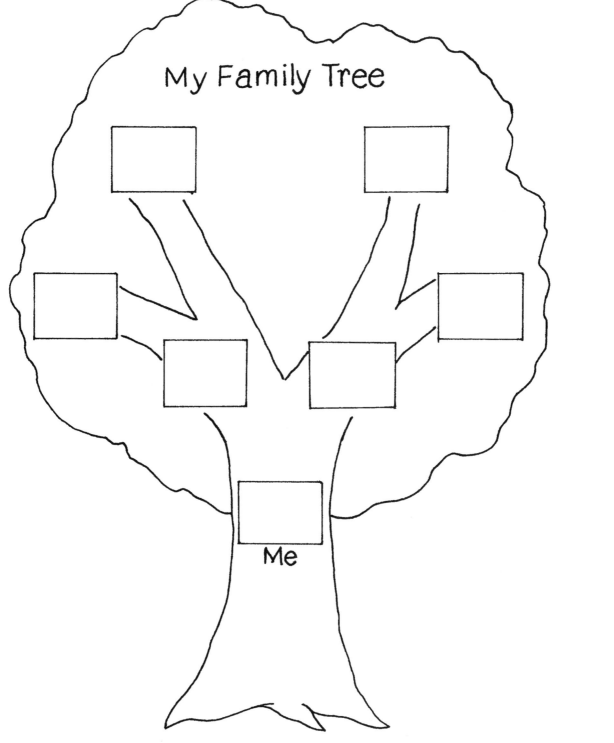

My Family Tree

Me

Copy, color and cut out. Glue to center of paper plate. Stick a brad through the end of the spinner and then through the center of the paper plate.

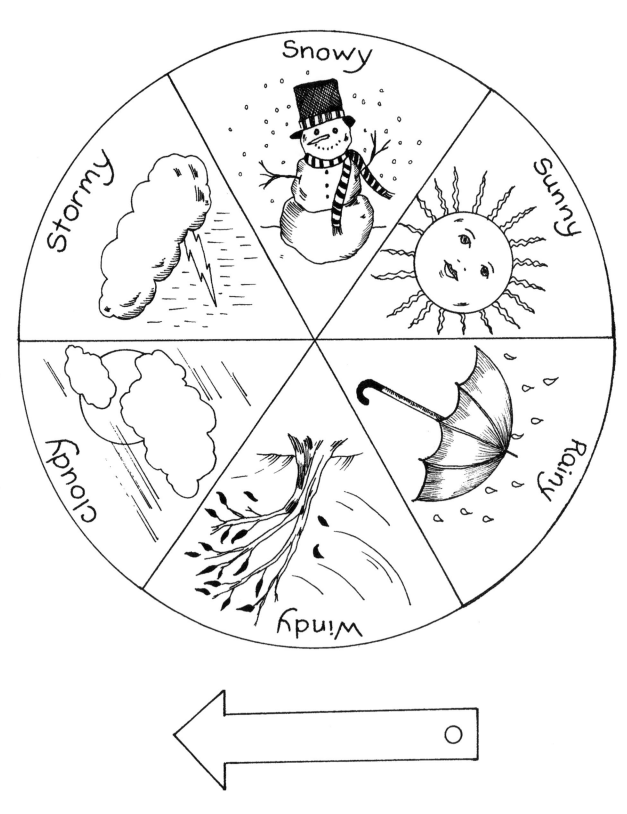

Conservation Game Board

Copy or enlarge. Color and laminate. Children roll a number cube and move a coin or large button the corresponding number of spaces. When they land on a reminder square, ask them to name what kind of conservation it represents. If they answer correctly, they continue. If they don't, they go back to the beginning. First one to the end wins.

You Need:

Spread butter on
your bread.

Sprinkle on cinnamon
and sugar.

Toast it in the toaster oven.

Enjoy!

Spiral Snake

Make one copy for each child. Have children color and then cut it out along the dotted line. Lift the end in the center of the circle.

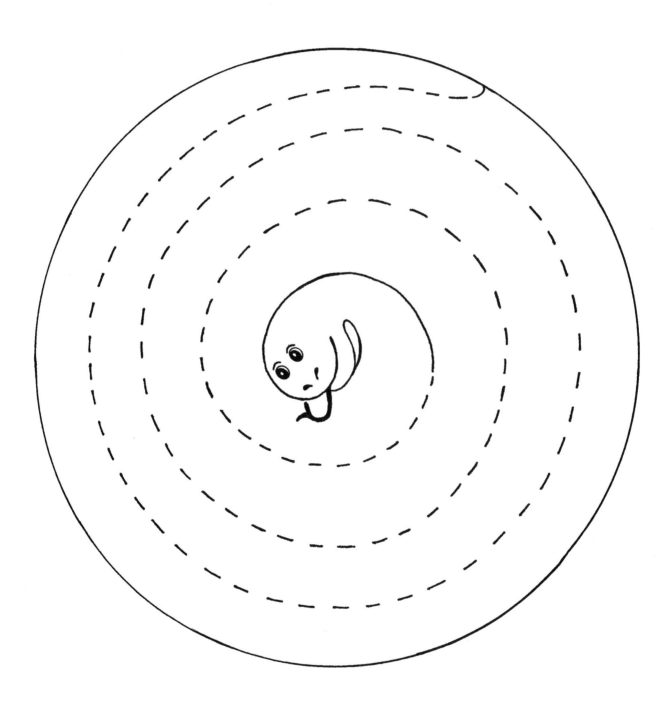

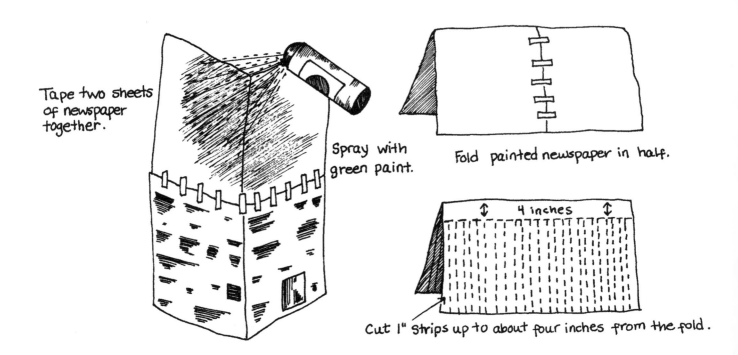

Tape two sheets of newspaper together.

Spray with green paint.

Fold painted newspaper in half.

↕ 4 inches ↕

Cut 1" strips up to about four inches from the fold.

Place a double strip of masking tape along fold.

Wrap the skirt around the child's waist. Fasten with velcro or tape.

Make one copy for each child.
Color and cut out.
Cut along dotted lines.
Fold in half; join together at slits.
Drop from waist or shoulder height.
Watch it twirl.

Hat for Firefighter, Cowpoke and Smoky Bear

Enlarge to fit 12″ X 18″ (30 cm x 45 cm) sheet of construction paper. Cut along solid outline and along dotted line. Stand flap up. Glue on shield for firefighter.

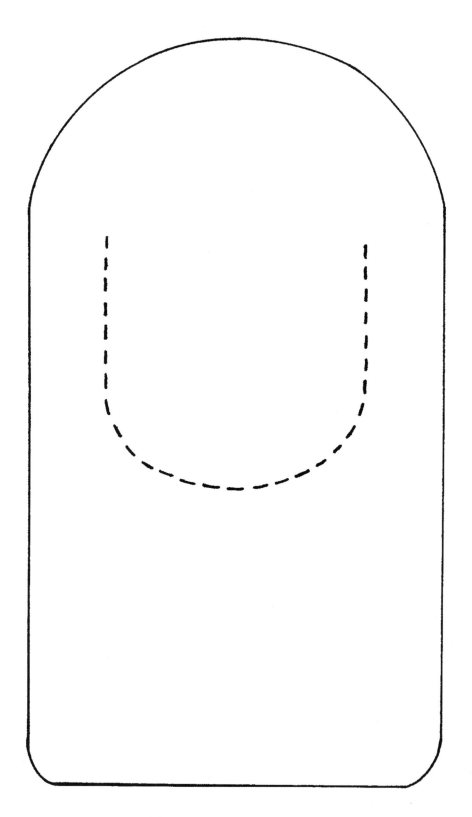

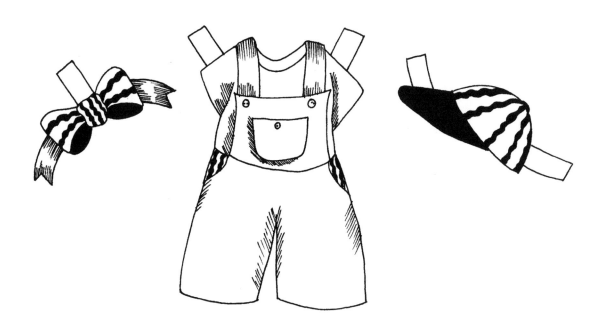

Horse Head and Torso

Attach clothespins for legs.

Glue a penny to each end of a 1″ X 8″ (3 cm x 20 cm) strip of poster board, fold the strip in half and paper-clip it over the end of a tongue depressor. Play the clappers to music.

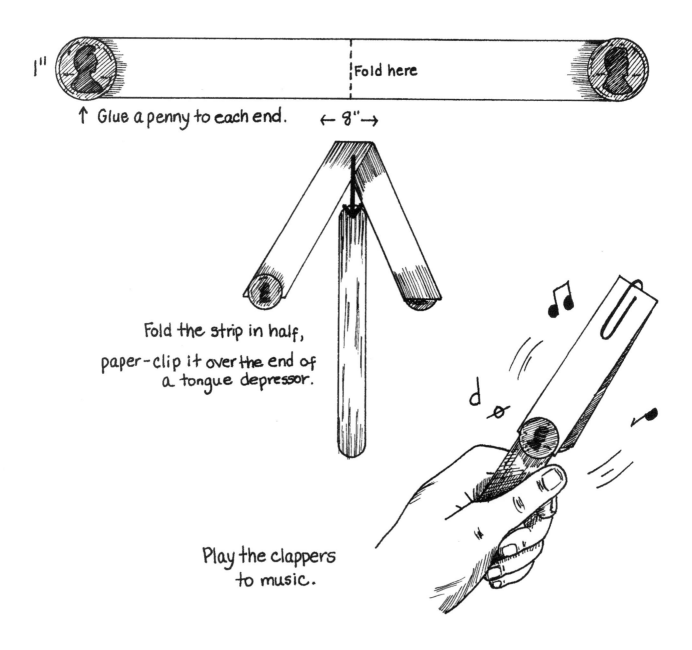

1″

Fold here

↑ Glue a penny to each end.   ← 8″ →

Fold the strip in half,
paper-clip it over the end of
a tongue depressor.

Play the clappers
to music.

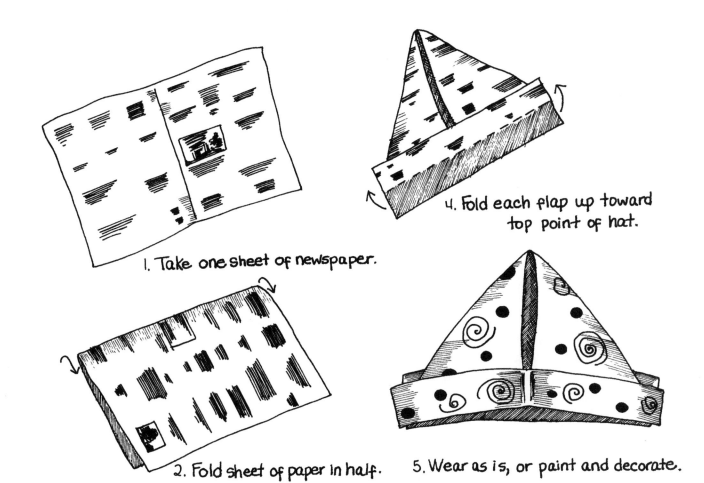

1. Take one sheet of newspaper.

4. Fold each flap up toward top point of hat.

2. Fold sheet of paper in half.

5. Wear as is, or paint and decorate.

leave this for bottom flap of hat.

Fold

3. Fold corners to meet in the middle about ¾ of the way to the bottom of the newspaper sheet.

You will need
a 9″ (23 cm) long square stick of wood, about ³/₈″ (9 mm) thick
ruler
pencil or pen
rasp or file
thin cardboard
scissors
thumbtack
straight pin with a large head
smooth, round pencil or pen

✓ Measure 2″ (5 cm) from one end and 3″ (8 cm) from the other.
✓ Make a mark at each measurement.
✓ Between these two points, mark off each ¹/₄″ inch (6 mm).
✓ File an indentation into each mark. Be sure the indentations cross the edge of the stick.
✓ Cut a 3 ¹/₂″ x ³/₈″ (9 cm x 9 mm) rectangle out of the cardboard. This will be the propeller.
✓ Make a mark in the middle of the propeller.
✓ Push the thumbtack through the mark on the propeller and into the end of the stick nearest to the notches.
✓ Remove the thumbtack.
✓ Push the large-headed pin through the propeller and into the hole in the stick. Be sure it fits snugly.
✓ Now for the trick. Hold the pencil or pen with your right hand, with forefinger extended and thumb at the back.
✓ With your left hand, hold the stick.
✓ If only your thumb tip touches the wood, the propeller will spin counterclockwise. If only the tip of your forefinger touches the wood, the propeller will spin clockwise. If both the thumb tip and the forefinger tip touch the stick at the same time, the propeller will not turn.
✓ You control the direction that the propeller spins!

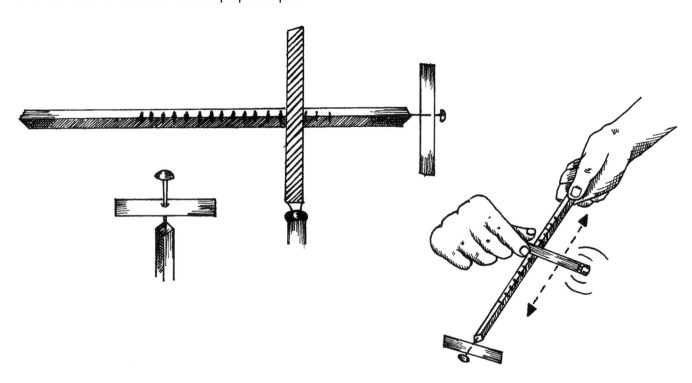

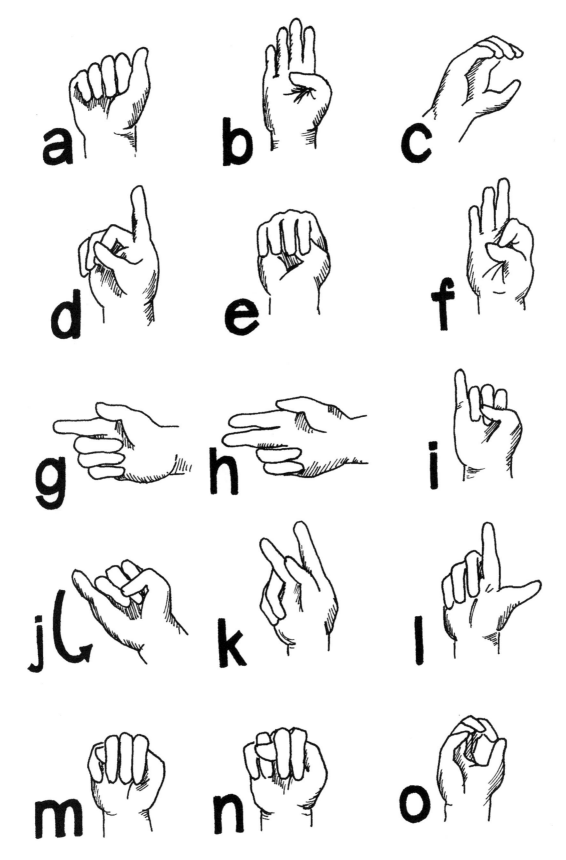

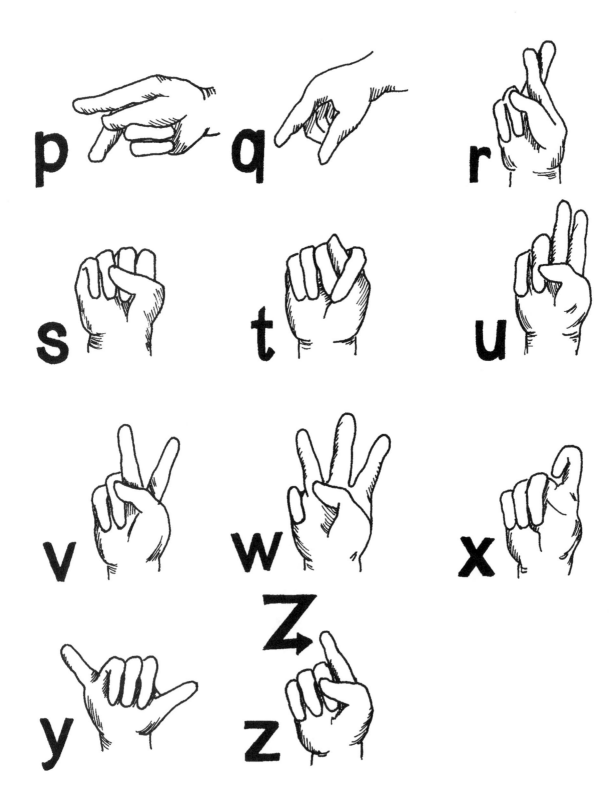

p q r
s t u
v w x
y z z

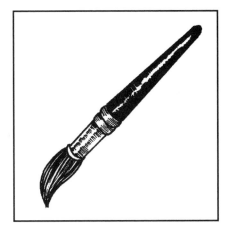

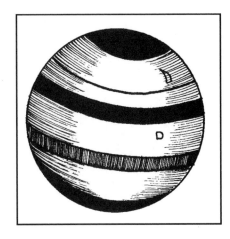

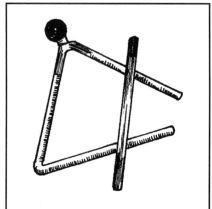

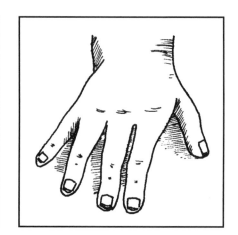

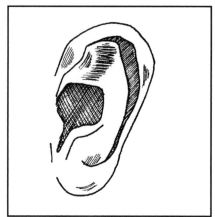

"My picture is about..."

Index

Book Index